Imagination and the Playfulness of God

DISTINGUISHED DISSERTATIONS IN CHRISTIAN THEOLOGY

Series Foreword

We are living in a vibrant season for academic Christian theology. After a hiatus of some decades, a real flowering of excellent systematic and moral theology has emerged. This situation calls for a series that showcases the contributions of newcomers to this ongoing and lively conversation. The journal *Word & World: Theology for Christian Ministry* and the academic society Christian Theological Research Fellowship (CTRF) are happy to cosponsor this series together with our publisher Pickwick Publications (an imprint of Wipf and Stock Publishers). Both the CTRF and *Word & World* are interested in excellence in academics but also in scholarship oriented toward Christ and the Church. The volumes in this series are distinguished for their combination of academic excellence with sensitivity to the primary context of Christian learning. We are happy to present the work of these young scholars to the wider world and are grateful to Luther Seminary for the support that helped make it possible.

Alan G. Padgett
Professor of Systematic Theology
Luther Seminary

Beth Felker Jones
Assistant Professor of Theology
Wheaton College

www.ctrf.info
www.luthersem.edu/word&world

Imagination and the Playfulness of God
The Theological Implications of Samuel Taylor Coleridge's Definition of the Human Imagination

ROBIN STOCKITT

☙PICKWICK Publications • Eugene, Oregon

IMAGINATION AND THE PLAYFULNESS OF GOD
The Theological Implications of Samuel Taylor Coleridge's Definition of the Human Imagination

Distinguished Dissertations in Christian Theology 6

Copyright © 2011 Robin Stockitt. All rights reserved. Except for brief quotations in critical publications or reviews, no part of this book may be reproduced in any manner without prior written permission from the publisher. Write: Permissions, Wipf and Stock Publishers, 199 W. 8th Ave., Suite 3, Eugene, OR 97401.

Pickwick Publications
An Imprint of Wipf and Stock Publishers
199 W. 8th Ave., Suite 3
Eugene, OR 97401

www.wipfandstock.com

ISBN 13: 978-1-61097-347-2

Cataloging-in-Publication data:

Stockitt, Robin.

    Imagination and the playfulness of God : the theological implications of Samuel Taylor Coleridge's definition of the human imagination / Robin Stockitt, with a foreword by Christoph Schwöbel.

    Distinguished Dissertations in Christian Theology 6

    xiv + 186 p. ; 23 cm. Includes bibliographical references.

    ISBN 13: 978-1-61097-347-2

    1. Imagination—Religious aspects—Christianity. 2. Imagination. 3. Coleridge, Samuel Taylor, 1772–1834—Criticism and interpretation. 4. Coleridge, Samuel Taylor, 1772–1834—Religion. 5. Coleridge, Samuel Taylor, 1772–1834—Philosophy. 6. God (Christianity)—Attributes. I. Schwöbel, Christoph. II. Title. III. Series.

BR115.16 S70 2011

Manufactured in the U.S.A.

For
Joni, Anna, Jonny, and Caz

Contents

Foreword by Christoph Schwöbel | *ix*
Acknowledgments | *xi*
Abbreviations | *xii*

PART 1 Coleridge and the Human Imagination
1. Introduction | 3
2. The Formative Influences on Coleridge's Views Concerning the Imagination | 18
3. Coleridge's Definition of the Imagination | 63
4. Key Features of Coleridge's View of the Imagination | 69

PART 2 Imagination and the Playfulness of God
5. Imagination and the Ontology of God | 93
6. Conclusion: Imagination and the Playfulness of God | 171

Appendix: Coleridge, the Imagination, and George MacDonald (1824–1905) | 177
Bibliography | 181

Foreword

SAMUEL TAYLOR COLERIDGE (1772–1834), poet, philosopher, translator, literary critic, opium addict, and amateur theologian, is one of the most enigmatic and fascinating figures in the history of Christian thought. A genius of receptivity, he could appropriate ideas from a seemingly unlimited diversity of sources, process them through the labyrinthine capacities of his mind, adapt them relentlessly to the self-reflective dynamics of his personal experience, and reproduce them in novel and imaginative combinations in a sprit of creative spontaneity. The world of his thought and writing is at the same time characterised by a bewildering multi-layered complexity, often *prima facie* contradictory, and an unstoppable desire for unity and dynamic harmony, relating the One and the Many in novel and surprising schemes of polyphonic integration. Eclectic to the point of outright plagiarism, Coleridge's recombination of appropriated sources reveals an astonishing originality. While in his poetry the sheer abundance of ideas and images could be tamed by poetic form and a unique atmospheric density, in his prose writings the reader must be prepared to follow his aids to reflection along the circuitous route of tiresome detours and surprising short cuts, often ending in intellectual cul des sacs, only to be surprised by liberating escape routes from the maze—true occasions of the *ekstasis* of the mind. A nightmare for an orderly associationist like David Hartley, whose philosophy and psychology Coleridge at one period embraced, his writings can offer disclosure experiences for those who are prepared to follows Coleridge's uncompromisingly inquiring spirit until one can discern systematic patterns in the consistently unsystematic modes of reflection.

If one looks at the sources he appropriated, Coleridge's philosophy appears at first as a remarkably random collection of ideas, freely combining classical Neo-Platonism with theses from empiricist philosophy and various forms of transcendental idealism, gleaned from Kant and the German Idealists. If one turns one's view to the logic of development in the writings themselves as well as in the overall route of Coleridge's philosophical thinking, and attempts not to grasp his thought but to follow the meandering route of his thinking, patterns emerge and insights can be gained. Like its often-chaotic inception, the reception of Coleridge's thought has been ambiguous. What appears to some as the random imaginings of a mind befuddled by opium, reveals itself to others as an imaginatively ordered cosmos in the dynamics of Coleridge's intellectual and spiritual development.

Coleridge's theology is equally perplexing. Born as the son of the vicar of Ottery St. Mary, educated at Christ's Hospital in Greyfriars, London, and Jesus College, Cambridge, Coleridge was for a time attracted to Unitarianism, even standing in for the Rev. Joshua Toulmin in taking services at Mary Street Unitarian Chapel at Taunton. Deeper reflection led him to a staunch defence of orthodox trinitarian doctrine, however, often by rather unorthodox routes. Similarly, Coleridge could argue for a "strong" view of the authority of the Scripture, while approaching it with an equally strong free approach to its interpretation, warranted, for him, so its seems, by the content of Scripture itself. The outcome is what could be termed *imaginative orthodoxy*, often moving in its spiritual depth and demanding in its high-flying speculative elaboration.

With this book Robin Stockitt offers a "Guide for the Perplexed" to the perplexing world of Coleridge's theological thinking. Choosing as his approach the central notion of the imagination, he traces this trajectory through the development of Coleridge's thinking, underlining the links by which the imagination is related to the other elements in the rampantly fertile forest of Coleridge's world of ideas. Submitted and accepted as a doctoral dissertation for the degree of Dr. theol. in the Faculty of Protestant Theology at Tübingen University, the book unearths the different strata of influences on Coleridge's view of the imagination, notably the influence of Kant, Fichte, Schelling, and Schiller, whose drama *Wallenstein* he also translated. The German influence is compared and contrasted to the influence of Hartley and Plotinus, thereby emphasising many connections between Neo-Platonism and German Idealism which have been a prominent feature both of the history of reception of neo-platonic thought and of the presuppositions of idealist systems in recent research.

This provides the backdrop for a skilful and economic presentation of Coleridge's views on the dynamics of imagination, relating it to the rationalist strand of reflection on reason and to the empiricist engagement with perception and experience, overcoming the shortcomings of both traditions. Stockitt offers a clear and sympathetic account of Coleridge's view of the imagination which he describes fittingly as "God's co-worker on earth, both mirroring and sharing in the activity of the Divine," providing the ground for Coleridge's thesis of the consubstantiality of the symbol with the divine reality it conveys in symbolic form. This presentation of Coleridge's views on the imagination is a rare achievement in the interpretation of a writer whose thought becomes lucid only by grappling with the apparent obscurities of its expression.

Yet, this is not just another study in critical intellectual history but also an exercise in constructive systematic theology. "What," Stockitt asks, "might happen if one approached conventional theological questions concerning the nature of the being of God through the lens of the imagination?" How would the "ontology of God" have to be conceived if the imagination in the created realm is the mirror of God's own imagination expressed in the creative agency of God. How does the imaginative playfulness of God, displayed in the free response to the events in a contingent creation, relate to the inner Being of God which Coleridge understood as the Trinity, conceived as the Idea Idearum, the dynamic enactment of the One and the Many in the perichoretic relationships of the three persons? Is the Trinity thus the root of the dynamic interplay between the three persons in their immanent relations and in the imaginative engagement with creation in the economic relations?

Robin Stockitt explores the theological inspirations offered by Coleridge constructively and suggestively, offering an account of the "playfulness" of God which seeks firm scriptural foundation and, at the same time, employs the wealth of scriptural images to develop an understanding of God who in his trinitarian being and in his interrelations with the world is not merely good for something but beautiful in himself, a God who is not in need of rational justification because he is his own purpose, true to himself as the "Eternal Self-Affirmant" (OM Lxxiv). To engage with the imaginative engagement of *this* God with his creation requires creaturely imagination, which Coleridge defined "as a repetition in the finite mind of the eternal act of creation in the infinite I AM" (BL, 202). Following the route of theological imagination one can understand creation as the imaginative letting be of creatures other than God, capable of responding to him. Even in the Incarnation and in the cross and resurrection of Christ one can detect the element of divine playfulness, misleading and overcoming the powers of evil in the liberation of the Son of God from death through the actualisation of new life freely granted by the eternal I AM. The victory of the playfulness of God over the deadly serious and seriously deadly powers of evil is celebrated by the *risus paschalis*, the laughter of the Christian church at Easter, joyfully echoing God's victory over death, the ultimate enemy. This victory opens up new vistas into the life of the kingdom of God, the consummated community of God with his liberated creation when playful enjoyment and joyful celebration will take the place of strenuous work, pain and tears.

Theologically daring, as Robin Stockitt's exploration appears at times, it is always conducted in a spirit of responsibility to the "subject-matter" of theological reflection and to the believing community whose life is enriched by the vision of a God who freely invites his human images to join in the play of divine goodness, truth, and beauty, overcoming the captivity of finite minds in the ugly and self-seeking addiction of self-deception in estrangement from God. The style of writing reflects Robin Stockitt's background in missionary work, in the world of education, and in the pastoral ministry. The result is a very readable book, inviting its readers to follow Coleridge's own invitation to explore faithfully and playfully the vision of an imaginative trinitarian God.

Christoph Schwöbel
Tübingen, Palm Sunday 2011

Acknowledgments

I WISH TO THANK THE following people:
Professor Christoph Schwöbel for being so willing to become my "Doktorvater" and offering me encouragement in pursuing this project; Professor Jeremy Begbie for being my "door-opener" so often; George Norwood for his patience in helping me with Hebrew and Greek; Martin Hermann for helping me to put the manuscript in some kind of order; Dr. Martin Wendte for guiding me through the mysteries of Tübingen University; Dr. Nick Zair for coaching me in Latin; Professor Trevor Hart for unwittingly inspiring me to take an interest in the imagination; Sheila Scheer for help with German translations; my family for believing in me; and the wonderful community at the Anglican Church in Freiburg for patiently and enthusiastically listening to me, as many of the ideas contained in this book were first offered to them.

Robin Stockitt

Abbreviations

Works by Samuel Taylor Coleridge:

AR	*Aids to Reflection*
BL	*Biographia Literaria*, Vols. 1 and 2
CL	*Collected Letters*
CN	*The Notebooks of Samuel Taylor Coleridge*
CIS	*Confessions of an Inquiring Spirit*
LL	*Lectures on Literature 1808–1819*
LS	*Lay Sermons*
OM	*Opus Maximum*
PL	*The Philosophical Lectures*
PW	*The Complete Poetical Works of Samuel Taylor Coleridge*
SM	*The Statesman's Manual*
TF	*The Friend*
TT	*Table Talk*

PART I

Coleridge and the Human Imagination

CHAPTER I

Introduction

WHY THEOLOGIZE ABOUT THE imagination? Why take something as beautiful, mysterious, creative, and wild as the human imagination and subject it to intellectual scrutiny? Surely its very essence resists taming; it needs the freedom to roam our mental and spiritual spaces where it can dream, pretend, play, and create, unchecked by rules or convention? Are we not in danger of the very interference, against which William Wordsworth warned in his poem "*The Tables Turned*"?[1]

> Sweet is the lore which Nature brings;
> Our meddling intellect
> Mis-shapes the beauteous forms of things:
> We murder to dissect.

My hope is that this book will not murder this precious gift of God—for that is what the imagination is—but rather it will seek to understand and appreciate its power, significance, and function more fully. I begin therefore with the familiar account of the meeting between the prophet Nathan and King David,[2] occasioned by the act of adultery that David had committed with Bathsheba. Here is a cameo portrait of the imagination in action, *par excellence*. In order to facilitate a genuine act of repentance Nathan visits the king and recounts a tale.

> The LORD sent Nathan to David. When he came to him, he said, "There were two men in a certain town, one rich and the other poor. The rich man had a very large number of sheep and cattle, but the poor man had nothing except one little ewe lamb that he had bought. He raised it, and it grew up with him and his

1. Wordsworth, *Selected Poetry of William Wordsworth*, 79–80.
2. 2 Sam 12: 1–13.

children. It shared his food, drank from his cup and even slept in his arms. It was like a daughter to him. Now a traveler came to the rich man, but the rich man refrained from taking one of his own sheep or cattle to prepare a meal for the traveller who had come to him. Instead, he took the ewe lamb that belonged to the poor man and prepared it for the one who had come to him."

David burned with anger against the man and said to Nathan, "As surely as the LORD lives, the man who did this deserves to die! He must pay for that lamb four times over, because he did such a thing and had no pity."

Then Nathan said to David, "You are the man! This is what the LORD, the God of Israel, says: 'I anointed you king over Israel, and I delivered you from the hand of Saul. I gave your master's house to you, and your master's wives into your arms. I gave you the house of Israel and Judah. And if all this had been too little, I would have given you even more. Why did you despise the word of the LORD by doing what is evil in his eyes? You struck down Uriah the Hittite with the sword and took his wife to be your own. You killed him with the sword of the Ammonites. Now, therefore, the sword shall never depart from your house, because you despised me and took the wife of Uriah the Hittite to be your own.' This is what the LORD says: 'Out of your own household I am going to bring calamity upon you. Before your very eyes I will take your wives and give them to one who is close to you, and he will lie with your wives in broad daylight. You did it in secret, but I will do this thing in broad daylight before all Israel.'"

Then David said to Nathan, "I have sinned against the LORD."

Nathan replied, "The LORD has taken away your sin. You are not going to die."

I begin with this extraordinary narrative for it opens up a number of significant questions concerning the nature and function of the imagination in the divine human encounter.

The approach adopted by Nathan in order to expedite David's repentance is an oblique one. He does not confront David head-on with his misdeeds, but adopts a narrative style that, by its very nature, demands much of both the speaker and the listener. Nathan is highly imaginative in his storytelling skills for he is required to perfect his art in such a way that the imagination of the listener is fully engaged. As the story is told, David, the listener, is required to enter into the story imaginatively as a passive observer of the protagonists. Yet as the tale unfolds this passive observation gradually metamorphoses into a far more active engagement.

David's participation becomes so intense that in his furious reaction to the tale, he appears to be barely able to distinguish fiction from reality. "David burned with anger against the man and said to Nathan, 'As surely as the LORD lives, the man who did this deserves to die!'" This "entering in" on the part of David is crucial for the success of Nathan's venture. Without David's complicit participation in the act of storytelling the narrative intention would fail, for his participation is dependent upon his capacity both to imagine and truly inhabit the story. David listens with intense interest but is unable on his own to configure the meaning of the tale. His indignation is aroused but Nathan's work is not yet done. His concluding task is to reconfigure the parable enabling David to connect the narrative of the two sheep farmers with the narrative of his own life. A synthesis occurs and it is at this very moment of synthesis that a new paradigm of perception is reached. David is enabled, through the prophetic skill of Nathan, to align the story of the two farmers with his own autobiography. It is a short step from there to a place of genuine repentance.

This mutual giving and receiving within the imaginative realm is suggestive perhaps of a broader principle, namely, that the way in which humankind receives *any* kind of divine revelation rests upon the usage of imaginative paradigms of perceptual reception. David arrived at a new understanding of truth, albeit the truth about himself and his relationship to God, through the process of imaginative encounter. Far from being drawn towards a fictional reality, his sudden sense of conviction about the true nature of his own condition stemmed entirely from his ability to inhabit the story that was being recounted to him. This points to the possibility that the imagination can be construed as the *Anknupfungspunkt*—the point of contact—of divine human interaction.

But the narrative from 2 Sam 12 quoted above raises further questions about the very ontology of God. Nathan comes to David in his capacity as a prophet of the Lord and dares to speak the word of the Lord to David. The form of this divine human communication, couched in a highly imaginative narrative, can legitimately be described as "playful." Nathan effectively entices David into the story, much as a fisherman entices fish to a hook. Once David has accepted the bait, he feels the full impact of the prophetic word. Nathan in effect "plays" with David, but with a highly serious intent, namely to bring about the repentance of the King. In so doing, he embarks on a risky venture for he cannot be sure of the outcome and potentially puts his own life in danger.

If Nathan is communicating something of the mind and character of God during this encounter, then one is compelled to consider; who is this God who engages with his creation in this manner? "God is who he is in the act of his revelation," states Barth in *Die Kirchliche Dogmatik*.[3] If God accommodates himself to the culture of David's time and to the particular psychological constitution of David, then this posits an imaginative empathy on God's behalf. Can we claim therefore that God is intrinsically imaginative, that imagination is one of his core attributes? And can we go further and claim that this imaginative attribute of God issues forth in a "playfulness" with which he engages with creation? Moltmann has proposed such a depiction of God in his book *Die Ersten Freigelassenen der Schöpfung*,[4] where he asserts that God plays with his own possibilities. Such an imaginative and playful depiction of God raises further questions about the extent to which God's actions in relation to the world bear the hallmark of improvisation; a dynamic and open-ended interchange between God and humankind that may have a clear intentionality but not necessarily a clear path to achieve that purpose. Can we therefore liken God to a jazz musician who plays within a clearly defined musical structure, yet improvises within that framework?

The Scope of the Project

This book will attempt to address these questions by placing them within a theological framework. MacIntyre addresses the theological role of the imagination in his book entitled *Faith, Theology and the Imagination* where he quotes Baillie: "I have long been of the opinion that the part played by the imagination in the soul's dealings with God, though it has always been understood by those skilled in the practice of the Christian cure of souls, has never been given proper place in Christian theology, which has been too much ruled by intellectualist pre-conceptions."[5]

Baillie asserts that apprehension of transcendent reality can legitimately be achieved indirectly, almost obliquely, through an appeal to the variant forms of the imagination. It is through this "inner eye" that we, as finite beings, may perceive the Divine. Baillie asserts that there is a form of knowing about God that is experienced through prayer and

---

3. Barth, *KD* 2/1, 288: "Gott ist, der er ist in der Tat seiner Offenbarung." All English translations of Karl Barth's *Die Kirchliche Dogmatik* are taken from *Church Dogmatics*, eds. Bromiley and Torrance.

4. Moltmann, *Die ersten Freigelassenen der Schöpfung*, 41.

5. MacIntyre, *Faith Theology and Imagination*, 1.

spiritual direction. This is what Jenson[6] would describe as a "first order experience." The task of theology, a secondary task, is to provide the grammar for the interpretation of such experiences. If Baillie's claim is to carry any weight then it behooves us to consider the biblical evidence for such an assertion.

When one looks at the biblical corpus however, it appears at first sight that we have a very slender foundation on which to build. In the King James translation of the Bible there are three Hebrew words used which are translated as imagination. These are:

(a) "God saw that the wickedness of man was great in the earth, and that every *imagination* (*yetser*) of the thoughts of his heart was only evil continually" (Gen 6:5).

(b) "At that time they shall call Jerusalem the throne of the LORD; and all the nations shall be gathered unto it, to the name of the LORD, to Jerusalem: neither shall they walk any more after the *imagination* (*sherirut*) of their evil heart" (Jer 3:17).

(c) "An heart that deviseth wicked *imaginations* (*machshevot*) feet that be swift in running to mischief" (Prov 6.18).

When we turn to the New Testament there are three further Greek words that are also translated in a similar way. These are:

(a) "Because that, when they knew God, they glorified him not as God, neither were thankful; but became vain in their *imaginations*, (*dialogismois*) and their foolish heart was darkened" (Rom 1: 21).

(b) "He hath shewed strength with his arm; he hath scattered the proud in the *imagination (dianoia)* of their hearts" (Lk 1:51).

(c) ". . . casting down *imaginations (logismous)*, and every high thing that exalteth itself against the knowledge of God, and bringing into captivity every thought to the obedience of Christ" (2 Cor 10:5).

What is most noticeable about each of these references is that all of them are used pejoratively. The "imaginations of a man's heart" is a synonym for evil inclinations totally unacceptable to God. It may be that we are simply faced with a somewhat clumsy English translation of carefully nuanced Hebrew and Greek terms, but such language, embedded in the English speaking world for centuries, has done little to endear the concept of the imagination as a valid theological category.

---

6. Jenson, *Systematic Theology Volume 1*, 3–22.

Not only is there apparent biblical justification for dismissing the imagination out of hand, there are other reasons which can be brought to bear on its eclipse in twentieth century theological enquiry. The challenge of the Enlightenment has inspired a range of responses to the key question of "how do we arrive at truth?" The empirical response, espoused for example by Hume and Hartley, insisted that reality consists merely in the aggregate sum of observable, verifiable particulars. The hidden matters relating to God and meaning will always remain just that—hidden—and therefore are, by definition, unknowable. Truth may be discovered but it is the fruit of a laborious process of logical, rational, analysis, which precludes any sense of mystery or otherness. The seventeenth century philosopher Thomas Sprat epitomized this view when he declared that, "It is our task to separate the knowledge of Nature, from the colors of Rhetoric, the devices of Fancy or the delightful deceit of Fables."[7]

Sprat stood at the entrance to the Enlightenment era and passed the baton on to subsequent thinkers of which Hartley, as we shall observe in due course, was highly significant. Such thinkers sought to drive a wedge between reason[8] and the imagination. The latter could not be trusted to provide access to truth being merely the stuff of fables and fairy tales, the province of artists and dreamers who, whilst they might entertain and delight, afford us with no new knowledge. Only reason could be counted upon to deliver truth in its purest form. One alternative response to this brash and confident rationalism was to retreat into a kind of religious apartheid, expressed at times by a strident fundamentalism, which insisted that truth could be found in the pages of Scripture alone on the condition that they were accepted as literally and completely true. Such an approach often failed to recognize the poetic, dramatic, enigmatic nature of divine revelation, and reveled only in certainty and absoluteness.

An alternative track is that offered by the Romantics, who reached their apogee during the nineteenth century. The English Romantics, epitomized by Coleridge, attempted to offer a robust defense of the Christian position in defiance of Enlightenment accusations, whilst simultaneously making strenuous efforts to engage with the cultural questions of the day. Theirs was an attempt to build from the raw materials of human

---

7. Taken from "A history of the Royal Society of London for the Improving of Natural Knowledge" (1667) newarkwww. Rutgers. edu/jlynch/Texts/sprat. html

8. Thinkers such as Hume and Hartley used the term "reason" in an equivalent sense to the word rationality. By this they meant that which is open to a logical rational process of reasoned deduction open to verification. Coleridge later took the word "Reason" and imbued it with an utterly different meaning, using it to embrace the whole abstract metaphysical realm of "Ideas."

experience and identify points of contact with the Divine. In attempting to build in this way they embraced the more opaque, aesthetic modes of utterance, allowing room for ambiguity and paradox. There was nothing neat and tidy about the Romantics in their philosophy or their theology and our chosen guide through the maze of thinking about the imagination was perhaps the most untidy of all. Yet despite this, the Romantics allow us to make a valid distinction between comprehension and apprehension, which, I believe, will be of invaluable help in approaching the question of the truth about God's imaginative nature.

This book will consist of two distinct parts. In the first part we will explore how one can give some content to our understanding of the word "imagination." How is this word to be defined? What is its function and place within human experience? What is its theological resonance? The second part of the book will make a shift away from epistemology towards ontology. If the human imagination is a reflection of, and a participation in, the divine imagination, then how does that influence our understanding of the nature of God? In so doing it will be necessary to avoid too great a degree of anthropomorphism, extrapolating upwards in a rather crude manner. Instead I will adopt a more conjectural position, asking what might happen if one approached conventional theological questions concerning the nature of the being of God through the lens of the imagination.

Introducing Samuel Taylor Coleridge (1772–1834)

To address this task we will accompany one key thinker who made a significant contribution to our understanding of the imagination. That thinker is the Romantic poet, philosopher, and theologian Samuel Taylor Coleridge (1772–1834). Coleridge possesses the reputation to this day of being a "true Bohemian, a feckless, unpractical genius."[9] He initially came to prominence in England as a poet, especially after the publication of the *Lyrical Ballads* in 1798 which he co-authored with William Wordsworth. The *Lyrical Ballads* came to represent a watershed in the development of an entirely new approach to poetry. Whilst studying at Jesus College, Cambridge, he met Robert Southey who later became the poet laureate and with whom he formed a lasting friendship. His time at Cambridge fostered a radical streak within him and he became consumed with the utopian notion of "Pantisocracy,"[10] hoping to emigrate to the New World with the intention of founding a new egalitarian society.

9. Simmons, *Letters from England*, x.
10. Meaning, "rule by all."

Eventually Southey and Coleridge fell out over the extent to which such a society could be truly equal.

After building an acquaintance with the Wedgewood brothers, Josiah and Thomas, an annual grant was made to Coleridge freeing him to pursue his literary career. The disappointment of the failed pantisocratic experiment drove Coleridge to look to continental Europe and Germany in particular for fresh inspiration. There he studied German, attended Göttingen University, and became familiar with the works of Immanuel Kant. For many years Coleridge kept copious notes in his Notebooks, recording his reflections upon life and plotting the development of his thinking. In 1809–10 he took editorial control of the literary and political magazine *The Friend* and from 1808 to 1818 he gave a series of lectures, most notably about Shakespeare.

Coleridge's addiction to opium is well documented, although at the time the drug—commonly known as Laudanum—was used primarily as a pain reliever and its addictive properties were not yet known. In his later years, partly as a result of his excessive opium use, he became somewhat reclusive and devoted his energies to writing. His most significant publication in the early years of the nineteenth century was the *Biographia Literaria*, a work which we will later consider in greater detail. After 1817, Coleridge's poetic output diminished and he concentrated more on works of a political and theological nature.

Coleridge is representative of the British Romantic Movement, which he—along with his friend and confidante, William Wordsworth—was largely responsible for shaping. The mid-twentieth-century author, poet, and Christian apologist, C. S. Lewis, once wrote a poem full of admiration for the legacy of Coleridge.

> In England the Romantic stream . . . flows I say
> from Scott and Coleridge too.
> A bore? A sponge? A laudanum addict? True;
> Yet Newman in that ruinous master saw
> One who restored our faculty for awe,
> who rediscovered the soul's depth and height,
> Who pricked with needles of the eternal light
> An England at that time half numbed to death
> with Paley's, Bentham's, Malthus' wintry breath.[11]

Romanticism appeared in the early nineteenth century as a reaction to the mechanical, precise, scientific pronouncements of the Enlightenment. For the Romantics such an approach to the search for true knowl-

---

11. Lewis, *The Collected Poems*, 80.

edge was dry, uninspiring, and devoid of any sense of mystery or unity. Enlightenment thinking was concerned with mechanistic interactions, with the gearing mechanisms of the world, but was unable, in the opinion of the Romantics, to address the deeper, more searching questions, which dealt with human consciousness, creativity, emotion and the underlying interdependence of all that there is. Richard Haven has articulated the Romantic dilemma in this way: "Blake said: 'the tree which moves some to tears of joy is, in the eyes of others, only a green thing that stands in the way.' For Blake, the first possibility was more revealing than the second. But the philosophy of the enlightenment took into account only the things that stand in the way."[12]

What the Romantics sought was a transformation in the way the world was perceived and understood, but it was not any kind of transformation that was desired. It was, as Cutsinger has observed, a search for "partnership, affinity, and participation."[13] The Romantics longed for a different way of knowing, for a way of piercing the apparent separation between the world and its Creator, for a way of *seeing through,* rather than simply *looking at.* It was above all a search for the unity of all knowledge that, inevitably given such a goal, was profoundly religious in character. Coleridge continually sought to expose what he perceived to be a fatal fault line in the philosophical position espoused by the prevailing materialist views of his day and his exposé is particularly evident in the fragments that have now been published in the *Opus Maximum.* Coleridge considered that materialism, as a philosophical position, possessed an inherent internal contradiction. It asserted that human judgments and actions were merely the result of a complex chain of cause-and-effect impersonal forces, subject effectively to the laws of natural science. Humanity was thus contained within the mechanical operations of nature itself, allowing no real place for human agency or will. Within this conceptual paradigm, the activity of "thinking" must logically be merely one part of a chain of non-rational forces. If this be the case then "thinking" does not deserve such an appellation and therefore cannot be trusted or given any credence. Yet within this materialist world, the human powers of reason are exalted as the arbiter and judge of truth. Philosophically this becomes nonsense by virtue of the materialist's own parameters or arbitration. If the universe is essentially one large interconnected machine, the human reason must, *a fortiori,* not be able to transcend its own location. It is logically impossible for the human mind to step outside of the machine

---

12. Cutsinger, *The Form of Transformed Vision,* 17.
13. Ibid., 16.

and stand in judgment over it. Coleridge, by contrast, argued that, "nature itself, as soon as we apply reason to its contemplation, forces us back to a something higher than nature as that on which it depends."[14] There is something mysterious about nature, averred Coleridge, that simply cannot be explained by recourse to materialism. Here he is pointing towards his deeply held Christian convictions.

Coleridge asserted that the deployment of reason in the contemplation of nature immediately pushes us to the limits of reason's powers and points in a metaphysical direction. It is simply "wilful perversity"[15] that prevents materialists from accepting this conclusion. The complex phenomena of Romanticism held strongly to the belief in the powerful, God-given, shaping influence of the human mind as the subject of perception. It was the mind that brought structures, shape, ideas, gestalt, to its perception of the world. This perspective stood in sharp contrast to those views that emphasized the essentially passive nature of human consciousness. If the mind was capable of possessing this "esemplastic"[16] power in the quest for unity, then the obvious corollary was that the mind could indeed shape knowledge. Whilst Coleridge had coined this phrase himself, he had clearly been strongly influenced, as we shall see in due course, by the Kantian notion of *Einbildungskraft*, the ability to make one.

This shaping function of the human mind in the search for truth can be illustrated perhaps by using the example of the rainbow. What exactly are we seeing when we see a rainbow? The question can be answered at a number of different levels. It can either be understood as the outcome of Newtonian optics, illustrating the way in which light is refracted through a prism. Alternatively, the rainbow could be understood and appreciated according to a theory of color such as that espoused by Goethe.[17] Finally, the rainbow could be viewed as a symbol of God's enduring mercy as expressed in the Genesis account of Noah's flood. All of these answers would, of course, possess their own validity and each reveals the diverse ways in which human perception can operate. In the example of the rainbow given above, there is a progression from the critical (Newtonian physics), to the artistic/poetic (the appreciation of color), to the philosophical/theological (which is concerned with ultimate meaning). Coleridge reflected deeply

---

14. Coleridge, *OM*, 140.

15. Masson, *Romanticism, Hermeneutics*, 145.

16. Coleridge, *BL* 1, 68. "Esemplastic. The Word is not in Johnson, nor have I met it elsewhere. Neither have I! I constructed it myself from the Greek words *eis em plattein*, i.e., to shape into one"

17. Goethe's theory of color was first published as *Zur Farbenlehre* in 1810.

on this diversity and his reflections drew him inexorably to explore how the imagination served as the central nervous system of his entire quest. But what exactly was that quest? Before delving into an analysis of the genesis of Coleridge's views on the imagination, we need to set the imagination in its correct habitat and to sketch the task that Coleridge had set himself.

Whilst Coleridge had not begun his life from an orthodox Christian position and did not initially embrace a Trinitarian faith, by the turn of the century he had begun to adopt a more conventional faith and became firmly committed to the Thirty Nine Articles of Faith of the Church of England. By then he had been exposed to Kant's *Critique of Pure Reason,* which he regarded as an attempt to construct one unified system of knowledge. Coleridge, inspired by Kant's example, aspired to build a single unified system that united all forms of knowledge, both philosophical and theological. In particular he wished to make this *Magnum Opus* an apologetic work that asserted the Christian faith and defended it against its detractors. In the epigraph to the *Rime of the Ancient Mariner* (1817), Coleridge penned these words: "I can readily believe that in the sum of existing things there are more invisible beings than visible. But who will explain this great family to us, their ranks, their relationships, their differences and their respective duties?"[18]

It was this great family of the sum total of human knowledge that Coleridge sought to explain and for which to provide a coherent framework. It was a bold—some might say naïve—initiative, which sought serious engagement with all branches of knowledge in such way as to demonstrate an intrinsic unity. In modern parlance, his was an attempt to construct a grand meta-narrative, which demonstrated the order of all things. Indeed, in his major work *Biographia Literaria,* he announced his intention to construct a total and undivided philosophy, in which "philosophy would pass into religion and religion become inclusive of philosophy."[19] Such a venture demanded a dialogue with current thinking and practice across a vast spectrum of domains, thus necessitating a broad and expansive understanding of a range of disparate disciplines. Daniel Hardy helpfully summarizes Coleridge's intentions by stating that they were "to discover the order of all things in relation to their source in God, and thus to recover what it is for them to be formed in their fullness by reference to the purposes of God."[20]

18. Quoted by Thomas Burnet in Empson and Pirie, *Coleridge's Verse,* 119.
19. Coleridge, *BL* 1, 282–83.
20. Hardy, *Harmony and Mutual Implication,* 35.

Whilst Coleridge acknowledged that it was impossible to conclusively demonstrate the existence of a good, wise, loving, and personal God, there were amply reasons to deduce that such a relational God exists. It was possible, according to Coleridge, to truly know some aspects of the truth about God and creation, without necessarily being able to offer conclusive proof. Both the merest speck of sand and the vast expanse of the universe alike declared the glory of God. It was because of this passion that Coleridge was able to assert the mutuality of all things. Each aspect of human knowledge, as well as the whole of the created order, was united in one common origin. His methodology thus demanded that close attention be paid to the particulars whilst simultaneously keeping an eye on the universal.

Such a dual attentiveness was unusual in his day, at an age when there was a tendency for thinking to become fragmented and atomized. By way of example, one could cite the separate disciplines to which he had been exposed. The list includes empiricism (sense-derived knowledge), Cartesian rationality, the moral cognition epitomized by Hume, the history of truth (associated with Lessing) and the gulf between noumenal and phenomenal knowledge espoused by Kant. Coleridge stood out against this trend by asserting that whilst each sphere possessed its own individual legitimacy, there was a mutual implication[21] in all things, which was waiting to be unearthed. Writing in the publication *The Friend*, Coleridge explained that his intention was not to provide an encyclopedia of the current state of knowledge but rather to refer his readers to a way of thinking, a mode of perception, directing them to absolute principles, thereby being able to discover something great, one, and indivisible. Such an approach placed him at odds with Descartes and his successors, who, in Coleridge's opinion, constructed arbitrary divisions around areas of human knowledge. For Coleridge, however, life was indivisible, such that *natura naturans* and the human mind were both partakers of a greater whole.

By 1814 this grand scheme had become Coleridge's *Logosophia*, which was to be divided into five distinct treatises. The first was called *Logos propaideuticos*, a work devoted to the science of logic. The second was known as *Logos Architectonicus*, concerned with the construction of natural theology. The third treatise, *Logos Theanthropos*, dealt with the divine logos incarnate and was intended to offer a commentary on the Gospel of John. The fourth treatise, *Logos Agonistes*, was aimed at countering the pantheism of Spinoza, and the final treatise, *Logos Alogos*, was

---

21. Ibid., 33.

devoted to a discussion of Unitarianism. It is the fragments from these different treatises that are now collected together in the *Opus Maximum*. Suffice to say that this *Opus Maximum* was never published in his own day and it took a further 170 years before the fragments were collected together and edited in one volume. Despite this apparent failure, Coleridge did publish significant volumes within his own lifetime. Some of the most important of these include *Biographia Literaria* (1815), *The Statesman's Manual* (1816), *Lay Sermons* (1817), and *Aids to Reflection* (1831). Each of these provide a rich resource for unearthing Coleridge's developing views on the role of the imagination within his grander project of constructing a unified system of knowledge under an orthodox Trinitarian framework.

Before exploring the nature of Coleridge's developing views of the imagination, two final observations need to be made as a postscript to this introduction. Firstly, Romanticism has sometimes been perceived as being characterized by a certain seriousness. It is my contention that whilst Coleridge's philosophical writings are dense to the point of impenetrability, they are not, in fact, serious at all and possess an inherent playfulness. One may cite the famous phrase of Hölderlin "weder im Scherze noch im Ernste"[22] ("neither in jest nor in seriousness") to depict the work of Coleridge which posits an alternative voice to these two poles, deploying in his poetic works the slippery language of seeming. A short excerpt from his collected works may suffice to illustrate this point. In an early version of his poem *Frost at Midnight*, Coleridge writes,

> Haply hence,
> That still the living spirit in our frame,
> Which loves not to behold a lifeless thing,
> Transfuses into all things its own Will,
> And its own pleasures; sometimes with deep faith,
> And sometimes with a willful playfulness.[23]

Here Coleridge proposes that giving life to "lifeless things" can sometimes be done with "deep faith" and sometimes with "wilful playfulness." Both approaches are deemed equally valid. It is this notion of playfulness that will form the substance of the second section of this book.

Secondly, it would be foolish to divorce Coleridge's philosophical and theological musings from his personal circumstances. At the centre of Coleridge's personal life was a lifelong struggle with his own addictions,

---

22. Santner, *Hyperion and Selected Poems*, 46.
23. Coleridge, *PW*, 241.

his troubled relationships, and his own deeply felt sense of sin and guilt. He was acutely conscious of his own need for redemption. Out of this milieu flowed a life of prayer that represented for him a real and personal encounter with a relational God. Coleridge did not dismiss this as mere pietism bearing no relation to his philosophical and theological enquiries. On the contrary, he firmly asserted that prayer was an entirely legitimate source of true knowledge about the world in which we inhabit. As Claude Welch has put it, "for Coleridge (in contrast to Hegel), 'let us pray' represented a higher level of activity than 'let us think about God.'"[24] Or, to use Coleridge's own words, "an hour of solitude passed in sincere and earnest prayer . . . will teach us more of thought, will awaken the faculty and form the habit of reflection than a year's study in the Schools without them."[25]

Such sentiments can be found expressed not only in his philosophical writings but also in his poetry. Here is an excerpt from the *Rime of the Ancient Mariner*.

> Farewell, farewell! but this I tell
> To thee, thou Wedding Guest!
> He prayeth well, who loveth well
> Both man and bird and beast
>
> He prayeth best, who loveth best
> All things both great and small;
> For the dear God who loveth us
> He made and loveth all.[26]

Coleridge here expresses the view that prayer and love are inextricably linked. The more one possesses the capacity to love, the more one is able to pray. And this love is intended not simply for fellow human beings, but all of nature, both man, bird and beast, all things both great and small. In other words, there is no essential difference between loving one's neighbor and loving all that God has made, for in all things there is a mutual origin found in the love and goodness of God and therefore, by implication, an intrinsic unity. All things are mutually implicated and this very interconnectedness can best be perceived and apprehended through prayer. We are most attuned both to the complexity and implicit simplicity of the world when we are most attentive to the creative love of the God who made all things. All things cohere together, but they only do so in God. Without doubt such comments betray a confidence in

---

24. Welch, *Samuel Taylor Coleridge*, 5.
25. Coleridge, *AR* 1, 120.
26. Coleridge, *PW* 1/1, 419 (lines 610–17).

both the accessibility of God by humankind and the nature of knowledge that can be derived from such divine encounters. This confidence placed him at a radical disjuncture with both his neo-platonic teachers and his contemporary thinkers. It is to these that we must now turn.

CHAPTER 2

The Formative Influences on Coleridge's Views Concerning the Imagination

GIVEN THAT COLERIDGE STANDS four square in the stream of English romanticism, it is now time to turn our attention more fully to the man himself. A poem that is of critical importance in understanding the development of Coleridge's theory of the imagination is the "Aeolian Harp" written in 1795. Here is an extract.

> O! the one Life within us and abroad,
> Which meets all motion and becomes its soul,
> A light in sound, a sound-like power in light,
> Rhythm in all thought, and joyance every where—
> Methinks, it should have been impossible
> Not to love all things in a world so fill'd;
> Where the breeze warbles, and the mute still air
> Is Music slumbering on her instrument.
> And thus, my Love! as on the midway slope
> Of yonder hill I stretch my limbs at noon,
> Whilst thro' my half-clos'd eye-lids I behold
> The sunbeams dance, like diamonds, on the main,
> And tranquil muse upon tranquility;
> Full many a thought uncall'd and undetain'd,
> And many idle flitting phantasies,
> Traverse my indolent and passive brain,
> As wild and various, as the random gales
> That swell and flutter on this subject Lute!
> And what if all of animated nature
> Be but organic Harps diversly fram'd,

That tremble into thought, as o'er them sweeps
Plastic and vast, one intellectual breeze,
At once the Soul of each, and God of all?[1]

The Aeolian Harp is a musical instrument that is "played" by the wind rather than by human intervention. As such it is a passive instrument entirely dependent on the wind to give it life. Due to Coleridge's affinity with nature, it is easy to see how the Aeolian harp could capture his imagination. Both music and nature possess a mystical, timeless quality which Coleridge knew could not adequately be captured in rational ways. Coleridge drew on the metaphor of this harp to articulate his view that the divine *pneuma* breathes through all of creation giving it vitality. Witness his exultant declaration in the opening lines of the quoted section; "O! The one Life within us and abroad, which meets all motion and becomes its soul." The apparently passive instrument was in reality fully alive with the very breath of God. Likewise the poet, the artist, and those who deal in the aesthetic are likewise in touch with the life-giving wind of the Spirit of God. This infusion of the divine is not restricted however solely to the province of artists. The whole of creation throbs with the very life of God, provided one develops the capacity to perceive it. From where did Coleridge develop such views? What is the genealogy of his concept of the perceptive imagination?

Coleridge was a voracious reader and it was this very openness of character that brought him into contact with a wide and eclectic range of formative influences that served to shape his world. His views on the imagination dominate his thinking over several decades and it is possible to track the developments that occur as he matures. When pondering issues of aesthetics, language, and symbolism, Coleridge engages with Addison, Burke, Kant, and Schiller. His work on the imagination is influenced by Leibnitz, Akenside, Fichte, and Schelling. His early years were dominated by works by Gerard, Tetens, and Hartley and at times he owes a debt to Hobbes, Johnson, and Hume.[2] When considering the nature of sympathy he reveals influences from Shakespeare, Boehme, Blake, and Shelley and in the theological realm he had clearly immersed himself in the patristic writers, Augustine, and the Puritan divines. His views change and evolve over time, so it is with some degree of provisionality that any assertions can be made about the guiding influences and underlying themes in his thinking.

1. Coleridge, *PW*, 100.
2. Engell, *The Creative Imagination*, 328.

Notwithstanding the panoply of sources from which Coleridge derived his inspiration, it is possible to identify four distinct streams which fed his development. Our starting point shall be his friendship with William Wordsworth. Although this may seem a strange place to begin when attempting to understand someone so deeply rooted in the abstractions of Greek philosophy and German idealism, it provides us with an insight into the way in which Coleridge thought, which is as important as what he thought. Coleridge's reflections often began with *experience* and it was from experience that he extrapolated his theories. When Coleridge read the poetry of his Lakeland friend he observed within him a response being evoked that was at once both deeply unnerving and profoundly energizing. Wordsworth's poetry drew him into another world and in that world he was put in contact with the mystery of awe. It proved to be of pivotal significance in the development of his thinking. His emotional engagement with this new poetry spurred him to re-examine the philosophical basis of such profoundly moving literature.

The second influential stream is represented here by the Neo-Platonist, Plotinus. Despite that fact that in his major work, *Biographia Literaria*, he adamantly defends himself against charges of being overly influenced by Platonic metaphysics, Coleridge's debt to Neo-Platonism is unquestioned. We shall sketch the contours of that influence. The third stream, which characterized his early years, was marked by a fascination with the mechanical philosophy of Hartley, known as associationism; to such an extent that his first son was named after the eighteenth century thinker. The fourth and final stream concerns Coleridge's engagement with German philosophy. Towards the end of the eighteenth century, Coleridge was drawn inexorably towards the emerging transcendental thinking coming out of Germany, spending time in the country and learning the language. These four streams, whilst not pretending to be the only sources, were amongst the most influential upon Coleridge's intellectual development. Without prior consideration of all four, it will not be possible to assess the validity and scope of his theory of the imagination. Only after having done this, will we be in a position to examine how his theory can usefully be deployed to enhance our understanding of the ontology of God.

William Wordsworth (1770–1850)

Coleridge met William Wordsworth for the first time in 1795 and the two of them became friends immediately, although their friendship had begun to cool by 1810. For a time they lived in close proximity to each other in

Somerset and in 1798 Coleridge and Wordsworth published a joint volume of poetry, *Lyrical Ballads*, which proved to be the catalyst for English romanticism. Coleridge experienced an epiphanic moment when encountering the genius of Wordsworth. Wordsworth's poetry elicited within Coleridge an emotional response that simply could not be explained using Hartley's associationist schema. Wordsworth touched on something of the sublime—even the divine—which Coleridge was quick to recognize. It is worth pausing here to savor the nature of Wordsworth's poetry. The first extract is taken from Wordsworth's poem *Ode to Immortality*.[3]

> Ye blessed Creatures, I have heard the call
> Ye to each other make; I see
> The heavens laugh with you in your jubilee;
> My heart is at your festival,
> My head hath its coronal,
> The fullness of your bliss, I feel—I feel it all.
> Oh evil day! if I were sullen
> While Earth herself is adorning,
> This sweet May-morning,
> And the Children are culling
> On every side,
> In a thousand valleys far and wide,
> Fresh flowers; while the sun shines warm,
> And the Babe leaps up on his Mother's arm:
> I hear, I hear, with joy I hear!
> —But there's a Tree, of many, one,
> A single Field which I have looked upon,
> Both of them speak of something that is gone:
> The Pansy at my feet
> Doth the same tale repeat:
> Whither is fled the visionary gleam?
> Where is it now, the glory and the dream?

In this poem Wordsworth reflects on lost childhood innocence, of a time when he was able to wonder at the beauty of nature and experience a metaphysical presence imbued in all that he saw. That sense of the divine had become dimmed with advancing years, yet the search for significance, so typical of Wordsworth, remained undiminished for it was only significance that lightens, "the heavy and weary weight of this unintelligible world."[4] Such poems evoked the imagination so powerfully in Coleridge that he was compelled to revise completely his earlier em-

---

3. Wordsworth, *The Poetical Works of William Wordsworth*, 354
4. Wordsworth, *Selected Poetry*, 99–103.

piricist philosophy. In chapter 4 of *Biographia Literaria*, Coleridge waxes eloquently over the genius of Wordsworth, praising his ability to evoke a mood, an atmosphere, which echoed the depths and heights of an ideal world. Wordsworth was capable of contemplating the "Ancient of Days" in all his works with a freshness of feeling that was deeply compelling. In his *Biographia*, Coleridge acknowledged his debt to Wordsworth when he wrote, "it was the balance of deep feeling with profound thought; the fine balance of truth in observing with the imaginative faculty in modifying the objects observed; and above all the original gift of spreading the tone, the atmosphere, and with it the depth and height of the ideal world around forms, incidents and situations, of which, for the common view, custom had be-dimmed all the lustre, had dried up the sparkle and the dew drops."[5]

In the period from 1795 to 1800 Wordsworth crossed a significant threshold in the style and manner of his poetic output. Robert Barth refers to this shift as the move from the "poetry of reference" to the "poetry of encounter."[6] This sense of poetry as encounter rather than something which was merely referential, signified a seismic shift in the way in which poetry had hitherto been enjoyed. Barth illustrates this in his book *The Symbolic Imagination*, where he demonstrates the shift by examining two different poems. One, *Lines left on a seat in a Yew tree*, was written in 1795 and is representative of the earlier style; the other, *A night piece*, was written a mere three years later and illustrates the "new" poetry of encounter. Here is an extract from the 1795 poem.

> Nay, Traveller! rest. This lonely Yew-tree stands
> Far from all human dwelling: what if here
> No sparkling rivulet spread the verdant herb?
> What if the bee love not these barren boughs?
> Yet, if the wind breathe soft, the curling waves,
> That break against the shore, shall lull thy mind
> By one soft impulse saved from vacancy.
> —Who he was
> That piled these stones and with the mossy sod
> First covered, and here taught this aged Tree
> With its dark arms to form a circling bower,
> I well remember—He was one who owned
> No common soul. In youth by science nursed,
> And led by nature into a wild scene
> Of lofty hopes, he to the world went forth

---

5. Coleridge, *BL*/I, 80.
6. Barth, *The Symbolic Imagination*, 96.

> A favoured Being, knowing no desire
> Which genius did not hallow; 'gainst the taint
> Of dissolute tongues, and jealousy, and hate,
> And scorn, against all enemies prepared,
> All but neglect.[7]

Here the poet is contemplating a beautiful yet melancholic scene where the central figure is the passing stranger. The opening phrase bids the reader to observe the rural idyll by pausing to rest. In so doing one is able to enjoy the lonely yew tree, the sparkling rivulet, the barren boughs and the soft breath of the wind. The poet remains detached from the poem pointing towards another person, or to a place in space and time. We, the readers of the poem, are merely observers of the unfolding description. We are not invited to be involved. The reader is not expected to resonate with the poem emotionally, but merely to look and learn from a discreet distance. All that is required is that the reader can observe the picturesque scene.

By 1798, Wordsworth's poetry had moved on apace. It is as if a decisive turn had been made and a far more engaged, emotionally intense form of poetry had emerged. The following lines from "A Night Piece" illustrate this.

> The sky is overcast
> With a continuous cloud of texture close,
> Heavy and wan, all whitened by the Moon,
> Which through that veil is indistinctly seen,
> A dull, contracted circle, yielding light
> So feebly spread, that not a shadow falls,
> Chequering the ground from rock, plant, tree, or tower.
> At length a pleasant instantaneous gleam
> Startles the pensive traveller while he treads
> His lonesome path, with unobserving eye
> Bent earthwards; he looks up—the clouds are split
> Asunder—and above his head he sees
> The clear Moon, and the glory of the heavens.
> There, in a black-blue vault she sails along,
> Followed by multitudes of stars, that, small
> And sharp, and bright, along the dark abyss
> Drive as she drives: how fast they wheel away,
> Yet vanish not!—the wind is in the tree,
> But they are silent—still they roll along
> Immeasurably distant; and the vault,

---

7. Wordsworth, *Selected Poetry*, 54–56.

> Built round by those white clouds, enormous clouds,
> Still deepens its unfathomable depth.
> At length the Vision closes; and the mind,
> Not undisturbed by the delight it feels,
> Which slowly settles into peaceful calm,
> Is left to muse upon the solemn scene.

There is a distinct shift of style between these two poems. In *The Night Piece*, Wordsworth plays with the relationships between light and dark, earth and heaven. At first sight this poem is simply about the sky, shrouded in cloud, with a rather feeble muted moonlight. The dominant movement in the poem is that of the sluggish clouds. Initially they are of "texture close," and later they "split asunder." Gradually the traveler is introduced and we, the readers, begin to accompany him. We have already started to enter the poem for ourselves and cease to be mere observers. Yet the poem is not simply about a journey through the night, it hints at another type of journey altogether, an inner one, where the mind discovers a "peaceful calm" and is "not undisturbed by the delight it feels." Here is the strength of this new style of poetry. Wordsworth enables his readers to encounter something of mystery through their own indwelling of the poems for themselves. This quintessentially romantic emphasis on mystery points to the belief that there is far more to human knowing than can be accounted for through empiricism. If mystery is such a vital, intriguing and powerfully magnetic force, then it is only through linguistic symbols that one can enter into it. This is what Robert Barth describes as the shift from the Poetry of Reference to the Poetry of Encounter. It heralded the beginnings of the Romantic Movement. For Coleridge such poetry encapsulated the essence of his project. It enabled the reader, via the imagination, to encounter the divine within and through the finite, thus realizing the true oneness of the universe.

Coleridge resonated with Wordsworth's longing to find significance. When John Stuart Mill, the great Victorian philosopher, compared the philosophical approaches of Bentham with Coleridge, he made the astute observation that for Bentham the key question to be addressed was always "is it true"? For Coleridge the inquiry was always "what does this mean"? The first of these questions was representative of a religious rationalism, epitomized perhaps most noticeably by the works of Paley, from whom Coleridge strenuously sought to distance himself. The latter question, concerned with meaning and significance, carried with it, however, the attendant danger of a lapse into individual subjectivity. Whilst Coleridge was passionate about discovering significance, he was at the same time concerned to place the search for ultimate meaning within an accountable, rational framework, one that could not be accused of subjectivism.

By the turn of the century Coleridge had overthrown his earlier mechanical views of the imagination. He was searching for a faculty capable of actively producing a oneness out of the many, something that was able to diffuse a tone and spirit of unity. Instead of the human mind being regarded as a mere passive and aggregative faculty, Coleridge sought for a far more active and assimilating role for the mind, something that was able not to simply to weld together, but to fuse into one. For fusion to be achieved, Coleridge needed a more synthetic and magical power which the empiricists could not provide. The imagination for Coleridge was thus the key, crucial, vital, human capacity for experiencing the beauty and sublimity of the world and by its very constitution mirrored something of the divine. Ironically, Wordsworth himself remained wedded to associationism and outlined his position in the preface to *Lyrical Ballads*. Defending his poetry on theoretical grounds was never something that Wordsworth had any real taste for. He said of himself that "he never cared a straw for theory and the preface was written at the request of Mr. Coleridge out of sheer good nature."[8] By this stage Coleridge was firmly convinced that the empiricist position was profoundly inadequate to explain the sublimeness of Wordsworth's poetry. In the autumn of 1802 Coleridge set out his views on the imagination and in particular his distinction between imagination and fancy in a letter to his friend Southey. It was Wordsworth's poetry not his philosophy that had persuaded him to change direction. For Coleridge, Wordsworth was "the only man who has effected a compleat and constant synthesis of thought and feeling and combined them with poetic forms, with the music of pleasurable passion and with the imagination, or the modifying power, in that highest sense of the word in which I have ventured to oppose it to Fancy or the aggregating power."[9]

Wordsworth himself had articulated his own understanding of the imagination in his poem *The Prelude*.

> This spiritual love acts not, nor can exist
> Without imagination, which in truth
> Is but another name for absolute power
> And clearest insight, amplitude of mind
> And reason in her most exalted mood.[10]

---

8. Barth, *The Symbolic Imagination*, 65.
9. Coleridge, *CL* II, 1034.
10. Wordsworth, *Selected Poetry*, 168ff.

And yet despite this paean of praise ascribed to the imagination as reason "in her most exalted mood," for Coleridge, this was insufficient. In the original preface to the first edition of *Biographia*, Coleridge is at pains to point out that whilst he considered that his friend Wordsworth had "provided a master sketch of imaginations' branches and fruit," he wished to add the trunk and the roots too.[11] He was convinced that Wordsworth had failed to recognize the productive, creative power of the imagination, relegating it, in effect, to the realm of "fancy." This may have been the result of Wordsworth's insistence that poetry should be written in the language of the common man or woman thereby eschewing loftier forms of expression. Wordsworth remained wedded to Enlightenment semiotics which sought to reduce signs, especially linguistic ones, to pure functionality. It was because of this, that Wordsworth did not see any essential difference between poetry and prose from a linguistic point of view. It is at this point that Coleridge diverged from his great friend. Coleridge perceived that part of the genius of Wordsworth's poetic revolution lay not only in his diction but also in his subject matter.[12]

An example of the revolutionary nature of Wordsworth's subject matter can be drawn from his early life. As a young man of barely fourteen years of age, he noticed the beauty of a tree's bare branches against the evening sky and at that precise moment wanted to be the very first poet to celebrate its beauty. By early the following morning he had penned these verses,

> I made no vows, but vows were then made for me:
> Bond unknown to me was given, that I should be
> —else sinning greatly
> A dedicated spirit.[13]

What Wordsworth had noticed about himself was that he experienced "spots of time" where there appeared to be a sudden breaking in some greater reality, when time seemed to stand still and the world felt unified and strangely sacred. When Wordsworth contemplated the tree, he saw the oneness of life which filled him with inexpressible joy.

One significant feature of Coleridge's engagement with Wordsworth's poetry was his close attention to the affective responses that it elicited within him. Coleridge writes that, after reading Mr. Wordsworth's writings, "I no sooner felt, than I sought to understand."[14] This order of

11. Coleridge *BL* 1, 82–88.
12. Halmi, *The Genealogy of Romantic Symbol*, 60.
13. Plotkin, *Nature and the Human Soul*, 306.
14. Coleridge, *BL* I, 82.

events is highly significant. For Coleridge, experience was often prior to reflection and it was this attentiveness to his emotional responses that provoked a subsequent search for intellectual clarification. Coleridge believed that the emotions were the key that unlocked the secrets of God's created order. Only once these secrets were unlocked could they be scrutinized by Reason and the Understanding. As Coleridge ruminated on his moods whilst reading this new poetry, he arrived at a place of clarity with regard to the difference between "Fancy" and "The Imagination." He concluded that they were two distinct and widely different faculties rather than as had commonly been supposed synonyms for the same thing but to a greater or lesser degree. It was the imagination alone that was capable of reaching towards the desired Romantic goal of discovering the inherent unity of all things. Such an obsession for unification in human knowledge points perhaps to Coleridge's latent fascination with Neo-Platonism. It is to this influential source that we must now direct our attention.

Plotinus (204–270)

At first glance Platonic metaphysics seems to be an unlikely bedfellow for someone of the ilk of Coleridge who placed the imagination at the core of his philosophical theology. As a schoolboy, however, Coleridge had been drawn to Plato and his successor Plotinus, sensing perhaps in these ancient writers a source for some kind of spiritual illumination. In particular, Coleridge was profoundly influenced by Plotinus' seminal work, *The Enneads*. In chapter 9 of his *Biographia Literaria*, Coleridge acknowledges this debt as he writes, "the early study of Plotinus . . . contributed to prepare my mind for the reception and welcoming of the Cogito quia sum, et sum quia Cogito, a philosophy of hardihood, but certainly the most ancient and therefore the most natural."[15]

This admission compels us to ask in what way Plotinus had prepared the ground for Coleridge's understanding of what constitutes the essence of human existence. A cursory reading of Plato, however, reveals that he was scathing in his condemnation of the imagination, suspicious of its mimetic function and placed it at the lowest rank among the intellectual faculties of the soul. This was due, no doubt, to his positioning of the knowing faculty of reason (*nous*) in opposition to imitative faculty of *phantasia*. In Plato's *Republic* the image is likened to a mirror, capable only of reflection and imitation. Plato separated the original forms of Being

---

15. Ibid., 144–46.

from the changeable forms of Becoming. Being belongs to the realm of Ideas which are immutable, separate, and timeless. The only access to Ideas is through Reason and the imagination was thus duly relegated to a merely mimetic, representational role. This wariness of the imagination was due to the perception that it tends to lead astray, away from the secure and the rational. The Platonic suspicion of the imagination stemmed from the fear that it gave humanity the ability to erect images of the gods, such that mere mortals could attempt to rival the divine demiurge. Plotinus, following in the footsteps of Plato, held the imagination to be similarly devoid of real potentiality. "We cannot apprehend intelligible entities," writes Plotinus, "with the imagination (*phantasia*) but only with the faculty of contemplation (*noesis*)."[16]

Given these views, one might question why Plotinus exerted such an influence on Coleridge's intellectual development. If the Neo-Platonic estimation of the imagination was that it was a low level faculty and indeed one that must be regarded with some degree of suspicion, then there must be other strands of Plotinian thinking which resonated with the impressionable young Coleridge. One must exercise a degree of caution, however, in asserting too forcefully that Neo-Platonic philosophy adamantly rejected the imagination, for it is necessary to clarify how the term was used. For Plato and Plotinus, the imagination was associated with *phantasia*, which is closer in meaning to the German *Vorstellung*, giving it a primarily representative function. The *phantasia* was closely allied to memory, the capacity to represent before our eyes an object or event that is no longer present. Defined in this way, *phantasia* could do no more than record events and bring them to the fore when required. It was perceived therefore in purely mimetic terms.

The Neo-Platonists were not opposed, however, to philosophical intuition which is much closer to Coleridge's own understanding of what constitutes the imagination. Plotinus warned that if normal human perception was solely governed by the corporeal eye, rather than the intellectual eye,[17] then one was not able to truly pierce through the outer material shell and see the splendid original within. It was this aesthetic aspect of perception, the exaltation of beauty—epitomized by some strands of Neo-Platonic thought—that found resonance with Coleridge. Whilst Plotinus does not use the term "imagination" to describe this way of seeing, it is clear that Coleridge concurred with the sentiments expressed. When, for

---

16. Plotinus, *The Ennead*, 5,5.
17. Beer, *Coleridge's Poetic Intelligence*, 29.

example, Coleridge later refers to the "despotism of the eye,"[18] he is echoing a profoundly Plotinian concept. Indeed In his *Biographia Literaria*, Coleridge extols the virtues of "philosophic imagination, the sacred power of self-intuition"[19] drawing directly and explicitly, as a source of inspiration, from Plotinus. It is my view therefore, that it was not Plotinus' view of the imagination *(phantasie)* to which Coleridge was drawn, but to the broader Neo-Platonic trajectory of which Plotinus was a chief exponent. It was within this world that Coleridge sought to explicate a more robust role for the productive imagination. It is possible, I believe, to identify a number of Plotinian emphases, which will emerge repeatedly in the subsequent writings of Coleridge.

In first place there is the Plotinian emphasis on the creative role of the artist. Whilst Plotinus is considered to be the founder of Neo-Platonism, he diverged from Plato in defending the role of the artist, aligning himself in this respect with Aristotle. Plotinus believed that since artists possessed the capacity for beauty, they compensated for what was lacking in things. Art thus becomes a conduit through which philosophical knowledge may be acquired. In *The Enneads*, Plotinus states that the poet or sculptor does far more than reproduce nature but actively engages in shaping the material at hand according to an idea conceived in the mind. It is the imagination of the artist that is brought to bear on the raw, unformed resources that are available. Hear the words of Plotinus himself: "Now it must be seen that the stone thus brought under the artist's hand to the beauty of form is beautiful not as stone—for so the crude block would be as pleasant but in virtue of the form or idea introduced by the art. This form is not in the material; it is in the designer before ever it enters the stone; and the artificer holds it not by his equipment of eyes and hands but by his participation in his art."[20]

Plotinus held a theory of perception that proposed a selectivity of interest on the part of the subject. The one perceiving does not merely soak up sense impressions like a sponge but actively chooses to select those senses that are of interest. The mind is creative, therefore, even at the point of perception and not simply at the point of creation. For Plotinus there is in nature an immanence of the One, which interacts with the creative perception of the subject. There is thus a transcendental interchange between the subject and object. As Baker has observed, "the artist literally

---

18. Coleridge, *BL* I, 107.
19. Ibid., 241.
20. Plotinus, *The Ennead*, 5. 8. 1.

creates and makes malleable matter comply with divine ideas."[21] There are clear echoes of this approach to the creative role of the artist much later in the work of Michelangelo. After having completed his masterly sculpture of the crucified Christ being held by Mary, now installed in St. Peter's Basilica in Rome, Michelangelo is known to have stated that he "saw" the Madonna and Christ in the untouched block of stone and his task as an artist was merely to release the two "imprisoned" figures. His statement would have made Plotinus proud.

Secondly, the place of contemplation was central to the thinking of Plotinus. Within his system contemplation is raised to the status of a productive, constitutive principle and it is through contemplation that everything is united as a single, all-pervasive reality. This distinctly Platonic emphasis on the value of the contemplative consciousness, as distinct from pure rationalization, was the key that enabled the soul to ascend upwards out of "*The Cave*"[22] towards the Good. Whilst Plotinus did not eschew rationality, he placed it within the care of contemplation to shape and give form to the materials furnished from experience. One of the pivotal tenets of Neo-Platonism was the striving of the soul to make its journey from below upwards towards God. This journey is made from the visible world through images that are the window through which one passes in the direction of the invisible. For the Neo-Platonist, the material world is an intermediary state with nature being merely the expression of a "thickening" of the spiritual. Matter is likened to a solidifying of the spirit, much as ice is the solid form of water. Materialism is thus a derivative, a subset, of the spiritual. It belongs both to the spiritual world and is, paradoxically, its opposite. There is, therefore, an intrinsic unity within the cosmos with each particular belonging to and mirroring the far greater One. As Hedley puts it, "nature is a harmonious unity because it is an image or expression of the divine mind."[23] The soul's rise towards the divine is carried on the wings of the imagination as this citation from *The Ennead* illustrates.

> Bring this vision actually before your sight, so that there shall be in your mind the gleaming representation of a sphere, a picture holding sprung, themselves, of that universe and repose or some at rest, some in motion. Keep this sphere before you, and from it imagine another, a sphere stripped of magnitude and of spatial differences; cast out your inborn sense of matter, taking care not merely to attenuate it: Call on God, maker of the sphere whose

21. Baker, *The Sacred River*, 76.
22. Plato, *The Republic*, 227–30.
23. Hedley, *Living Forms of the Imagination*, 22.

image you now hold, and pray him to enter. And may he come bringing his own universe with all the gods that dwell in it—he who is the one god and all the gods, where each is all, blending into a unity, distinct in powers but all one god in virtue of that one divine power of many facets.[24]

Here Plotinus contemplates the omnipresence of the One through an invocation, conceived in the mind, of a sphere, which is subsequently stripped of its spatial and temporal qualities. This negative theology facilitates communion with the divine. Because the Neo-Platonic legacy bequeathed an emphasis on interiority, rather than simply the observation of nature, imaginative contemplation was always given a major part to play in the search for the One. The non-spatial, omnipresent One that is being sought is the centerpiece of the thinking of Plotinus. This form of contemplation undertaken by the soul is only made possible because the soul itself is godlike, partaking in the very essence of the divine. It is an intuitive ability within the human mind. All one can justifiably assert, however, about the true nature of God, according to Neo-Platonic thinking, is that God is who he is; he is unique and incapable of any further comparison.

The philosophic system that Coleridge attempted to construct was based on a transcendental—as distinct from a transcendent—consciousness. He defined transcendentalism as the capacity to arrive at true knowledge by an intuitive process which, bounded by the limits of reason and the understanding, was able to discern beneath surface appearances. Against this Coleridge was scathing of those philosophic approaches, epitomized by the materialists, which concentrated merely on reflection and representation. Likewise he abhorred those transcendentists who "abandoned distinct consciousness" by indulging in fights of lawless speculation.[25] Neither the pole of mechanical representation nor the opposite pole of uncontrolled fantasy could be trusted to deliver true insight. Instead Coleridge espoused a philosophic consciousness which bears the imprint of Plotinian thinking. He articulates his position in his *Biographia Literaria*, where he describes those who admire the beauty of the stars, the rolling hills and valleys, but who may never venture beyond these mere appearances. There are few, he claims, who have learned that the sources of such wonders are "far higher and more inward."[26] This is clearly an al-

---

24. Plotinus, *The Ennead*, V. 8.9.1–2.
25. Coleridge, *BL* I, 237.
26. Ibid., 239.

lusion to the divine immanence, perceptible within nature, which is not open to dissection and scientific reductionism. To bolster his argument Coleridge quotes approvingly from *The Enneads*, in which Plotinus writes about intuitive knowledge stating that, "we ought not to pursue it with a view of detecting its secret source, but to watch in quiet till it suddenly shines upon us; preparing ourselves for the blessed spectacle as the eye waits patiently for the rising sun."[27]

The kind of philosophic imagination championed by Plotinus found a deep resonance in Coleridge. He called this kind of intuition "sacred"[28] and it formed the basis of his subsequent views on the role of symbol. Coleridge articulates his description of the power of this intuitive faculty with graphic illustrations drawn from his observations of the natural world. Those who can intuit in this way can already see the wings of the air-sylph forming within the skin of the caterpillar. They both know and feel that whilst *actual* forces are at work, *potential* forces are just as real and active yet lie hidden from sight. In this respect Coleridge links the role of the imagination—or, to use more Plotinian language, the philosophic consciousness—to potentiality, to the world of possibilities.

The third major structural influence that Plotinus exerted over Coleridge concerns the resolution of the apparent dissonance between unity and particularity. Coleridge liked to quote the line from Plotinus, "never could the eye have beheld the sun, had not its own essence been soliform."[29] The human eye (the Many) is only capable of seeing the sun and appreciating its power and beauty, because its essence is sun-like (the One). It was this unifying of the One and the Many, central to the thinking of Plotinus, that would emerge repeatedly in the subsequent thinking of Coleridge. The principle of distinction-in-unity and unity-in-distinction, which he so admired in Plotinus's work, carried a resonance, as Coleridge perceived it, with some themes in John's Gospel. In the mid-1790s, Coleridge described himself as a Trinitarian in philosophy yet a Unitarian in religion. This philosophical Trinitarianism can be seen as having its origin in the Plotinian unification emphasis on the One and the Many. Plotinian thinking is characterized by two fundamental triads. The first of these is the Trinity of Divine principles, namely the Absolute, the Spirit and the Soul. The other tripartite division refers to human constitution of Spirit, Soul, and Body. Such a triadic schema was typical of much Greek

---

27. Plotinus, *The Ennead*, 3.8.4.
28. Coleridge, *BL* 1, 241.
29. Ibid., 115.

thought and not confined to Plotinus.³⁰ The spiritual boundary lines were however not rigid and fixed but dynamic and fluid. The bodily perception of the senses, also known as discursive thought, was considered by Plotinus to be the lower faculty and not truly in touch with reality. It was only the higher spiritual perception or intuitive knowledge (gnosis) that was capable of perceiving the world as it really is.

Plotinus insisted that whilst the relationship between the human spirit and the spiritual world were distinct, there is a participation of the two within each other. The spiritual world was not a mere expression of the human mind, a self-externalization of what has been internally constructed; rather it possessed an intrinsic, external, separate, existence. Yet the spirit and the spiritual world also possessed a unity within a duality, an interpenetration of one another. Here we witness that the origins of Coleridge's philosophic Trinitarianism lie in his immersion in Greek, and more specifically Plotinian, thinking. The Neo-Platonic struggle to articulate the relationship between change and permanence, between the universal and the particular and, most significantly of all, how unity can be found within diversity, represented the very issues which Coleridge perceived to be essential in his quest to construct a unified system of knowledge.

Inge compares the worldview of Plotinus to an eternal systolic and diastolic heartbeat pulsing from a divine source, going out into the world and subsequently returning to its origin.³¹ This Plotinian conception paints a picture of the world in which all things were united by a common originating source. Coleridge, clearly building upon such a foundation, was one of the first British theologians to assert that all of creation shared in the gift of life given by God. It is because of the giftedness of all things that one can claim that the highest form of endeavor is to strive to return to the divine spring from whence all things emerge. Coleridge later adopted this imagery of eternally circular motion to depict the true nature of the poet's craft. The artist, according to Coleridge, is capable of "converting a series into a whole, to see and create the great cycle, the circular motion of the world, which to our short sight appears as a straight line."³²

30. Triadic schemas are typical of Neo-Platonism and clearly exerted a strong influence on the way in which Coleridge thought. One example of this comes from an early notebook entry (circa 1795–1800) in which Coleridge divided human existence into three neat categories. In lowest place was Brute Life, in which mankind simply pursues sensual pleasures. The next step upwards is Human Life, marked by the pursuit of studies for our intellectual faculties. The highest stage is Divine Life whereby we become deiform by obedience to the divine command. (*CN* 1 256) This is clearly an adaptation of Plotinus's schema concerning the three planes on which a person may choose to live (*Enneads* 564–65).
31. Inge, *The Philosophy of Plotinus*, 104–63.
32. Vlasopolos, *The Symbolic Method of Coleridge*, 169.

Fourthly, Coleridge was profoundly influenced by the Plotinian notion of an Idea. In his work entitled *The Statesman's Manual* (1816), Coleridge toys with the philosophical conundrum concerning the nature of an Idea. For Coleridge, Ideas are found within the realm of reason and refer to abstract metaphysical notions such as freedom, love, and the divine—those things which are the product of the imagination actuated by pure reason without correspondence to the world of the senses. Whilst Coleridge often used the word "reason," he was keen to distance himself from definitions of the term which understood it simply as a rational human capability. In the *Opus Maximum*, Coleridge is at pains to make this distinction: "There is one point on which we are particularly anxious to prevent any misunderstanding. This respects the difference between two (possible) assertions, 'such as a truth may be known as truth by the light of reason' and 'the same truth was discovered or might have been discovered, by men by means of their reason exclusively.' We may assert the former, and in the course of this work shall find occasion to assert it without involving, nay, we altogether disbelieve and deny the latter."[33]

What Coleridge means by making such a strong statement is that human reason is a derivative of divine reason; it is the repetition of the infinite in the finite and thus is a form of divine revelation. This line of argumentation is derived from Coleridge's view that divine revelation, whilst being contained in Scripture, is not confined to Scripture. Indeed the light of God is shed on all of humanity regardless of creed, echoing the Johannine prologue that the light that shines on all is coming into the world. This logosophic construction runs throughout Coleridgean thinking and illustrates his view that there is a deep interconnectedness between Plotinian and New Testament conceptions of the Logos. If reason is God's gift to humanity and is the place where ideas are located, the key question that needs to be addressed is their status. Are they regulative in the Aristotelian and Kantian sense in that they shape and form sensory data and find their origin in human consciousness; or are they constitutive in the Plotinian sense in that they are one with the transcendent power which is intrinsic to creation?[34] Coleridge clearly favored the latter option, believing that Ideas were both constitutive and creative. This is a major theme in Coleridge's thinking to which we will later return.

Coleridge bears many hallmarks of Neo-Platonism throughout his writings. Indeed Perkins maintains that the Logosophic principle, so pervasive in Neo-Platonic thinking, runs like a red thread through the centre

---

33. Coleridge, *OM*, 12.
34. Coleridge, *SM*, 114.

of his thought.[35] Coleridge was a speculative metaphysical theologian, whose passion was the rehabilitation of reason as divine light, in sharp contrast to some strands of Enlightenment thought in which reason stood alone, apart from any divine initiative. This is the key determinant in the Logos doctrine, to establish the veracity of the Logos as the Creator, the Word, the Redeemer. Yet, whilst it is possible to identify the imprint of Plotinus in the thinking of Coleridge, he strongly diverged from him on one key point. Plotinus was known to espouse an emanationist theory of creation. By this he likened the emanations from the One to the rays of the Sun which constantly emit light and heat without any diminution of its potency. Plotinus' emanationism followed a graduated order. The first emanation was the *nous* or the Logos, the divine mind. In second place came the world soul followed by the human soul. In last and lowest place came the created material world, the least perfected of all the emanations. The material world of creation for Plotinus is merely the outflow, the emanation of the One. There is thus no intentional causality regarding any emanation and no distinct intrinsic integrity to creation itself. Coleridge was deeply suspicious of this strand of Plotinian thought. For Coleridge, creation itself is the product of an agency, an act of the divine will and not an impersonal emanation. The schema proposed by Plotinus offered no concept of intention or choice and for Coleridge this was utterly unacceptable. In particular, such a view could not address the pressing question concerning the nature of evil. How can the existence of evil be accounted for within a paradigm that contains no adequate concept of will? The failure of the Plotinian system for Coleridge was a thus failure of recognition of the reality of evil. The notion that everything proceeded by a mysterious, impersonal emanation from the One was, for Coleridge, simply inadequate.

Hartley (1705–57)

For a short time around the period 1793–97, Coleridge dallied with the influential eighteenth-century philosophy of David Hartley. By the end of the eighteenth century his utilitarian, mechanistic theory of the doctrine of associations had become the accepted British philosophy. This theory propounded the view that the brain received vibrations, the nature of which were determined by each person's experience and by the circumstances of the moment. These vibrations or sensations become associated together with others and the ideas corresponding to the sensations form

35. Perkins, *Coleridge's Philosophy*, 3.

what appear to be new ideas. Coleridge likened his views to a game of billiards.³⁶ When one ball is struck it moves across the billiard table bumping into other balls causing them to move. The human mind, according to Hartley, functions in the same manner, continually receiving sense impressions which collide with others in a somewhat random and haphazard way. Hartley, along with other empirical philosophers like Hobbes, Locke, and Hume, represented the mind as a *tabula rasa*—a blank slate or an unused hard drive—upon which sense impressions through experience are recorded. The mind functions, according to them, as a *passive receiver* of information. This information is stored in the memory and the process of reflection is nothing other than the recalling and combining of sense impressions by the faculty of association.

Hartley gave to the imagination a role, albeit a limited and somewhat diminished one. Within his empiricist framework, the imagination operated merely as a subset of memory and more robust role for the imagination was viewed with some degree of suspicion. Who knows what esoteric flights of fancy could be created via such a medium? The imagination does not deal with the real world and provides no access to truth or understanding. It takes as its object, not the establishment of verifiable truth but intentional falsehood. It was understood to be merely a mechanical activity devoid of any creative function and as such was diametrically opposed to the sovereign faculty of reason. Coleridge's early exposure to such views convinced him of their validity. In December 1794, shortly before his first meeting with Wordsworth, Coleridge wrote to his friend Southey to say, "I am a compleat Necessitarian and understand the subject as well almost as Hartley himself but I go further than Hartley and believe in the corporeality of thought namely that is motion."³⁷

Whilst Coleridge initially espoused an associationist view of the imagination, there were signs by the end of the 1790s that he was beginning to discard this position with some degree of dissatisfaction. What brought about this change? In part it was due to his poetic encounters with Wordsworth, but in addition to this his reading was showing signs of breadth and, in the autumn of 1796, records show that he borrowed Cudworth's *True Intellectual System* from Bristol library. Cudworth exposed Coleridge to a Neo-Platonic view of the world, such that he was, in effect, compelled to make a distinction between reason and the understanding, a distinction that marked a decisive shift away from associationism. He articulates this shift in this statement: "Mind in the associationists' system

36. Coleridge, *BL* I, 108.
37. Coleridge, *CL* 1, 137.

is always passive, a lazy Looker on an external World. If the mind be not passive, if it be indeed made in God's Image, & that too in the sublimest sense—the Image of the Creator—there is ground for suspicion, that any system built on the passiveness of the mind must be false, as a system."[38]

Hartley represented much that was typical of eighteenth century theology and religious philosophy. Three recurring motifs can be detected during this period. In first place was the supremacy of rationality. Only the natural, the measurable, and verifiable could be truly apprehended, thus rendering redundant any signs or perception of the supernatural. The human mind functioned merely as the passive recipient of information which could be stored and categorized. There was thus little difference between the work of a philosopher and the archival work of a historian. Secondly, there was a mistrust of, and a distaste for, mystery, whether it be the mystery of human sin, the mystery of freedom, or indeed the mystery of God. Finally, the rationalist conception of God was deist, a doctrine that understood God as the divine clockmaker who looks upon his finished creation from afar but is in no way involved or in relationship with it. The net result of these three motifs was the banishment of the numinous or any kind of immanent presence. It is in essence the classic Enlightenment position. Once Coleridge was cognizant of this, the overthrow of associationism was swift. He realized that Hartley was able to provide neither an abiding place for his intellect nor afford shelter for his soul. Indeed, a short time after *Biographia Literaria* was published in 1815, a work which in significant part was devoted to Coleridge's dissatisfaction with Hartley's schema, he published the *Statesman's Manual* (1816) in which he penned the following lines: "The leading differences between mechanical and vital philosophy may all be drawn from one point: namely, that the former demanding every mode and act of existence real or possible visibility, knows only of distance and nearness, composition and decomposition, in short the relations of unproductive particles to each other; so that in every instance the result is the exact sum of the component qualities, as in arithmetical addition. This is the philosophy of death and only dead nature can it hold good."[39]

Perhaps the single most significant area of dissatisfaction for Coleridge was that associationism ensured that the mind always remained a passive recipient of external sensory data. Instinctively he knew that the mind needed to be given a far more *active role*, an instinct that drew him inexorably across the English Channel towards Germany. "Any system," he

38. Coleridge, *BL* 1, 221.
39. Coleridge, *SM*, 89.

wrote in one of his letters, "built on the passiveness of the mind must be a false system."[40] Notwithstanding this sudden swerve away from Hartley and all that he represented, it is possible to detect, as we shall see in due course, lingering influences upon Coleridge when he later turns to explain his distinction between imagination and fancy.

The German Influence

In the autumn of 1798 Coleridge traveled to Germany in order to pursue an intensive study of German philosophy. During the late eighteenth century the early Enlightenment ideas gave way to a Transcendental Idealism. The German thinkers had responded to the developments in modern science with far great flexibility than their British counterparts. German thought was very dynamic and could incorporate new ideas without losing its centripetal grip on the ideals of unity.[41] This German organicism was constantly in process. Foremost amongst the exponents of the new German Idealism was Immanuel Kant, whose shadow was caste over subsequent generations of thinkers. Two of these, Fichte and Schelling, we shall consider here together with Kant. Our task is not to explore the precise contours of their thinking but rather to assess the extent to which their views on the imagination shaped the development of Coleridge's project. The philosophical revolution propounded by Kant and his successors exerted a magnetic attraction for Coleridge who was eager to support his intuitions within a robust intellectual framework. In addition to these philosophers we shall also consider the part played by the poet and playwright Schiller, whose influence over Coleridge, whilst being perhaps less prominent, was nonetheless highly significant. We shall look at these four figures in turn.

Before doing so however, it is important to address the question as to whether Coleridge was merely the wholesale importer of German idealism into Britain. Is it true that Coleridge was an unashamed plagiarist who simply swallowed the thought of his German contemporaries whole and subsequently regurgitated it for an English audience? Whilst the influence of the Germans upon Coleridge was undeniable, he was highly selective as to which aspects he was prepared to assimilate into his own structural framework. His intentions were explicitly Christian in their articulation as this comment in *Biographia Literaria* illustrates. His desire was that, "philosophy would pass into religion, and religion

---

40. Coleridge, *CL* II, 709.
41. Engell in Coleridge, *BL* I, lxx.

become inclusive of philosophy."[42] In other words, he viewed the new philosophy emerging out of Germany as a useful tool, the handmaid as it were, for the apologetic defense of Christianity in the face of a militant materialism. For Coleridge this was always the order of priority, for religion could never be the servant of philosophy.

Immanuel Kant (1724–1804)

The influence that Kant's work exerted on Coleridge was highly significant. Kant's views articulated in his three major *Critiques*, dealt with subjects close to Coleridge's heart, namely the role of the human mind in shaping true knowledge, the nature and extent of creative human potential, and the perception of beauty and the sublime. Kooy claims that that, "one of the greatest lessons Coleridge learned from Kant was, in his own words, 'to treat every subject in reference to the operation of the mental faculties to which it specifically pertains.'"[43] This lesson was drawn from Kant's third *Critique* concerning the place of aesthetic judgment, the product of many years of previous work with which Kant had been engaged. In order to appreciate how Kant had arrived at his philosophy of judgment it is necessary to retrace some of his earlier footsteps.

Some years prior to Coleridge's visit, in 1781, Kant had published his first edition of *Critique of Pure Reason* in which he set out his views on the place of the imagination reclaiming for it a central position in human knowing. Kant's work proved to be a major watershed in the history of philosophy. Prior to this, the imagination had been considered in purely mimetic terms capable only of reproductive functions. Kant reversed the order of priority, claiming that human knowing was rooted, not initially in the processing of sensible data, but in the *a priori* subjective imagination. Imagination was presented by Kant as being a far more powerful and essential power. It was the imagination that was productive, creative, capable of shaping and forming knowledge and understanding. The imagination had the capacity to invent a world purely through the use of human resources. Kant's project was a self-proclaimed Copernican Revolution. Previously reality was perceived to be at the centre of the universe and the human mind revolved in orbit, as it were, around it. Kant inverted this order, placing the human mind at the centre, with reality or being pushed to the periphery. Henceforth "being" was no longer conceived as the transcendent origin of meaning but was simply

---

42. Ibid., 283.
43. Kooy, *Coleridge, Schiller and Aesthetic Freedom*, 100.

the representation of the subject, namely the mind, the *a priori* imagination. The ripple effects of this reorientation would prove to be immense. Kant had, in short, displaced the divine from its originating position and replaced it with the transcendental human imagination.

Kant developed a highly sophisticated philosophy of the imagination through his three *Critiques* and his search for a way of describing the relation between subject and object located his argumentation firmly within the epistemological field. Using a building metaphor he set out to construct a home for reason's powers. Kant suggested that humanity naturally possesses instinctive non-rational capabilities which drive our creativity and the development of our cognitive faculties. He associates these drives with the imagination which he understood to be, "A blind, albeit indispensable, function of the soul without which we would have no awareness but which we are however only seldom aware of."[44]

What, however, did Kant mean by the phrase "transcendental imagination"? Hannah Arendt renders this phrase, as articulated in the second edition of *Critique of Pure Reason* (1787), as "the art concealed in the depths of the human soul."[45] It was the presuppositions of human experience, which provided the grid that we place over the natural world and through which we interpret and construct meaning. Previously the articulation of meaning was considered to be the prerogative of a transcendent divine being. Kant maintained that meaning was, in reality, located in the transcendent properties of the human mind. The means by which Kant justified this radical reshaping of an understanding of the place and function of the imagination are rehearsed in *Pure Reason*. Arguing there that the manifold of sensibility, the raw data that we daily receive from the world around us, and the understanding, that faculty which processes that data into categories are united or synthesized into one. This process, which he termed *Einbildungskraft*, is carried out by the imagination. Without the imagination no synthesis can take place.

It is not hard to see why Kant's view held such an influence over Coleridge. The new direction of Coleridge's thinking stemmed from a dissatisfaction with Cartesian methodology and philosophy. In Kant, he had discovered someone who articulated a view of the imagination that gave it a far more active role in human perception. Coleridge expresses this in one of his notebook entries: "Our sense in no way acquaint us

---

44. Kant, *Kritik der Reinen Vernunft*, (A78/B103): "einer blinden obgleich unentbehrlichen Funktion der Seele, ohne die wir überall gar keine Erkenntnis haben würden, der wir uns aber selten nur einmal bewußt sind."

45. Arendt, *Lectures on Kant's Political Philosophy*, 82.

with the Things, as they are in and of themselves, which we attribute to Things without us, yea . . . this very Outness, are not strictly properties of the things themselves, but either constituents or modifications of our own minds."[46]

After the first printing of *Pure Reason* in 1781, Kant appeared to retreat from the startling conclusions that he had arrived at such that by the second printing in 1787 he had softened some of his argumentation and imposed some degree of limit on imagination's prowess. By the time he wrote his third *Critique of Judgement*, Kant turned his attention to a consideration of aesthetics and considered there what it meant to make an aesthetic judgment. In dealing with this issue he appeared once more to give a free role to the imagination by drawing a sharp distinction between the consideration of beauty and that of the sublime.

Beauty, according to Kant, stemmed from a recognition of a pattern or shape that displayed a finality of form. Something that is considered beautiful does not require or demand anything outside of itself for it is, in effect, a completed, final object that exists without purpose of function. It possesses what Kant describes as "purposefulness without purpose."[47] Art has no utilitarian function, it does not *do* anything, it simply *is*. For something to be beautiful, we cannot ask the question, "what is it for?" but rather its beauty depends on our capacity to behold it with our imagination in pure freedom. When one views Van Gogh's famous painting of his bedroom for example, one observes the bed not as a useful piece of furniture but as an admirable, albeit functionally useless work of beauty. It matters not whether the dimensions of the bed are correct or whether this particular bed actually exists. It is enough to know that in Van Gogh's hands this bed is beautiful.

Kant thus celebrated that self-referential, impractical quality of beauty. In such a celebration, the imagination was afforded the privilege of free play. When we wish to discern if something is beautiful or not, the reference point is not the object being considered but the emotional response that the object elicits in the subject. The judgment of taste is therefore not a cognitive judgment open to logical analysis; rather it is aesthetic and belongs solely to the subjective realm. The free play of the imagination is drawn to whatever in nature is in the state of process, possessing movement, such as the shapes that the tongues of flame make in a fireplace or the rippling surface of a pond. Such things engage the imagination so that it is captivated by the life and dynamism observable

---

46. Coleridge, *CN* III, 3605.
47. *Zweckmässigkeit ohne Zweck*.

in the world. Art is the process of imitation of that life force. For Kant, the imagination was a powerful agent in creating secondary material out of that which was supplied to it by nature. It provided a source of entertainment and could be used to remodel our own experiences. In essence, the imagination was the origin of human freedom.

Whilst Kant affirmed the pivotal role of the imagination in aesthetics, he asserted that this was something that could not be conceptualized but only felt. This dissociation between reason and emotion emerged most forcibly in his treatment of the sublime. Whilst beauty could be apprehended by the imagination, the sublime pushed the imagination to the extreme. The sublime plumbs the depths and soars to the heights of what the imagination is capable of perceiving. It provokes the imagination to venture into strange new territory, a land of super abundance. Whereas the judgment of beauty produces the response of pleasure, the judgment of the sublime only leads to awe. Kant's discussion of the sublime moves away from art towards nature. The danger with any discussion about the role of the artist, in Kant's view, is the ascription of intentionality or purpose which can always be contested. With nature, however, purpose is altogether removed. One can discuss sublimity with regard to nature without reference to any supposed divine purpose more readily than one can when discussing the works of Milton, Byron, or Shakespeare. To observe the majesty of Mont Blanc, for example, and to notice the response of awe within ourselves is to depict the human imagination as simply possessing a self-referential capacity telling us nothing about the existence or otherwise of God. It was this conception of the self as the first principle, so evident in Kant, that Coleridge strongly objected to. The human imagination, according to Coleridge, needs to be located within an overall theological anthropology defined in terms of "I" and "you" relationships. We will return to the subject of Coleridge's anthropology in a later chapter.

Jeremy Begbie helpfully encapsulates the nature of Kant's aesthetic philosophy.[48] He asserts that Kant effectively drove a wedge between the physical material world and the inner world of the mental experience of the individual. Form and order are imposed upon creation by the disinterested human observer and are not inherent within it. Order, and therefore beauty, is a human construct and is placed like a grid over what we see, hear, taste, and touch. That order is not intrinsic to the object being considered but comes to it from without. Given that in Kant's view the judgment of taste is an entirely subjective experience and makes no

---

48. Begbie, *Voicing Creation's Praise*, 191.

universal cognitive claims, the corollary of this is that aesthetic judgments are limited to the particularity of their own contexts. One cannot abstract from a judgment of beauty in a particular case to generalized statement about the true nature of beauty with universal validity.

The rupture which Kant opened up between aesthetic experience and cognitive knowledge is articulated by Colin Gunton when he writes that Kant "set up an *a priori* criterion of rectitude which, by excluding aesthetic judgements entirely from the realm of the objectively knowable, opens a breach between different kinds of judgment about the world. What begins as a distinction becomes an epistemological and ontological chasm."[49]

The freedom accorded to the creative imagination drove Kant to consider in his final work, *Opus Posthumum*, questions that touched on the attributes of God and the art and mystery of creation. It suggests that his explorations into the dynamic, creative functions of the imagination led him to investigate what this might mean for the ontology of God. The notion of God as a creative artist complements Kant's reflections on aesthetics, genius, and art espoused in the *Critique of Judgment*. Engell explains: "In the *Opus*, Kant makes the human imagination the condition of the constitution of space. God, the original creator and hence the original condition of all things becomes 'eine Dichtung,' a prototype of art."[50] Kant's theory of the imagination in *Critique of Judgment* presents itself with some degree of ambiguity. When the question of beauty is considered, imagination is presented as playful and autonomous yet when the sublime is in view it would appear that the imagination has reached its limit and is powerless to explain the sense of awe that is experienced. Kant appears to oscillate between loyalties, at times giving the imagination a free role and at others seeking to constrain its capacity. This tension which Kant struggled to resolve was swept away however by the Romantics who followed him.

Kant's legacy to Coleridge was to show how *a priori* judgments were possible. The faculty of reason possessed a synthetic function that was far greater than simply the analysis that the understanding provided. Where Coleridge differed from Kant was in his identification of what he deemed to be a fatal flaw in Kant's scheme. Coleridge averred that Kant's attempt to bridge the gap between subject and object betrayed an assumption that the two were distinct and separate entities. Kant's presupposition was that there was a duality of subject and object with reason, imagination,

---

49. Gunton, *The One, the Three, and the Many*, 4.
50. Engell, *The Creative Imagination*, 138.

and ideas existing in one realm and objects existing in another. The mind was thus portrayed as having an independent existence from the world in which reason becomes the absolute subject with the noumenon being the absolute object. This radical division of subject and object was viewed by Coleridge as Kant's great failing. For Coleridge no such chasm existed, as both subject and object existed in relational tension with one another and their individual entities were subsumed within a greater sum, which he called "the I AM." Coleridge claimed that the foundational principle of his philosophic method was to "be found therefore neither in object or subject taken separately . . . it must be found in that which is neither subject or object exclusively, but which is the identity of both . . . This principle . . . manifests itself in the SUM or I AM; which I shall hereafter . . . express by the words spirit, self and self-consciousness."[51]

Coleridge's scheme was far more dynamic and fluid than Kant's. Kant's error, according to Coleridge, was to posit the validity of fixed subject-object categories. Coleridge questioned this assumption and in so doing raised the possibility that there could be a single organic framework of experience that exists within the infinite I AM. Coleridge entered the contemporary controversy concerning the relation between the understanding and reason, heavily influenced as it was by Kant, with characteristic vigor yet chose to diverge from Kant. Coleridge maintained that reason and understanding were two different beasts. Whilst both were regarded as modes of being, they each performed very different functions. Judgments of the understanding were solely concerned with making sense of the objects before us, what we can see, touch, taste, feel, and measure. The understanding orders these sense impressions into meaningful categories. Here is Coleridge in his own words. Understanding is "the faculty of the finite, that which reduces the confused impressions to their essential forms—quantity, quality, relations . . . Without it, man's representative powers would be a delirium, a chaos, a scudding of cloudage of shapes."[52]

By contrast, the world of ideas was, for Coleridge, the domain of reason. It was in this realm that notions of justice, holiness, freewill, and morals have their origin. Such ideas were not static or fixed concepts but dynamic and concerned with ultimate aims. All of these ideas, belonging as they do to the category of reason, possess a revelatory quality. They reveal something of the divine, which is eternal and not confined to a particular time or place. Coleridge here moves well outside Kant's carefully constructed limitations on humankind's reasoning powers. Kant had

---

51. Coleridge, *BL* I, 182–83.

52. Ibid., 122.

always maintained reason's regulative properties; Coleridge moved those properties to the constitutive sphere. Coleridge wrote in *Lay Sermons*, "whether Ideas are regulative only, according to Aristotle and Kant; or likewise constitutive and one with the power and life of nature, according Plato and Plotinus, is the highest problem of philosophy."[53] To exalt reason to this high and lofty position demands that a power or engine be found. Coleridge ascribed this motor to the imagination.

Not only did Coleridge diverge from Kant here, but he also became dissatisfied with Kant's emphasis on duty and morality, the accompaniments of his practical reason. For Coleridge such emphases were dry and barren and merely served to reinstate a religion of legalistic obedience. What Coleridge searched for was reconciliation of individual freedom of conscience with the objective laws of reason. Coleridge's dissatisfaction with Kantian ethics can be observed when he makes a link between aesthetic pleasure and moral interest, a link that Kant would never have made. Kant believed that judgments of taste in the aesthetic realm needed to remain entirely free, unfettered by any moral claim or boundary limitation. Such judgments referred solely to the subjective responses and as such offered no true knowledge or information about the world. The aesthetic realm must have its independence preserved. A judgment of taste is simply and only the disinterested pleasure in the form of the object. At one level Coleridge concurred with such Kantian views and wrote to this effect in his notebooks: "Have nothing to do with the action as determined by law, but only with the feelings leading to and accompanying it . . . To the poet Adam Bell or Robin Hood are as good men as Alexander or the Duke of Marlborough. The poet lives in an element, in which Property is no further recognized than as it affects the Imagination, or produces states of moral Activity."[54] Here Coleridge sounds decidedly Kantian in separating the craft of the poet from the constraints of moral orthodoxy. In the playful world of the artist anything becomes possible, yet this apparently bears little or no relation to the harsh realities and dilemmas of the real world. It was Wordsworth who profoundly epitomized this potentiality for Coleridge: He was able through his poetry to "excite a feeling analogous to the supernatural, by awakening the mind's attention from the lethargy of custom," so wrote Coleridge about his great friend in *Biographia Literaria*.[55] The poet was, in effect, inhabiting

---

53. Coleridge, *LS*, 114.
54. Coleridge, *CN* III, 3956.
55. Coleridge, *BL* II, 7.

another world outside of moral limitations or the boundaries of reason calling readers to be awakened and to learn to perceive afresh.

Thus far Coleridge is a true Kantian. Yet Coleridge pushed Kantian ideas to their limits and was unwilling to maintain such a strict divorce between the aesthetic world and moral feeling. In another notebook entry, Coleridge proposed that such a marriage is not only possible but is indeed advantageous: "Suppose the presence [of moral feeling], and then there will accrue an excellence even to the quality of the pleasures themselves, but not only of the refined but also the grosser—in as much as a larger sweep of ideas will be associated with each enjoyment, but with each idea will be associated a number of Sensations—and consequently each pleasure will become more the pleasure of the whole Being."[56] Here Coleridge is proposing a radical addition to the Kantian scheme. The presence of moral feelings need not be dismissed as irrelevant but rather needs to be incorporated into the entire process of aesthetic perception. The addition of a moral imperative is not a constraint or an intrusion but an enhancement of the aesthetic process. What Coleridge demonstrates here is his insistence on the unity of the process of human knowing. All the faculties of understanding, reason, emotion, moral intuition, and imagination combine to contribute to our perception of the world and our capacity to shape it. Whilst Coleridge displays many of the characteristic hallmarks of Kantianism he remains his own man and was unafraid to chart new territory where Kant himself was loathe to tread.

Johann Gottlieb Fichte (1762–1814)

Although Kant's influence on subsequent generations of philosophers was immense, his project contained some unresolved issues that were subsequently taken up by other German idealists. The ambiguity of Kant's position was that he appeared to retreat from the implications of some of his own conclusions. When dealing with the question of the nature and perception of beauty in his *Critique of Pure Judgement*, Kant granted to the imagination freedom and autonomy. When dealing with the sublime, however, which surpasses beauty, the position of the imagination in Kant's scheme is one of powerlessness. He wished to remain faithful to the primacy of imagination set forth in his first edition of *Pure Reason* but also wished to establish the limitations of that same imaginative power in *Pure Judgement*. This conflict of loyalties remained an unresolved dilemma. No such hesitancy was displayed by Fichte however, who seized up

---

56. Coleridge, *CN* III, 3584.

the notion of the imagination from Kant and magnified its importance considerably.

Whilst Kant strove to keep in place the boundary markers between scientific, moral, and aesthetic theory, Fichte brushed them aside and saw no reason to keep a division between the phenomenal world that could be known and the noumenal world that could not. In his work, *Die Bestimmung des Menschen* (1800), Fichte hails the imagination as the very possibility of our consciousness, the source of our life and our being. Whilst he acknowledged the rapport between the imagination and the transcendental ego that Kant had discovered, he extrapolated from this that all the syntheses of human subjectivity could be achieved by "the productive imagination" (*die Produktive Einbildungskraft*). The foundation of his philosophical system was that human self-consciousness, empowered by the productive imagination, was capable of synthesizing the finite and the infinite. The reconciliation between subject and object which had so engaged Kant could be overcome in one leap, namely by an imaginative act of self-consciousness.[57]

Coleridge's reading of Fichte enabled him to engage with two dilemmas. In first place Kant's "Copernican Revolution" had left an apparent vacuum in human knowing. If the self is the centre of all perception, the framework of the world, then one is led into a deadlocked position. The world as it is, the *Ding-an-Sich*, can never be truly known at all and one is left in a land of pure subjectivity. In second place, Fichte's writings permitted Coleridge to counter what he perceived to be the pervasive and dangerous threat coming from Spinoza. At the turn of the century the work of Spinoza had been re-introduced into Germany through the publication of Jacobi's *Letters to Mendelssohn upon Spinoza's Doctrine*. This publication was the stimulus for a re-awakened interest in Spinoza's pantheistic determinism and was highly influential in determining the mood and culture of the day. In one of the few references that Coleridge made regarding Fichte, he is alarmed by this threat and writes in his *Biographia Literaria*, 'Fichte's *Wissenschaftslehre* or *Lore of Ultimate Science*, was to add the key-stone of the arch: and by commencing with an act, instead of a thing or substance, Fichte assuredly gave the first mortal blow to Spinozism as taught by Spinoza himself."[58]

The mortal blow that Coleridge considered that Fichte had dealt to Spinoza was entirely necessary because the essence of human freedom was under threat. Spinoza's doctrine questioned the freedom of the human

57. Perkins, *Logic and Logos*, 5.
58. Coleridge, *BL* I, 158.

subject claiming that the exercise of choice was illusory. The truth lay, according to Spinoza, in a deterministic view of nature that controlled all human action. All human choice was the product of cause and effect such that there was an infinite regression backwards to the ultimate cause of all being. Spinoza thus totally denied the independence of the subject and subjugated it entirely to the absolute object or primal cause, *causa sui*. The irony of this position was that Spinoza was unable to construct a system of ethics despite this being the title of one of his major works. If all human choice is merely the product of mechanistic causes then one is left with a universe governed by impersonal forces and ethical moral choices become an impossibility once all human action is determined by external objectivity. It is not hard to see why Coleridge regarded the pantheism of Spinoza as being tantamount to atheism.

Fichte's attack on Spinoza was to invert this whole process. He was wary of the power that Spinoza devolved to the absolute object which he stigmatized, according to Coleridge, by referring to it as "the unruly violence of nature."[59] Schelling too was acutely aware of this and in his *Zur Geschichte der Neueren Philosophie* asserted that Fichte's idealism was the complete opposite of Spinozism or was an inverted form of it. The reason for this lay in Fichte's opposition to Spinoza's absolutizing of the object which destroys everything subjective. Coleridge considered that there were really only two consistent philosophical systems; one which emphasized the priority of the subject and the other which gave precedence to the object. In one of his notebooks Coleridge makes this point. "Only two systems of Philosophy are possible. 1. Spinoza, 2. Kant, i.e., the absolute and the relative. Or 1. Ontosophical. 2. The Anthropological."[60] What Coleridge had identified in Spinoza was the view that the whole world is seen as an expression of the divine being from which everything else is directly derived in a strictly causal manner.[61] The objective world is the divine world, the absolute being, with no distinction between God and nature.

Fichte wrestled with the question of the interface between the self, *Ich*, and external reality which he defined with reference to the self by naming it *Nicht-Ich*. Fichte asserted that it was only the imagination that was capable of mediating between these two poles. Imagination was portrayed as a kind of power or elemental force that, like gravity or magnetism, was always present and continually exerted its invisible influence. Everything

---

59. Ibid., 159.
60. Coleridge, *PL*, 53.
61. Hurtrez, *Nature and Subjectivity*, 3.

was located therefore within the imagination leaving little or no room for the *Ding-an-Sich*. For Fichte no such external reality existed. By the time he published the *Versuch einer neuen Darstellung der Wissenschaftslehre* (1797), he had virtually excised objective reality altogether and placed everything within the realm of transcendentalism. "The main principle of the dogmaticians," he wrote with reference to the empiricists, "is that the 'thing-in-itself' is nothing and has . . . no reality." By contrast, he stressed, "it is being asserted here that all reality . . . is merely generated by the imagination."[62]

For Coleridge, Fichte's emphasis on the act of self-consciousness was profoundly attractive. The influence which Fichte exerted upon Coleridge lay in his assertion that a reconciliation between subject and object could be afforded by an insistence on the primacy of a self-conscious act of declaration—"I am." Fichte's philosophy began therefore with an act rather than a thing. The unification between the *Ich* and the *Nicht-Ich* was made possible through the exercise of the imagination but this action takes place only within the *Ich*. The role of the *Nicht-Ich* is as a postulate of the *Ich* on the basis that the *Ich* requires an opposite force with which to struggle. When the two poles are bound together there is an oscillation or hovering (*schweben*) of the imagination. Fichte was so determined to elevate the role of the imagination that he went much further than Kant dared to go. He equates the *Produktive Einbildungskraft* with *Geist* and considers them virtually synonymous. The productive imagination facilitates all human endeavor from artistic expression, technological advance, religious perception, and philosophical enquiry—all flowed from the same spring, namely the philosophical imagination.

The influence which Fichte exerted upon Coleridge was ambivalent yet significant. Coleridge resonated with Fichte's assessment of the productive capability of the imagination according it a similarly pivotal role in the operation of the human spirit. The hovering, mediating role between subject and object (*Ich* and *Nicht-Ich*) articulated by Fichte finds its natural counterpart in Coleridge too, the difference being that Fichte placed almost the entire weight on one end of the polar spectrum which Coleridge was loathe to do. Coleridge's later work placed a great deal of emphasis on "Will" as the primary expression of the human condition. It is when we act, claimed Coleridge, that we make an "I AM" statement about ourselves. In this respect Coleridge mirrors an aspect of Fichte's

---

62. Fichte, *Versuch einer neuen Darstellung der Wissenschaftslehre*, 24: "Das Princip der Dogmatikers, das Ding an sich, ist nichts, und hat . . . keine Realität . . . es wird demanch hier gelehrt, dass alle Realität . . . bloss durch die Einbildungskraft hervorgebracht werde."

system in which great priority was placed on the self-conscious assertion of the *Ich*. Where he diverged was in claiming that the foundation for the *Ich* was in the divine absolute *Ich* of God and not in an internal subjectivism which Fichte appeared to espouse. Coleridge also did not consider that the *Nicht-Ich* was a threat to the existence of the *Ich*. On the contrary, the relationship between the two formed the cornerstone of his views on personality which we shall consider in due course.

Whilst both Coleridge and Fichte could be called subjectivists, they each propounded a fundamentally different expression of what that term could mean. Coleridge considered that the value Fichte placed on the subjective *Ich* amounted to nothing less than idolatry. In his *Aids to Reflection* he makes reference to Fichte, albeit somewhat covertly, when he links the (Fichtean) subjective idolism with (Hartleyan) materialism as twins which together only produce confusion. The former, claims Coleridge, only leads to a "Mazy Dream" and the latter to "a World of Spectres and Apparitions."[63] Whilst Coleridge was impressed by Fichte's systematic philosophical method which required that all truths be demonstrated and was grateful to Fichte for his attack on Spinoza, he was highly critical of the results of Fichte's deliberations. In the same passage from *Biographia Literaria* which praises Fichte, Coleridge goes on to make this damning indictment: "But this fundamental idea he overbuilt with a heavy mass of mere notions and psychological acts of arbitrary reflection. Thus his theory degenerated into a crude Egoismus, a boastful and hyperstoic hostility to Nature as lifeless, godless and altogether unholy: while his religion consisted in the assumption of a mere ordo ordinans, which we were permitted to call God; and his ethics in an ascetic and almost monkish mortification of the natural passions and desires."[64]

The heart of Coleridge's critique of Fichte lay in what he considered to be the idolatry of the *Ich*. Once everything is located subjectively in the *Ich* with a corresponding suspicion of the *Nicht-Ich*, then one is left open both to the twin charges of crude egotism and a denigration of all that does not belong to the *Ich*, namely nature itself. In Coleridge's view, Fichte had fallen into the trap of overemphasizing the subject to the detriment of the object. Fichte's completion of the Kantian revolution had only succeeded in placing the *Ich* where God alone should dwell thereby relegating God's created order into a lifeless, godless, and altogether unholy position. For Coleridge, Fichte's exaltation of the *Ich* made it into

---

63. Coleridge, *AR*, 399.
64. Coleridge, *BL* I, 158.

a lawless tyrant intent on the destruction of the *Nicht-Ich* which always stood in its way.

Coleridge's great project to construct a unified system of knowledge was, as has already been noted, profoundly Christian in character and intent. Fichte by contrast wrote not as a Christian theologian but as a philosopher with an interest in religion. Both characters deployed a similar method yet gave a very different content to their deliberations. By way of example, one may observe the way in they dealt with the concept of Christ. For Fichte, the longing of the *Ich* for self-fulfillment and actualization was evidence of the finite straining towards the infinite. This yearning is made possible because of the Christ. The infinite *Ich* is an absolute epitomized by Christ; the finite *Ich* possesses a yearning that constantly tends towards the absolute *Ich*. Yet this infinite *Ich*, namely Christ, does not dwell in an external heaven. There could, of course, be no such objectivity, certainly nothing that was truly knowable. Heaven was therefore an internal construct of the human subject with the Christ figure being the unifying focal point of all human yearning. In doing so Fichte adopted Christian language but effectively interiorized the Christian creed excising its external historicity.

In similar fashion Christ, or the Logos, was the point of unity for Coleridge. The hidden, mysterious unity that lies behind and within all things was none other than the Logos made flesh in the person of Christ as revealed especially in the Johannine Gospel. On this point there is a structural analogy between Fichte and Coleridge with both men deploying the same approach to the quest for unity between subject and object. Yet for Coleridge the term "Christ" held a very different content. Christ was not an idealized symbol of humanity, the object of all our longings; nor was Christ an internal human construct existing purely within the mind. For Coleridge, Christ was the Logos principle made flesh, the penetration of the finite by the infinite, transcendence in immanence. Both thinkers wrestled with the subject-object dichotomy; both deployed the unifying Christ principle, yet the meaning that each gave to those same concepts proved to be very different.

Friedrich Wilhelm Joseph Schelling (1775–1854)

In addition to his exposure to Kant, Coleridge was profoundly influenced by the work of Schelling. Indeed, it is widely known that Coleridge plagiarized Schelling unashamedly in *Biographia Literaria* where large sections of unabridged Schelling appear. In chapter 9 Coleridge admits that in discovering Schelling's *Naturphilosophie* and his *System des Transcendentalen*

Idealismus, he had "found a genial coincidence with much that I had toiled out for myself, and a powerful assistance in what I had yet to do."[65] His admiration for both Fichte and Schelling was expressed in his view that both of these successors to Kant had virtually completed the Kantian revolution in philosophy. "It is to Schelling," he wrote in his *Biographia*, "that we owe the completion and the most important victories of this revolution in philosophy."[66] He strongly refutes the charge of plagiarism insisting that much of what he had read in German philosophy he had already had in mind before he had even learned a word of German. Yet despite his undisguised borrowing from Schelling, Schelling himself was an admirer of Coleridge and had only kind words to say about him.

It would be misleading to claim that Coleridge was merely the vehicle for transporting Schelling's ideas across the Channel to England. Recent Coleridgean scholarship contends that Coleridge imbibed the thought of Kant, Fichte, and Schelling yet, by a syncretic process, made it uniquely his own adopting some parts of German idealism and rejecting others. In the first volume of *Biographia* Coleridge appears to build extensively upon Schelling's thought yet in the second volume he decisively moves away from what he perceived to be the dangers of Schelling's incipient Pantheism contained within his *Naturphilosophie*. A mere three years after the publication of *Biographia*, Coleridge reflected on this work and concluded in a letter to H. Green in 1818 that he had been seduced by Schelling's system and that in so doing had abandoned his better judgment. By the end of 1818 he regarded Schelling's thought as little more than Behemism, which in essence was nothing other than pantheism.[67]

Whilst Kant had neatly partitioned his *Critiques* into three divisions, namely the scientific (*Pure Reason*), the moral (*Practical Reason*) and the aesthetic (*Judgement*), Schelling took his ideas much further than Kant was prepared to go and blurred the boundaries between these three. Schelling's thought rested upon two key principles. The first of these was that whatever exists is knowable because it is an embodiment of rationality or a manifestation of the Absolute. The second foundation of his thought turned upon the relation between subject and object. Although Kant had placed these two in opposition to each other, Schelling perceived no such duality. Rather, he considered that they were in fact united in a kind of magnetic embrace precisely because they were held in the identity of the Absolute. For Schelling, there were two realms of the knowable. One was

---

65. Ibid., 160.
66. Ibid., 163.
67. Coleridge, *CL* IV, 883.

nature itself where things were distributed in space with their intelligibility consisting in the relations between them. A higher form of knowing, however, is in history, for history, according to Schelling, consists in the thoughts and actions of human minds over time. Collingwood expresses Schelling's position in this way, "nature, qua intelligible, demands a knower to understand it and exhibits its full essence only when there is a mind that knows it."[68]

Yet if nature is indivisible then the mind too is part of nature and must be subject to the process of being known; the mind cannot only be the knower, it must also be the known. This continuous process of self-knowledge means that history is the ongoing self-realization of the Absolute, of knowing and being known. Schelling had clearly moved on apace from where Kant had stopped. The dilemma which Kant had been unable to resolve concerned the way in which the sensuous realm of nature, bound by deterministic laws, related to the realm of the subject's cognitive and ethical self-determination. If the subject is part of nature there would seem to be no way of explaining how nature which we can only know as deterministic can give rise to a subject which seems to transcend determinism in its knowing and in its ethical actions. Schelling elevated the productive power of the imagination to much greater heights and made extravagant claims about its capacity to reconcile these age-old knotty, theological and philosophical conundrums. The oppositions of, for example, freedom and necessity or being and becoming or the relation between the universal and the particular could all be resolved and redeemed, according to Schelling, by the transcendental imagination. The imagination became, in his hands, the panacea for everything. In contrast to the careful, rational argumentation of Kant, Schelling peppered his writings with the poetic, the mystical, the Gnostic. In the words of Kearney, he sought to "produce a form of conscious poetry which articulates the unconscious poetry of being itself. And this unconscious poetry or poiesis (creation of everyday existence) is one in which all men participate as possessors of the 'productive imagination.'"[69]

Schelling was effectively attempting to dismantle the distinctions between nature and art through the productive imagination. In so doing Schelling collapsed the distinctiveness of God's ontology and creation, the two becoming practically indistinguishable. The task that Schelling gave himself was to unify transcendental philosophy with a philosophy of nature. These two systems were understood to be twin aspects of

---

68. Collingwood, *The Idea of History*, 113.
69. Kearney, *The Wake of Imagination*, 179.

the one worldview which was held together by an "aesthetic act of the imagination."[70] Schelling's thought progressed from a starting point with Fichte's subjective idealism, to *Naturphilosophie*, followed by transcendental idealism, then to an *Identitätssystem*, and finally ending with an existential theology. Schelling considered that the Enlightenment philosophies, epitomized by the Cartesian *cogito ergo sum*, had created a split between humanity and nature. Descarte's insistence on self-affirmation had done nothing to verify the existence of the external world. Schelling addressed this issue by taking the subjective, transcendental world of *ich bin* and the objective world of *es gibt* and attempted to show how the imagination, as *In-Eins-Bildung*, could function as a productive, unifying power. Schelling took the polarities of humanity and nature, the real and the ideal, perception and reality, and set out to demonstrate that it was the imagination alone that was capable of illuminating the inherent unity between these apparent opposites. Behind all of reality was God's divine imagination, *die göttliche Einbildungskraft*, the generating power within the whole universe. As a philosopher he asked the most basic questions of all—why is there something instead of nothing? Why is this world so rich in its diversity and multiplicity of forms? In what way is everything connected? The answers lay, for Schelling, in the imagination. It is God's imagination that shapes humanity and the universe. Mankind's imagination is a derivative of this on a smaller scale and the highest expression of the human imagination is found in the aesthetic realm. Divine creation can be presented through art since it is founded on the notion of the infinite ideal dwelling in the real. The German word *Einbildungskraft*, meaning the power of forming into one, describes an act on which all creation in based. It is the power through which the ideal becomes real.

Imagination for Schelling acts like a mysterious invisible force similar to electricity or magnetism. This imaginative force is capable of creating a dialectic between what is infinite and ideal with what is finite and real. Nature, belonging to the realm of the finite and real, is nothing other than the general or ideal finding expression in the particular. The diversity of the natural form is simply the manifestation of a prior unity. This is the realm of the ideal or the spiritual where all things originate and subsequently find their articulation in the real and the finite. As Engell states, for Schelling, "imaginative creation thus involves both a centripetal force of unification and a centrifugal force of differentiation. The presence of God and the static existence of ideas are at the center of these forces."[71]

70. Engell, *The Creative Imagination*, 301.
71. Ibid., 305.

The process of unification is thus the joining together of the universal and the particular such that they arrive at a point of unity or *Indifferenzpunkt*. The outcome of these two forces—centrifugal and centripetal—is a third force (*eine Dritte*). The influence of Schelling upon Coleridge on this point is clear. Chapter 13 of *Biographia Literaria* is devoted to a discussion of the imagination. In it, following Schelling, he asserts that the unifying purpose of the imagination acts as two counteracting forces that both differentiate and reconcile simultaneously. These two forces interpenetrate one another producing a third by-product which he termed *tertium aliquid*,[72] bearing the same name that Schelling had earlier devised. Schelling's enthusiasm for the imagination took him far beyond the limits that Kant had imposed on his own philosophy of the imagination. In Schelling's consideration of the role and function of art he reserves his highest esteem for the creative powers of the imagination. The task of art and philosophy, he claimed, was to produce a form of conscious poetry which was the articulation of the unconscious poetry (or *poiesis*) of being itself. The poet and the artist do far more than interpret the creative design of the world but participate in the on-going creativity of the Creator. In making such a claim, Schelling effectively collapsed the distinction between divine and human creation, thereby elevating imagination to the rank of the divine. This was a lofty claim indeed for the imagination and ran counter to the insistence of earlier Enlightenment thinkers who insisted that the imagination remained both peripheral and subservient to rationality. The distinction that Kant had maintained between legitimate thought and metaphysical speculation had now been swept aside. The danger inherent in Schelling's thought, according to Coleridge, lay in the trajectory that it had taken. If everything could be known and unified by the all-encompassing power of the imagination, how could anything be truly understood? Are we not left with the endless playfulness of the imagination creating and re-creating itself? Is not the very existence of the objective world placed in jeopardy?

Schelling developed a theory of the imagination that contained a series of levels or stages. The simplest form of the imagination he named the *ursprüngliche Anschauung*, or *erste Potenz*. This is the human capacity to receive sensory stimuli from the outside world deploying the five senses of touch, taste, hearing, smell, and taste. Once we receive these sense impressions passively we order them actively. We know, for example, that a strawberry can be grouped under the categories of either food (an edible fruit), or color (red) or taste (pleasure). The second phase employing both

---

72. Coleridge, *BL* I, 198.

active and passive components is the *produktive Anschauung* or *zweite Potenz*. This is the attempt to reconcile together the perceiver and the perceived. This assimilation continues as the mind struggles to provide an intellectual synthesis of knowledge. It is an inwardly directed activity and one which makes no further connections with an objective form outside of the mind itself. This level of functioning of the imagination Schelling described as *intellektuelle Anschauung*.

In order to step beyond this boundary and allow the imagination to unify internal subjective knowledge with external reality Schelling deployed the imagination in its *höchste Potenz*. This usage of the imagination was *eine aesthetische Anschauung* or *Kunstvermögen*. By way of illustration, one may point to Schelling's views on myth. Schelling makes reference to myth most noticeably in his *Philosophy of Art* (1802–3), although there are hints of his interest in this area as early as 1795 in his *Philosophical Letters on Dogmatism and Criticism*. In turning to myth as a powerful cultural influence, Schelling sought to demonstrate how the "I" and the external world are indissolubly connected in so far as there is a transcendental part of the ego. For Schelling, myth was a work of art in which the natural and the historical are joined together in narrative.[73] Myth was capable of providing a synthesizing role for apparently opposing polarities. But in order for myth to exert this power the imagination needed to be deployed. Smart asserts that for Schelling, "the astonishing faculty of the imagination is the intermediary which ties together theoretic and practical reason."[74] The strong symbolic element contained in mythological stories to which Schelling was attracted bears similarities with Coleridge's emphasis on symbol which we will later explore. Perhaps it was this element of Schelling's thought above others that Coleridge adopted and incorporated into his developing views on the imagination.

Friedrich Schiller (1759–1805)

Coleridge's engagement with Schiller appears at first sight to be tangential at best. He barely cites Schiller's work and does not actively either refute or endorse his theoretical formulations in the way that he does with Hartley or Fichte for example. It is due to this apparent reticence that Coleridgean scholarship has been reluctant to link him too closely with Schiller. And yet it would be remiss to ignore Schiller's more oblique influence on Coleridge. Michael Kooy has persuasively put forward the

---

73. Smart, *Nineteenth Century Religious Thought*, 57.
74. Ibid., 56.

case that Coleridge had read Schiller before his exposure to Kant, Fichte, and Schelling.[75] His acquaintance with Schiller's writings is evidenced by the fact that his personal library contained a copy of his *Musenalmanach* together with his *Versammelte Gedichte* and *Kleinere prosaische Schriften*. A further indication of the esteem with which Coleridge held Schiller is attested by the fact that he chose to translate into English the trilogy *Wallenstein*. Coleridge had been offered a contract by a publisher to translate the play into English and did so with characteristic enthusiasm. In part this may have been driven by Coleridge's financial circumstances but he would not have undertaken such a challenging project without a high view of the work. Indeed as a dramatist, Coleridge compared Schiller to the genius of Shakespeare, high praise indeed.[76] *Wallenstein* was written in the aftermath of Schiller's work entitled *Aesthetic Letters*, and exhibits Schiller's preoccupation with the moral and social out-workings of the *Spieltrieb*.

It is likely that Coleridge's earliest encounter with Schiller took place when he read *Die Rauber* soon after its publication in 1792. He was instantly captivated. In a letter to Southey written in 1794 Coleridge exclaimed, "My God! Southey! Who is this Schiller? This convulser of the heart?"[77] Later in the same year Coleridge penned a sonnet entitled "*To the author of the Robbers*," in which he addresses Schiller as "Ah! Bard tremendous in sublimity!"[78] Without doubt Coleridge had discovered a kindred spirit in this German poet and playwright. His magnetic pull stemmed from his ability to capture a sense of the sublime without resorting to the convention of introducing ghosts, goblins, and other features of fantasy. Schiller's works entailed the merely human but it was his deft handling of this mundane subject matter that so inspired the young Coleridge.

What precisely however was the nature of the Schillerian influence upon Coleridge? Is it possible to detect any structural similarities between the two men and in what way did Schiller's views shape the unfolding development of Coleridge's conception of the imagination? An answer to this question requires an appreciation of Schiller's *Aesthetic Letters*.[79] Schiller writes about the notion of freedom in these letters where he links aesthetics to moral action. He addresses the question as to whether one

75. Kooy, *Coleridge, Schiller and Aesthetic Freedom*, 1–8.
76. Coleridge, *PW* II, 724–25.
77. Coleridge, *CL* I, 122.
78. Coleridge, *PW* I, 73.
79. Schiller, *Briefe über die ästhetische Erziehung des Menschen*. Online: http://www.dreigliederung.de/gliederung/schillersbriefe.html.

can live in freedom in a way that is most fully human where we are most true to ourselves. He claims that we must be able to exercise free choice in a rational way for we are creatures both of sense and reason. By what route however do we take to arrive at a place of rational free choice? In his early letters Schiller averred that we possess two distinct drives; the *Stofftrieb* and the *Formtrieb*. The former sense drive is directed towards the phenomenal material world and is concerned with the apprehension of matter and substance. When one yields entirely to the *Stofftrieb* one is given over to physicality of reality, eschewing the more abstract, hidden aspirations towards love, joy, and freedom.

The other basic drive—*Formtrieb*—is far more subjective and deals with the realm of forms, ideas, and shape. This corresponded in similarity to Fichte's *Ich*. The *Formtrieb* is *geistlich* and *innerlich*, and pays less attention to the savage, beautiful, sensual world around us focusing instead on issues of self-determination and liberty. For Schiller singular attention to either one of these extreme alignments was dangerous. One might have expected Schiller to favor the more internal *Formtrieb* yet he was aware that an acute detachment from the real world could lead to compassionless self-absorption which did nothing to achieve true free humanity. Ideally both the *Stofftrieb* and the *Formtrieb* need to be sublimated within each other to avoid the dominance of either the external, physical world or the internal, moral world. This mutual submission however is a delicate balancing act and thus Schiller posited a third drive, a *tertium aliquid*, which he named the *Spieltrieb*, a drive which unified the other two.[80] This unification brings together the "permanence and self-sustaining identities of the ideal world with the individual processes and flux of material existence."[81] In effect it unites together the feelings, passions and impressions which are the product of our engagement with physical reality with the ideas of reason. The desire and capacity to play sets us free from the constraints of both physicality and morality.

Schiller's *Spieltrieb* thus performs much the same function as Kant's *Einbildungskraft*, yet it would be a mistake to equate the two entirely. The *Spieltrieb* is the highest level of imaginative functioning and was associated in Schiller's view with the perception of the aesthetic. The object of the play instinct was the identification of the *lebendige Gestalt*; a term that served to describe all the aesthetic qualities of phenomena and what is termed in the widest sense "beauty." Schiller chose his terms carefully and explained his reasoning in letter XV: "The choice of this term is totally

80. Engell, *The Creative Imagination*, 231.
81. Ibid., 232.

in accord with language usage because the word play can be applied to everything that is by accident neither subjective nor objective neither outward nor inward."[82]

The *Spieltrieb* brings together sense impressions (*Gefühl*), derived from the objective world, into harmony with reason, which inhabits the subjective world. The classic Cartesian division between object and subject, which had for so long been a stumbling block in post-Enlightenment thinking, is brought into harmonious unity via the *Spieltrieb*.

To substantiate these claims Schiller asks, "what is the *Ziel* of each of the three drives?" For the *Stofftrieb* it is the actual experience of the content of life itself, the sensual experiences that make life what it is.[83] The *Ziel* of the *Formtrieb* is totally other than this. It is concerned with the drive to find form, shape, and indeed meaning in life and this drive, of necessity, contains an ethical dimension to it. By contrast the purpose of the *Spieltrieb* is entirely non-utilitarian. It has no destination other than the enjoyment and contemplation of beauty. The use of the term *Spiel* carried with it the sense of activity and process and conveyed a greater sense of movement than Fichte's *Schweben der Einbildungskraft*. It suggested an active, beautiful, yet somewhat random interplay between two different drives bringing them to a place of harmony. The rhetorical shock that this produced lay in the claim that it was via play—not reason or duty—that humanity could find its highest fulfillment. By placing play and the perception of the aesthetic in such a central position, Schiller contradicted Kant's emphasis on ethics and duty as a moral obligation. Was there any place for ethics therefore in the playful scheme of Schiller? The connection between aesthetic contemplation, play, and morality was, for Schiller, an indirect one. The enjoyment of aesthetic pleasure as an end in itself carries with it its own integrity and does not need to be validated by moral imperative. If there is to be an ethical result of such playfulness then it comes as a by-product and not as an intention. Aesthetics for both Schiller and Coleridge thus demanded its own autonomy and could not be subjugated to serve a higher moral purpose. The anthropological implication of this claim is that humankind is most fully human when at play.

---

82. Schiller http://www.kuehnle-online.de/literatur/schiller/prosa/aestherzieh/15.htm: "Diesen Namen rechtfertigt der Sprachgebrauch vollkommen, der alles das, was weder subjektiv noch objektiv zufällig ist und doch weder äußerlich noch innerlich nötigt, mit dem Wort Spiel zu bezeichnen pflegt."

83. Kooy, *Coleridge, Schiller and Aesthetic Freedom*, 108.

We can witness this reversal of priorities in *Biographia Literaria* where Coleridge discusses the poet's craft with reference to his critique of the work of William Wordsworth. Coleridge raises an objection to the philosophy lying behind the poetry of Wordsworth, "inasmuch as it proposes truth for its immediate object instead of pleasure."[84] Coleridge claims that this order—truth first, then pleasure—is fundamentally flawed and needs to be inverted. He goes on to write, "but here is unfortunately a small Hysteron-Proteron. For the communication of pleasure is the introductory means by which alone the poet must expect to moralize his readers."[85] This assertion clearly bears the hallmarks of Schiller's *Spieltrieb*. Schiller's concern was to maintain the independence of art and morality, for once art becomes shackled to a utilitarian purpose it loses its freedom. It is precisely because of this freedom that it possesses the power to produce pleasure. Art needs the space in which to play unfettered by any supposedly higher moral intent. Neither Coleridge nor Schiller were seeking to divorce aesthetics from morality in a Kantian manner. Rather they were attempting to assert the profound connection between the two but only as long as aesthetics remained autonomous and free. It is only by way of *indirection* that the connection is maintained. As Kooy states, "the aesthetic must be autonomous in order that it may indirectly provide that (i.e. moral) benefit."[86] Whilst Schiller explicitly espoused the notion of play as being fundamental to both art and human anthropology, Coleridge was somewhat more reluctant to deploy such a term. Yet despite this we can witness the Schillerian emphasis on *Spieltrieb* in the poetry of Coleridge. Here is an excerpt from his poem *Ad Vilmum Axiologum*, written to commemorate Wordsworth's "*Song*" in *The Prelude*.

> This be the meed, that thy song creates a thousand fold echo!
> Sweet as the warble of woods that awake at the gale of the morning!
> List! The hearts of the Pure like caves in the ancient mountains
> Deep deep in the Bosom and from the Bosom resound it
> Each a different tone, complete or in musical fragments
> Al have welcom'd thy Voice and receive and retain and prolong it
> This is the word of the Lord! It is spoken and beings eternal
> Live and are born as an infant—the eternal begets the immortal
> Love is the spirit of life and music the life of the spirit.[87]

84. Coleridge, *BL* II, 130.
85. Ibid., 131.
86. Kooy, *Coleridge, Schiller and Aesthetic Freedom*, 118.
87. Coleridge, *PW* I, 391–92.

This poem is filled with emotion, resonance, and the celebration of aesthetic encounter in art. The poetry issues forth in a thousand fold echo, which is elicited from the heart of the reader of the poem. This is art that truly engages in the fullest most imaginative way. There is a playful reciprocation between the poet, the reader, and the unreal world that the poem creates. Yet this very freedom whilst being at one level purposeless, begets something eternal and life giving within the human spirit. No one could remain unchanged after such an encounter; at least that is the implicit claim in such poetry. The name of Schiller never appears as a footnote to this poem yet his shadow is clearly cast. To substantiate this assertion one can turn again to the *Biographia Literaria*, where Coleridge discusses the liberating effects of art. With reference to the great French and British playwrights of his day, he writes, "Their tragic scenes were meant to affect us indeed, but yet within the bounds of pleasure, and in union with the activity both of our understanding and imagination. They wished to transport the mind to a sense of its possible greatness and to implant the germs of that greatness during the temporary oblivion of the worthless 'things we are.'"[88]

The temporary oblivion to which Coleridge refers is the freedom from external restraint, a state of free aesthetic pleasure. It is only from within that place of freedom that the possibility of greatness can emerge. The *Spieltrieb* offers an area of free space where one can play with possibilities without any obligation to commit oneself either to sensuous experience or to any moral responsibility. In his *Lectures* Coleridge tried to articulate this very Schillerian view when he wrote, "to reconcile opposites and to leave a middle state of mind more strictly appropriate to the imagination than any other when it is hovering between images: as soon as it . . . is fixed on one it becomes understanding and when it is waving between them attaching itself to neither it is imagination."[89]

Coleridge's engagement with Schiller thus provided him with the impetus to explore the notion of the imagination as inhabiting this free space where the possibility of play could unite both the objective and subjective worlds and lead indirectly to a renewed moral purpose. By revering the place of play, Coleridge was echoing the Platonic view that play was indeed a religious activity. Coleridge noted in one of his notebooks that the search for truth is sometimes, perhaps often, found in the most surprising places. "Amid the profoundest and most condensed

---

88. Coleridge, *BL* II, 46n.
89. Coleridge, *LL*, 311.

constructions of hardest thinking, the playfulness of the Boy starts up, like a wild Fig tree from monumental marble."[90]

Having explored some of the key influences on Coleridge's theoretical paradigms, as well as his poetic practice, we are now a position to turn to his definition of the imagination outlined most clearly in chapter 13 of his *Biographia Literaria*.

---

90. Coleridge, *CN* IV, 4777.

CHAPTER 3

Coleridge's Definition of the Imagination

COLERIDGE'S *BIOGRAPHIA LITERARIA* IS a substantial work covering his views on politics, religion, and philosophy, which includes his reflections on thinkers such as Hartley, Kant, Fichte, and Schelling. Yet his primary motive for the work was not philosophical but rather he was seeking "a settlement of the long continued controversy concerning the true nature of poetic diction."[1] His epiphanic moments of insight concerning the nature and power of poetry to which we have already alluded caused him to distance himself from Wordsworth's poetic philosophical position. In his view, Wordsworth had entirely missed the opportunity to re-define the poetic venture. Coleridge sought for a framework that could contain his own theories, the new insights he had gained from German Idealism, and his own deepening Christian conviction. In pursuit of his aim of settling the poetic controversy he wrote what, in effect, became a literary and philosophical autobiography.

The Three Forms of the Imagination

The heart of his views on poetry was founded upon a particular role for the imagination. Coleridge was persuaded that the poet "diffuses a tone, and a spirit of unity, that blends, and as it were fuses, each into each, by that synthetic and magical power, to which we have exclusively appropriated the name imagination."[2] The artistic imagination was neither the passive receptor of sense impressions nor the untamed expression of emotional forces. Rather it was something intensely intentional, held

1. Coleridge, *BL* I, 1.
2. Coleridge, *BL* II, 15–16.

within the power and control of the subject. The artistic imagination was, for Coleridge, an endeavor, a discipline, the engine of creativity. By the time Coleridge wrote *Biographia* in 1815 he had come to the conclusion that the imagination could be defined with some degree of precision. He outlined this in chapter 13 of his book, although some years later he expressed some dissatisfaction with his own definitions, considering them to be too heavily influenced by the pantheism of Schelling. Notwithstanding this caveat, the definitions he offers illustrate a stage in the ongoing development of his thinking. He divided the imagination into three categories: the primary, the secondary, and fancy. We will examine each one in turn.

The Primary Imagination

After twelve chapters of brilliant, insightful, obscure, literary and philosophical criticism, Coleridge offers this well known definition.

> The primary imagination I hold to be the living power and prime agent of all human perception, and as a repetition in the finite mind of the eternal act of creation in the infinite I AM.[3]

Here he ascribes to the primary imagination a profoundly metaphysical function. In its creative power the primary imagination is reflective of and participates in the very creative imaginative powers of God. It repeats in the finite realm what God performs in eternity. The allusion to the infinite "I AM" draws strongly upon biblical imagery. The imagination, for Coleridge, was not merely the human tool for perception, a "lazy Looker-on on an external world."[4] Rather, it possessed an active, creative, synthetic function of its own that mirrored the very actions of God.

All of these functions may be deployed, for example, as one gazes upon the beauty of an Alpine scene. A geographer or geologist may be concerned with the origin of the landforms and the shape of the contours. An artist may, by contrast, be far more aware of aesthetics of the scenery. A third option is to view a mountain scene as a place of majesty, awe, and terror, redolent with the numinous. Coleridge maintained that it is the primary imagination that enables us to adopt a range of perceptual standpoints and from each to derive a different facet of true knowledge. For Coleridge the primary imagination is quite simply an act of faith; it is the interpenetration of the divine. The primary imagination was the rightful inheritance of every human being and it participates in or

3. Ibid., 202.
4. Ibid., 202.

"repeats" the ongoing divine act of imaginative creation. When God created the world he brought cosmos out of chaos. The primary imagination likewise provides a gestalt ordering of our world. It is the means by which we perceive the symbolic nature of the world.

It is not uncommon however, in Coleridgean scholarship, to overlook the profoundly religious nature of this definition. The primary imagination is invested with sacramental qualities. It is a *living* power, capable of bringing to life, akin perhaps to the *ruach* that God breathed into Adam as described in Gen 2. It is a *prime* agent suggesting its priority in terms of importance as an instrument that fashions and creates. This imagination repeats in a finite way what God does in an infinite way. It walks the earth but touches the heavens as it does so. It is as if the human imagination is described as being God's co-worker on earth both mirroring and sharing in the activity of the divine.

It is a bold claim, given the Kantian environment in which Coleridge was writing, in which the prevailing view was that the phenomenal and noumenal worlds could not be bridged. His definition of the human imagination departed radically from the predominant Enlightenment concept of the human being. By positing a theological link with divine creativity Coleridge located the imagination not as an autonomous natural function but as a characteristic of the *imago Dei* in humankind. In doing so he made a daring assertion; that the divine imagination lodged within the human heart is a statement of human identity and not simply a description of human activity. To be fully human is to manifest the creative divine imagination of God's own self. A further corollary of this definition of the primary imagination is that it is to be understood as a human faculty that stands in relation to a divine attribute possessing therefore a pluriform quality. In Coleridge's mind there is no place for an individual autonomous imagination unconnected to anything or anyone else. Coleridge's definition demanded a significant "other", namely God, to be continually present. This conception correlates well with the later development of his theologically grounded anthropology.

The Secondary Imagination

Coleridge believed that the secondary imagination was an echo of the primary and as such was particularly found in those artists and thinkers who possessed a creative instinct. It was an ability not necessarily fully developed in everyone. This he defined as follows: "The secondary imagination I consider as an echo of the former (the primary), coexisting with the conscious will, yet still as identical with the primary in the kind of its agency, and differing only in degree and in the mode of its operation. It dissolves, diffuses, dissipates, in order to create; or where this process is rendered impossible, yet still at all events it struggles to idealize and to unify. It is essentially vital, even as all objects (as objects) are essentially fixed and dead."[5]

The secondary imagination works by breaking down, only to re-fashion, original perceptions into a new form. Without such a facility the world around us would remain a confusing mixture of shapes, sounds, and experiences with nothing to give any shape or meaning. The imagination provides the means by which order and meaning are found. It is the means by which we make symbols in order to shape our understanding of the world.

Fancy

Coleridge termed the lowest form of the imagination as "Fancy." The definition that he offers, exhibits a remaining influence of Hartley's associationism.

> Fancy on the contrary, has no other counters to play with, but fixities and definites. The Fancy is indeed no other than a mode of memory emancipated from the order of time and space; while it is blended with, and modified by that empirical phenomenon of the will, which we express by the word choice. But equally with the ordinary memory the Fancy must receive all its materials ready made from the law of association.[6]

For Coleridge fancy was merely a mechanical operation, akin to the moving around of pieces on a chessboard or the re-arrangement of goods wagons in a railway station yard. It was nothing more than a repositioning of data and as such carried no creative functions and no contact with the divine. All that fancy can do is to use the limited materials at hand, namely that which is provided by sensory data, and gather them together in a series of constellations. Fancy is not a creative, shaping, forming activity. It can only use what is seen, measured, and touched and does not deal with newness and innovation. In chapter 24 of *Biographia Literaria*, which forms the conclusion of this great work, Coleridge describes Fancy in disparaging terms. It is "always the ape, and too often the counterfeit and adulterer of our memory."[7] The exercise of choice that is open to

---

5. Ibid., 202.
6. Ibid., 202.
7. Ibid., 235.

Fancy is deliberate and intentional but the raw materials available to it are limited to what the human mind can remember or has experienced. It is a strange irony that Wordsworth maintained this "lower" view of the imagination even though it was through his poetry that Coleridge was exposed to the "translucency of the divine," the hallmark of the more exalted primary imagination.

The Relative Significance of the Three Forms of the Imagination.

There is considerable scholarly dissension concerning the relative importance that Coleridge attached to the primary and secondary imaginations. Engell[8], for example, adopts the orthodox view that it is the secondary imagination that possesses the higher function. He asserts that the primary imagination is a spontaneous, involuntary, reflex capability, similar to what Kant would call an empirical imagination. Engell argues that the primary imagination is more primitive in that it is comparable to one of the primary colors from which other colors may be blended. "There is no originality in the primary imagination," he claims, it merely "repeats and copies."[9] It is therefore the secondary imagination, according to Engell, that possesses the higher, more transcendent function. It alone can dissolve, diffuse and dissipate.

The argumentation that Engell deploys to prove his assertion however could appear as somewhat simplistic. The argument that one moves from the lower function (primary) to the higher function (secondary) could equally well be turned on its head. One could also claim that the very word "primary" is indicative of a priority of importance over and above something that is "merely" secondary. Furthermore, J. Wordsworth makes a persuasive case that it is the primary imagination that Coleridge had in mind when defining the most exalted mode of imagination's role.[10] His case rests upon an analysis of Coleridge's literary form. The primary imagination is described in lofty terms with rich use of adjectives; "*living* power," "*prime* agent," "*all* human perception," and the progression from "*finite*" to "*eternal*" to "*infinite*." It is exultant prose proclaiming the presence of the eternal dwelling in the finite, the ongoing creative power of God poured out in continual creativity in humankind. By contrast, the secondary imagination is described in comparatively pedestrian, businesslike terms. It is the primary that appears to have the more impressive

---

8. Coleridge, *BL* I, lxxxix.
9. Ibid., xci.
10. Gravil, Newlyn & Roe, *Coleridge's Imagination*, 24.

definition. The primary imagination is concerned not only with perception but also participates in the ongoing eternal act of creation. To claim, with Engell, that there is no originality in the primary imagination is extraordinary if this imaginative function participates and mirrors God's own creative originality. There is a twofold function, both perception and creation, such that the imagination possesses the capability of opening up and exploring the possible, the new, the innovative. It is the imagination that can make that which is absent, a present reality. It possesses what Ricoeur was much later to refer to a "passion for the possible."[11] Clearly the primary and secondary imaginations are never set in a competitive relationship with one another and to dispute which is the higher function is ultimately of little benefit. Both possess the power to "dissolve, diffuse, dissipate, in order to create . . . to idealize and to unify." Most crucially, both participate in the imaginative activity of God.

It is the word "unify," however, that identifies the Coleridgean definition of the imagination as essentially Romantic. The search for unity, the ability to see the Cause in the Effect, the perception of the divine in all things, that was the hallmark of the Romantic Movement. The unifying capacity of Coleridge's imagination functioned at three different levels of reconciliation. These were represented in perception, in art, and in philosophy. As Engell explains, "the imagination performs three syntheses that are the same kind but that differ in degree."[12] These synthetic functions are enabled via the deployment of "esemplastic" symbols that possessed the power to shape into one. At the most mundane level, symbols of perception are used so habitually that they are scarcely recognized as symbols for they include such things as language and number. Artistic symbols are of a higher order for they represent an ideal form and by implication, a divine shaping. The highest expression of symbolic usage comes within the philosophical sphere for philosophy offers a means of communicating linguistically what art achieves materially.[13] This synthesizing reconciling agency, achieved through symbol, is demonstrative of the living power that resides within the imagination.

Having sketched the contours of Coleridge's definition of the imagination as it is presented in *Biographia Literaria*, we are now in a position to examine in more detail the precise content of Coleridge's imaginative world. This discussion will form the substance of chapter 4.

---

11. Ricoeur, *Rule of Metaphor*, 3–8.
12. Coleridge, *BL* I, lxxxii.
13. Ibid., lxxxiii.

CHAPTER 4

Key Features of Coleridge's View of the Imagination

Whilst Coleridge's definition of the imagination can readily be located, contained as it is within a small section of *Biographia Literaria*, what is not so plain is the identification of some of its key features. Commenting on the *Biographia* definition, Engell makes this observation: "Imagination belongs neither to the purely subjective nor to the purely objective, neither to the ideal nor to the real, to the spiritual or the concrete. Reconciling and harmonizing these opposites, it partakes of both. Coleridge designated it as a force or power or energy that transforms and blends ideas, images, thoughts, and things."[1]

How, in the mind of Coleridge, does this unifying, reshaping process take place? In what context? By what means? To what end? To answer these probing questions we will examine four distinct but related themes. None of these are spelled out in a logical, chronological manner in the often dense and obscure writings of Coleridge but they are nevertheless repeated streams of thought that run underneath his convoluted argumentation. We will look at four of these features in turn.

Polar Unification

The late eighteenth and early nineteenth centuries were times of great change and intellectual foment. New discoveries in the field of magnetism and electricity, for example, opened up an entirely novel way of perceiving how the forces of attraction and repulsion could be held in tension rather than as polar opposites. Of critical importance for Coleridge was the search

---

1. Engell in Coleridge, *BL* I, lxxxi.

to find a unity between theoretical and practical sciences, albeit one that was not based on utilitarian ideas. Could there be one harmonious body of knowledge? The issue for Coleridge therefore was to determine how differing realities are constituted and the nature of their mutual interaction. Coleridge's conception of the imagination was built on the idea of polarity, upon a balance of opposites: the old and the new, the same and the different, real and ideal, sensuous and spiritual, temporal and eternal, immanent and transcendent. These apparent dichotomies were not seen as being in opposition to one another but were regarded as being in polar tension within the same force field. The task that he set himself was to find a way that brought such polarities into an organic unity. The search for unity within or behind all things was the abiding pre-occupation of Coleridge. Indeed Cutsinger maintains that Coleridge cannot rightly be understood apart from an appreciation of this quest. It is necessary, however, to define carefully what is understood by Coleridgean unity. Unity was not understood to be the mere amalgamation of disparate individual entities forming a larger whole. Rather it was a unity that was perceived prior to any attention to particular entities. Indeed Coleridge emphasized the necessity of excluding the particular precisely so that the general could be apprehended. This is not to say that Coleridge despised or ignored diversity. On the contrary, he welcomed and embraced it but only as part of the One which does not exist at the expense of the Many. He was profoundly interested in difference but not so much in differences. He celebrated the *fact* of particularity and individuality rather than the actuality of difference.

By way of example, one may consider the case of a bowl of apples. If Coleridge were to contemplate the fruit he would not be so much concerned about their individual differences of shape, size, texture, and taste. He would be much more taken with the notion or the idea of apple as a symbol of something that participates in a far greater whole. Apples thus became, as did everything else for Coleridge, "protophaenomon," in that they possessed a translucent quality that opened a window onto another world, the eternal world of the One. This profoundly Platonic view with clear Plotinian strains of thinking placed him at odds with Kant whom he considered to be locked into an Aristotelian world. For Coleridge, Aristotle and Plato represented two totally different ways of perceiving the world and he asserted that humankind could be placed in one or other camp. "Every man is born an Aristotelian or a Platonist. I do not think it possible that any one born an Aristotelian can become a Platonist, and I am sure no born Platonist can ever change into an

Aristotelian. They are the two classes of men, beside which it is next impossible to conceive a third."[2]

This distinction manifested itself in a difference in methodology. Aristotelians were, according to Coleridge, concerned with particulars, with measuring, categorizing, placing into compartments, and from these initial observations, by a process of induction, drawing generalizations. These natural philosophers, of whom Locke and Hartley were representative, took the objective raw material of passive natural phenomena as their starting point. It might conceivably be possible to abstract universals from these particulars but the thorough-going Aristotelian knows that universals are not really there.

Platonists like Coleridge, by contrast, begin with the universals. They begin with Ideas which are universal in their application and existence. They are profoundly real and are metaphysically prior to the particulars. The subjective philosophers considered self-conscious intelligence as being antecedent to all knowledge. It is what the mind brings to external data that is key. In his *Philosophical Lectures* Coleridge explained the distinction between the two positions in this way. The natural philosophers "give the whole to the object and make the subject, that is the reflecting and contemplating, feeling part, merely the result of that. The transcendentalists give the whole to the subject and make the object a mere result involved in it."[3]

Coleridge described these two poles of perception as being akin to two rivers, both of which flow into one lake. Initially, as we have seen, Coleridge had espoused only one of these sources, the associationism of Hartley, but quickly came to realize that this natural system made no room for any metaphysical, transcendent reality. Within this framework the mind was merely a machine composed of vibrations which ordered and re-ordered sense impressions. Associationism was, in effect, an expression of a latent atheism and as such was totally inadequate to represent Coleridge's emerging thinking. It was epitomized in the phrase, *es gibt* ("there is"), which, for Coleridge, was utterly insufficient.

The alternative subjective pole, to which Coleridge was later drawn, placed the locus of control within the individual. It was the place of being, *ich bin* rather than *es gibt*. His was an attempt to find an intimate union between inward intelligence and external substance. It was the unity of the perceiver that he perceived, the conjoining of the conceiver and conception. This unification of polar principles lay at the heart of

---

2. Coleridge, *TT*, 125.
3. Engell, *The Creative Imagination*, 330.

all of Coleridge's thinking. In a letter written to a young doctor, James Gillman, Coleridge outlined his mature philosophy: "An idea contemplates the Alpha and Omega (one-all; Finite-Infinite, Subject-Object, Mind-Matter, Substance-Form, Time-Space, Motion-Rest, Futuration-Presence , etc.) and it is indifferent towards which of the pairs you take, for they are symbols of the same truth produced by different positions."[4]

The engine room of this polar unification for Coleridge is the inward "I." Yet we must be careful to be clear concerning Coleridge's understanding of this. Coleridge defined the understanding as that faculty which receives sense impressions from the external world and then orders them. The understanding (Kant's *Verstand*), is capable of grasping the two poles of perceptions, the subject and the object, but the understanding cannot unify them. It cannot create the images upon which that unification depends. Reason, by contrast, is that faculty which operates within the realm of ideas. Ideas do not originate from sense impressions but are dependent on the external material world to provide the symbolic material in order to be articulated. It is reason therefore and not the understanding which is the higher capability, for it is reason that originates the world of ideas.

The key question that this schema presents therefore is how to determine the true status of ideas. Are they, following Kant, regulative and merely the product of the mind of an individual and thus limited in their scope? Or, are they constitutive, representing and reflecting something of their divine origin? It was this latter constitutive position that Coleridge held, pointing to his profoundly metaphysical, indeed biblical roots. The understanding and reason were, however, never to be understood as being in competition with one another. The understanding includes and subsumes the senses just as reason includes and subsumes the understanding. Coleridge envisaged these as expanding concentric circles. So what place within this schema did Coleridge accord to the imagination? For Coleridge, the imagination was the means by which this polar unification was facilitated. How can ideas generated by reason be expressed in a coherent way? Only through the use of symbol and image. It is the imagination that takes symbols drawn from the external world of the senses and unites them with ideas proposed by reason. Imagination has therefore an inter-connecting instrumentality, "the laboratory in which the thought elaborates essence into experience," so wrote Coleridge in one of his notebooks.[5] The imagination integrates the understanding, reason, ideas, and the senses at times being active and at others passive.

---

4. Coleridge, *CL* III, 1033.
5. Coleridge, *CN* III, 4398.

It possesses the capacity to translate this process into images and symbols which provide the mind with a language to express itself.

Coleridge's conclusion that the imagination possessed this capability caused him to search for appropriate language to articulate his views. He described the imagination as having a modifying, co-adunative, fusive, unifying, and esemplastic power. It alone was capable of shaping and forming into one. His search for the unity that lay behind all things shows traces of his early fascination with neo-Platonism. Polar unification however was not the only quality that Coleridge's imagination possessed. We have already hinted that the unifying operation of the imagination displayed both active and passive components. This was the second key hallmark of Coleridge's imaginative project which we shall now explore in more detail.

The Passive-active Imagination

In a notebook entry, Coleridge wrote that the imagination "must receive something from nature and something from the mind's own self-reflection as well, before it can produce a symbolic bond between the two."[6] There are two possible ways of defining the active and passive relationship that Coleridge had in mind here. One sense is that of gift and reception. The citation above makes mention of the act, undertaken by the imagination, of receiving something as a gift from the created world, before anything can be returned in a newly reshaped form. There is a reciprocal mutuality implied here even if the relationship may not be entirely symmetrical. The other sense is that of the distinction between activity and rest which implies that the imagination cannot and does not always function like the continuous stream of direct electrical current. The pairing of activity and rest is suggestive of an energy or power that pulses, much like a human heartbeat, with moments of output interspersed with pauses.

Yet there is a third strand that one can add to this description. In his *Biographia Literaria*, Coleridge muses on the way in which inward experiences are processed. He writes, "Our inward experiences were . . . arranged in three separate classes: the passive, or what our school-men call the merely receptive quality of the mind; the voluntary; and the spontaneous, which holds the middle place between both."[7]

Coleridge asserts here that imagination is both active (voluntary) and passive (involuntary) and therefore is also spontaneous. This spontaneity carries the sense of something that is intuitive, child-like, even playful, and bears similarity with Schiller's *Spieltrieb*. Whilst Coleridge

6. Coleridge, *BL* I, xxxiv.
7. Ibid., 90.

uses the term "spontaneous," he does so in a quite different manner to Kant who likewise sought to make sense of the notion of freedom. The dilemma that Kant faced was how to locate freedom in relation to reason, for freedom, by definition, cannot not be the end product of progression of rational causality. Writing with reference to Kant, Andrew Bowie explains: "Reason, involves something which is infinite, in the sense that it cannot in any way be determined by anything finite we know about the world. It shows a spontaneity so pure that it goes beyond everything with which sensuousness can provide it.[8]

The spontaneity which Coleridge insisted upon belonged to the heart of what it means to be human and was of an altogether different order. Coleridge did not share the Kantian suspicion of the divine inhabiting the finite world of human experience. For Coleridge, the occupation of the middle ground by the spontaneous imagination was only made possible by a reciprocal relationship with God. The notion of the imagination as something that functions in a spontaneous manner demands that there be a something, or someone, who elicits a spontaneous response. Spontaneity in its very essence demands reciprocity which, in the world of Coleridge, makes perfect sense.

In December 1809 Coleridge spent Christmas beside the Lake of Ratzenburg. One evening there was a thunderstorm which broke with great intensity over the place where he was staying. Musing upon this experience he felt that some kind of breaking in of the sublime had occurred. He recorded his reflections about this in his publication *The Friend*. "There are sounds more sublime than any sight can be, more absolutely suspending the power of comparison, and more utterly absorbing the mind's self-consciousness in its total attention to the object working upon it."[9] Whilst this self-conscious attentiveness was directed at the majesty of a thunderstorm, one feels that Coleridge could equally have been describing sublime music created by human means. Coleridge's search for contact with the sublime could be likened to a courtship. For him the search possessed an elusive quality about it. At times there is a leaning forward, a straining to touch and then at others a drawing back to wait and observe. Both the passive and the active forms of engagement are required. He knew for certain that the actual point of contact, the *Anknupfungspunkt*, required total attention to the present moment.

The following two citations from Coleridge's works are illustrative of not only the fecundity of his thinking but the struggle with which he

---

8. Bowie, *Aesthetics and Subjectivity*, 21.
9. Coleridge, *TF* I, 367.

was continually engaged, namely to articulate the nature of the relationship between subject and object. In particular, one can observe here the tension between the passive reception of sensory information and the subsequent active processing. The first citation recounts the common human experience of forgetting a person's name.

> I feel that there is a mystery in the sudden by-act-of-will-unaided, nay, more that that, frustrated recollection of a name. I was trying to recollect the name of a Bristol friend . . . I began with the Letters of the Alphabet—A, B, C, etc. and I know not why, felt convinced that it began with H. I ran through all the vowels and with all the consonants, in vain. Three minutes afterwards, having completely given up, the name Daniel, at once stared up, perfectly insulated, without the dimmest antecedent connection. There is no explanation of this fact. The name Daniel must have been a living Atom-being in my mind . . . and there it is! Not assisted by any association, but the very contrary—by the suspension and sedation of all associations.[10]

This next excerpt, which refers back to the difficulty of remembering the name Daniel, takes the discussion of the active-passive nature of the imagination a stage further.

> Now let a man watch his mind while he is composing; or, to take a still more common case, while he is trying to recollect a name (remember Daniel) and he will find the process completely analogous. Most of my readers will have observed a small water insect on the surface of the rivulets, . . . how the little animal wins its way up against the stream, by alternate pulses of active and passive motion, now resisting the current, now yielding to it in order to gather strength and momentary fulcrum for a further propulsion. This is no unapt emblem of the mind's self-experience in the act of thinking. There are evidently two powers at work, which relatively to each other are active and passive. In philosophical language we must denominate this intermediate faculty in all its degrees and denominations, the imagination.[11]

Coleridge concludes that the imagination functions in this bipolar fashion, at times being a passive recipient and at others being the active agent. He is considering the way in which the unconscious undergirds all human mental activity and in particular the imagination. Coleridge was acutely aware that if there was no modulating power between the

10. Coburn, *Inquiring Spirit*, 30–31.
11. Coleridge, *BL* I, 124–25.

two poles of activity and passivity, inherent dangers lay lurking. If the flow of energy were simply in one direction—for example, from the self-conscious mind towards the external world—then the temptation would be that the human mind would become a self-enclosed, self-referential, solipsistic, even tyrannical, entity. The alternative pole of temptation was equally dangerous. If energy only flows from nature towards the human mind then the mind becomes a mere passive receptor of stimuli, a device for recording and measuring information. These two extremes permit either gross self-delusion or significant self-deprecation both of which are to be strenuously avoided. A mediation between these two—the active and passive nature of the imagination—is necessary, according to Coleridge, in order to keep the mind healthy.[12] In his *Shakespeare Lectures*[13] of 1811–12, Coleridge acknowledges that it is when the mind relaxes into a kind of *reverie*, floating between two or more images, that the imagination is most productive. When it is fixated on simply one option the tendency is that merely the understanding is deployed. With two images to consider, both the passive and active imaginative faculties are required often at the same time.

Coleridge was not alone in making such assertions about the nature of the imagination and it is difficult to attribute the origins of this view to Coleridge alone. Notwithstanding the relative obscurity of the origins of these views, it is pertinent to note the conclusion to which Coleridge came after having remembered the missing name and having spent time considering a water insect. He muses: "There are evidently two powers at work, which relatively to each other are active and passive; and this is not possible without an intermediate faculty, which is at once both active and passive. In philosophical language, we must denominate this intermediate faculty in all its degrees and determinations, the imagination."[14]

This is how Coleridge observed the imagination in action; at times very active in forming, shaping, and creating, whilst at other times apparently dormant and still. The moments of inactivity are as significant and potentially creative as the times of greatest action. One of Coleridge's poems, "*To Nature*" illustrates well this oscillation between the active and passive modes of perception.

> It may indeed be phantasy, when I
> essay to draw from all created things
> deep heartfelt, inward joy that closely clings;

12. Ibid., lxxxiv.
13. Coleridge, *LL*, 311.
14. Coleridge, *BL* I, 124–25.

and trace in leaves and flowers that round me lie
lessons of love and earnest piety.[15]

This poem articulates the conundrum that Coleridge sought to resolve, namely the relationship between the narrator and Nature and its apparently active-passive pattern. The narrator in the poem seeks to draw from Nature that which only Nature can provide and which the narrator lacks. The narrator actively seeks but has to passively wait. However, the one thing that the narrator lacks is the feeling of inward joy which belongs to the abstract world of feelings and not to the phenomenal world of things. Joy is the by-product of the active-passive engagement of the two. As Hurtrez explains, "the activity of Nature and the corresponding passivity of the subject is counterbalanced by the activity of the 'I' and the corresponding passivity of Nature."[16]

The pattern of oscillation between the active and passive poles, bears some similarities with Fichte's *Schweben* between the *Ich* and *Nicht-Ich*, and Schiller's *Spieltrieb*. It describes a movement that possesses an ebb and flow, a giving as well as a receiving and points in the direction of the whole notion of improvisation, a subject to which we will later turn to consider in greater detail.

Symbol

The intellectual endeavor that absorbed the energies of Coleridge was directed for the most part at reconciling what appeared to be opposites in human experience, namely the relationship between subject and object. No doubt this quest either resonated with, or was influenced by, the same struggle that consumed the thinking of the German idealists. At one end of the philosophical spectrum, Coleridge was deeply convinced that the mind was profoundly active in the act of knowing and perceiving and was no mere recorder of received information. In this respect, Coleridge was a true Kantian. Yet he also knew that what we perceive as *things* are indeed *things*, and not merely the outward projection of the mind. There was, according to Coleridge, an objective reality out there and thus he was able to assert that when the ordinary person sees a table, what he sees, "is the table itself . . . and not the phantom of a table from which he may argumentatively deduce the reality of a table which he does not see."[17] But knowing that the table was really there posed a problem if all reality was simply

---

15. Coleridge, *PW* II, 1–5.
16. Hurtrez, *Nature and Subjectivity*, 13.
17. Coleridge, *BL* I, 179.

constructed within the mind, as Fichte would perhaps have claimed. How could this dilemma be solved? This was the Coleridgean quest that he addressed, in part at least, by recourse to a theory of symbol.

Coleridge's theory of symbol as a constituent part of the imagination did not emerge in a philosophical or theological vacuum. Brice argues that in formulating his theory, Coleridge was caught between the powerful influences of two intellectual forces. The first of these he labels "epistemological pietism," following in the Calvinist tradition, which emphasized the "noetic" effects of the Fall. Calvin averred that the consequences of the sin of Adam and Eve lay in the impaired, if not virtually destroyed, capacity of humankind to reason and perceive God aright. Whilst God revealed himself through Nature, humanity had lost the power to intuit this.[18] Human knowledge was situated in a vast abyss of ignorance and darkness. Calvin was thus both a representative and the main instigator of the drive to undermine any linkage between the triadic relationships of nature, divine revelation, and human reason. From a Calvinist/Augustinian interpretation of the Fall of humankind there was no analogy between human and divine reason, for man simply could not discern the mind of God via Nature.

Brice argues that this Calvinist stream had an undermining influence on Coleridge's confidence in his theory of symbol. Whilst he believed that symbolic knowledge was true knowledge he struggled to defend this position philosophically. In part, this may have been due the fact that in his personal life there was a considerable degree of resonance with the Calvinist description of fallen humanity. His opium addiction, his clandestine love for Sara Hutchinson, or even his own unhappy marriage no doubt contributed to his cry for charity to be extended towards him. Whatever the cause, Coleridge was acutely aware of his own fallen-ness, which was expressed at times through his notebooks in doubts that lingered over his capacity to perceive the divine.

The second intellectual force that constrained Coleridge's development of his theory of symbol was the "theological voluntarism" of thinkers such as Locke and Newton. This tradition emphasized the radical transcendence of God in relation to creation, a relationship that was arbitrary and contingent. Because God was so totally "other," the notion that the divine could be discerned symbolically within the created order was discounted. Human reason was totally inadequate to comprehend the mysteries of so transcendent a God. This Humean "fork" placed a radical disjuncture between two types of human knowing. In his work,

---

18. Brice, *Coleridge and Scepticism*, 4.

An Enquiry Concerning Human Understanding, published in 1748, Hume wrote, "All the objects of human reason or enquiry may naturally be divided into two kinds, to wit, Relations of Ideas, and Matters of fact. Of the first kind are the sciences of Geometry, Algebra, and Arithmetic . . . [which are] discoverable by the mere operation of thought . . . Matters of fact, which are the second object of human reason, are not ascertained in the same manner; nor is our evidence of their truth, however great, of a like nature with the foregoing."[19] Hume's suspicion of any brand of Natural Religion in which one sought to extrapolate truth about God through the deployment arguments from design offered a forceful critique of the kind of theological approach to which Coleridge was drawn.

Given these two impinging philosophical and theological forces, the emphasis that Coleridge sought to place on symbol derived from his attempt to find a unifying power that existed between the underlying laws within nature, human reason and the divine. There was a triad of relationships in need of a connecting power, illustrated in this simple diagram.

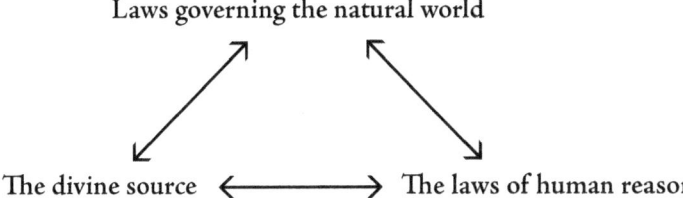

Brice articulates Coleridge's intentions in seeking to find appropriate connections between these three poles. His theory of symbolism was an effort to connect human language and reason to the intelligible language of divinity incarnate in the natural world, and to try to explain the relationship of reciprocity that exists between poems about nature and the divine poetry in nature, that they are ideally mirrored.[20]

How did Coleridge approach this task, which he had set himself? Coleridge was both a keen observer of the natural world around him and also highly attentive to the shifting moods, thoughts, and affections, which he observed within himself. Whilst there was an intellectual rigor in his argumentation his theories often began from spontaneous intuition. It is no surprise therefore to discover that one Saturday evening in April 1805, we find Coleridge staring up at the moon from his study window in Malta. He jots down what he observes.

19. Hume, *An Enquiry Concerning Human Understanding*, 24.
20. Brice, *Coleridge and Scepticism*, 1.

> In looking at objects of Nature while I am thinking, as at yonder moon dim-glimmering thro' the dewy window-pane, I seem rather to be seeking, as it were asking, a symbolic language for something within me that already and forever exists, than observing anything new. Even when that latter is the case, yet still I have always an obscure feeling as if that new phenomena were the dim Awakening of a forgotten or hidden truth of my inner nature. It is still interesting as a Word, a Symbol! It is the Logos the Creator![21]

Here Coleridge expresses vividly how an ordinary, dare we say mundane, experience of observing moonlight caused him to engage in an act of self-reflection. It is as if the phenomena that he perceives, combined with the feeling of awe felt inwardly, evoked an ancient memory. The symbol of the moon uncovers what lies hidden or dormant within for it connects with, reveals, and exposes what already is, rather than creating something new. Coleridge articulates here what was to become a central component in his theory of the imagination, namely the place of symbol. The exalted position that Coleridge afforded to symbol reflects his concern to define the nature of the copula between the notion of "Idea" and its expression or embodiment. Can there be in reality a fusion between thought and form? Coleridge's persistent concern to uncover the inherent underlying unity in all things extended to his theory of symbol such that form and its symbolic manifestation were both derived from a single piece of fabric.

His intuitive theory, founded in experience, was that the poetic imagination—so sublimely expressed in the works of Shakespeare, Milton, and Wordsworth—was an echo of the divine imagination lodged deep within the human soul. This divine residual, evident in the Book of Nature too, must be in some way joined or linked together and it was Coleridge's conviction that symbol provided just such a bridge. In a notebook entry, Coleridge reflects on the curious phenomena of Coralline Zoolithe (Coral). The root of coral is rock and its stem is stone, yet its branches are flesh, teeming with life itself.[22] Coral was thus a perfect symbol of the true experience of human regeneration or redemption, whereby humanity is transformed, by the grace of God, from lifeless stone to living breath.

Coleridge explores the significance of symbol, by placing it in contrast with allegory. "By a symbol I mean, not a metaphor or allegory or any other figure of speech or form or fancy but an actual and essential part

---

21. Coleridge, *CN* II, 2546.
22. Coleridge, *CN* IV, 4717.

of that, the whole of which it represents."[23] Coleridge gives an example of what he means by such figures of speech. They are attempts to communicate the principle of a higher dignity in a more known form. So, when John writes, "that which is born of the flesh is flesh; and that which is born of the Spirit is spirit,"[24] he is using analogous language that reveals something through subjects that are different from each other, yet which also bear a resemblance. With metaphorical language, on the other hand, the illustration is made by means of similarity rather than difference. Paul, for example, explains the act of redemption in Christ by reliance on metaphors such as the repayment of a debt or the reconciliation of an estranged parent and child. The metaphorical benefit is the establishment of sameness in order to articulate a higher truth. Symbol, by contrast, is of a wholly different order. In Coleridge's own words it is, "characterized by the translucence of the Special in the individual or of the General in the Especial or of the Universal in the General. Above all by the translucence of the eternal through and in the temporal. It always partakes of the reality which it renders intelligible; and while it enunciates the whole, abides itself as a living part in that unity of which it is the representative."[25]

Whilst Coleridge presents symbol and allegory as being in radical opposition to each other, he does not denigrate either but simply points out that they operate in different ways just as the understanding and reason or imagination and fancy. The tree of the knowledge of good and evil was, for Coleridge, an example of allegory, the meaning of which is limited and quickly exhausted. By contrast, symbols are more fertile and diffuse in their meaning. An example of this can be drawn from Matthew's Gospel where Jesus declares that, "The light of the body is the eye."[26] The eye is a symbol of vision simply because it participates in the whole that it represents. It is therefore not *allegorical* but *tautegorical*.[27] The primacy that Coleridge accorded to symbol is related to his definition of reason in relation to the understanding. Reason, being the higher faculty, is capable of *a priori* ideas, which are constitutive in their nature. Understanding is capable simply of working with sensory data and organizing it into an intelligible whole. Reason, however, cannot operate unilaterally and requires expression in concrete, linguistic terms. It is the imagination that enables this process to occur and it is here that Coleridge insists

23. Coleridge, *LS*, 79.
24. John 3:6.
25. Coleridge, *SM*, 30.
26. Matt 6:22.
27. Coleridge, *CN* IV, 4711.

that the truths of reason cannot but be communicated except by symbol. As Engell states, "reason must be transformed into a symbolic sensual language before it can inform other faculties or communicate truth."[28]

Imagination thus gives reason a language of its own and an ability to appear in forms that can be apprehended. Imagination is given a mediating role between the reason and the understanding. Coleridge states as much unequivocally in his *Biographia Literaria* where he claims, "an Idea, in the highest sense of that word, cannot be conveyed but by a symbol and except in geometry, all symbols of necessity involve an apparent contradiction."[29] Here Coleridge is making a couple of claims in one highly condensed sentence. In first place, he allocates a huge responsibility to symbol. If ideas are constitutive, as he insisted, then they are the essential shaping forces within all human knowledge. When those ideas are in need of articulation they require a vehicle for that to happen. That vehicle, according to Coleridge, is symbol. A symbol possesses the property of "Outness," or externality. At one level, it is the outward expression of an inward mental image, yet it is in fact far more than that. It also correlates directly with and participates in the external reality that the internal image has initiated. By judicious and creative use of the imagination humankind is capable of forming something that is truly new, a symbol that unites the oneness of all things within and behind the multiplicity of the many; what Coleridge referred to as "Multeity in Unity."[30]

This production of symbol is made possible because of the role of the secondary imagination. It is this power which, when activated by reason, can discern the hidden-ness of divine Ideas. The imagination can do far more than simply copy or repeat what is given to it by the senses. It can break down, dissolve, and reassemble, whilst all the time retaining hold onto that idea which lies at the core. A symbol thus refers simultaneously to that which is actually presented in front of the observer and that which remains unseen and obscured. As Hedley explains, "the presence of the symbol points to that which is otherwise absent."[31] The Coleridgean symbol is thus the reconciler of opposites, the individual and the representative, the particular and the universal.

In his book *Aids to Reflection*, Coleridge applies this theory of symbol to the scriptural narrative of the Fall (Gen 3). He interprets the nature of human sinfulness as that tendency to use only the understanding without

28. Engell, *The Creative Imagination*, 338.
29. Coleridge, *BL* I, 156.
30. Coleridge, *BL* II, 232.
31. Hedley, *Living Forms of the Imagination*, 132.

the modifying light of reason.[32] Understanding on its own leads simply to "the wily temper to evil and counterfeit good."[33] It does not possess any higher function, is concerned only with superficialities and thus cannot be trusted to seek the divine imperative. If this is how Adam and Eve sinned, then their story is symbolic of our story too. It is a symbol of all of human nature in that Adam "falls" in every human being each day.

In addition to this critically communicative role that symbol possesses, Coleridge states that there is also an inherent, or at least an apparent, contradiction. To what does Coleridge refer when he makes such a claim? Here Coleridge is asserting the "tautegorical" nature of symbol. The deployment of this term by Coleridge is highly significant and was first used by him in *The Statesman's Manual*, where he derives the term from the Greek phrase "*o estin aei tautegorikon*," meaning "that which is always tautegorical."[34] The Oxford English Dictionary attributes the English term directly to Coleridge who understood it to mean *expressing the same subject but with a difference*, in contrast to metaphors which are always allegorical and which express a different subject but with a resemblance. A tautegorical symbol possesses a form that is not accidental but essential to the meaning being conveyed. "The form is a necessary correlate of the content."[35] Schelling expressed great admiration for Coleridge for his usage of this very term claiming that, "Coleridge had expressed many things better than he could himself, that in one word he had comprised a whole essay, saying that mythology was not allegorical but tautegorical."[36] Coleridge does not denigrate allegory but merely recognizes that allegory functions in a different way to the tautegory of symbol. The use of allegory is about instruction, about fashioning "truth" into a particular package in order to elicit a specific educational intent. Its meaning is thus rapidly exhausted. Symbols, by contrast, possess the capacity to unify matter and spirit in that they simultaneously refer to what is seen and also to what is not visible. They therefore produce a cluster of related meanings with a beautiful, fertile imprecision. Hedley explains Coleridgean theory of symbol in this way: "The symbol of light conveys the productive bestowing of illumination without exhaustion or depletion of the source, but also joy; awe; insight; warmth; sustenance.

---

32. In this context Coleridge associates conscience and the laws of God with the term "Reason."
33. Coleridge, *AR*, 268.
34. Coleridge, *SM*, 30n.
35. Hedley, *Living Forms of the Imagination*, 141.
36. Coleridge, *SM*, 30n.

There is a continuum between the nature and effects of the symbol (e.g. the sun) and the object symbolized (God). The symbol presupposes the vital link between meaning and Being: between the visible and invisible coincidence between image and reality."[37]

Symbol makes that which is invisible, visible and that which is absent, present. Even literary characters can become symbolic figures with this dual potentiality. Hercules is symbolic of physical strength just as Don Juan is symbolic of strength of character. For both figures there is a balance of the generic and the individual making the symbol profoundly instructive.[38] Perkins maintains that Coleridge's theory of symbol stems from an acceptance of the Augustinian view that for fallen humanity divine truths are no longer fully translucent; that they can only be perceived partially as it were, through an opaque veil. The symbol presents spiritual truths through the fallen medium of sensible objects.[39] It uses the profane to speak of the sacred.

Notwithstanding these caveats, Coleridge made bold attempts to plot his own course through this philosophical and theological minefield and developed his theory of symbol mainly in a work entitled *The Statesman's Manual* incorporating his *Lay Sermons*. Coleridge was keen to make a sharp distinction between allegory and symbol. He defined allegory as merely "picture language," which was simply an abstraction from the senses. As such it was unsubstantial and worthless.[40] Symbols however were characterized, as we have already noted, by a "translucency of the Special." This distinction between allegory and symbol was a vitally important one for Coleridge. Symbol was capable of effecting a reconciliation between the universal and the particular and this was necessary if one is to perceive aright the distinction between the literal and the metaphorical. In the case of scriptural exegesis this is crucial in order to avoid "disastrous consequences" and other "miseries".[41]

Symbols thus possessed a sacramental quality, both pointing to and partaking in the very essence of divine truth. This view was founded on an assumption that objects in the natural world possessed an intrinsic significance of a poetic, philosophical, and religious nature. There was an inherently "numinous" quality about them. The translucency of the natural world capable of communicating the divine was something that Coleridge

---

37. Hedley, *Living Forms of the Imagination*, 135.
38. Coleridge, *BL* II, 214–15.
39. Perkins, *Coleridge's Philosophy*, 51.
40. Coleridge, *LS*, 30.
41. Ibid., 30.

was passionate to pass on to his children. In the final version of his poem *Frost at Midnight*, written in 1798 to his son Hartley, he longs that the beauty of nature would communicate something of the voice of God.

> Dear Babe, that sleepest cradled by my side,
> Whose gentle breathings, heard in this deep calm,
> Fill up the interspersèd vacancies
> And momentary pauses of the thought!
> My babe so beautiful! it thrills my heart
> With tender gladness, thus to look at thee,
> And think that thou shalt learn far other lore,
> And in far other scenes! For I was reared
> In the great city, pent 'mid cloisters dim,
> And saw nought lovely but the sky and stars.
> But thou, my babe! shalt wander like a breeze
> By lakes and sandy shores, beneath the crags
> Of ancient mountain, and beneath the clouds,
> Which image in their bulk both lakes and shores
> And mountain crags: so shalt thou see and hear
> The lovely shapes and sounds intelligible
> Of that eternal language, which thy God
> Utters, who from eternity doth teach
> Himself in all, and all things in himself.
> Great universal Teacher! he shall mould
> Thy spirit, and by giving make it ask.[42]

Coleridge writes here of the lakes, sandy shores, crags, and mountains speaking an eternal language which God himself utters. This is Coleridge's principle of consubstantiality by which he meant that symbols are "harmonious in themselves and consubstantial with the truths of which they are conductors."[43] Not only was this true of symbolic language, it was also true of the book of Nature by which God reveals himself to humanity. To "read" Nature is to find a complete correspondence with the spiritual truths that are located there. Coleridge reveals here the *Logosophic* framework of his thinking. The principle of all life and indeed of all knowledge is that behind and within all things there is the *Logos*, the Divine power, the ground of all phenomena. From this *Logos* the same principles that determine human subjectivity also govern the objective structure of the natural world. Coleridge's views rest on a belief in the inherent transcendent properties of all beings. Everything in the world is intrinsically transcendent and possesses therefore an underlying oneness. There is a

42. Coleridge, *PW*, 242.
43. Coleridge, *LS*, 29.

prevailing unity in all reality behind the appearance of great diversity stemming ultimately from the oneness of God's own being. When one observes, for example, the love between a man and woman, one learns something too about the nature of God's love. There is a oneness of being between human love contained in the symbolic union of marriage and the true eternal nature of divine love.

The principle of consubstantiality, which pervades so much of Coleridge's thinking, was not derived through a process of logical deduction. For Coleridge it was simply an act of faith. The process of symbol making and symbol perceiving could not be entertained apart from a faith decision; an act of the will. The consubstantiality of the world was, for Coleridge, akin to the consubstantiality of the three persons of the Trinity declared at the Nicene Council. There was an inter-penetration between the symbol and divine reality with the two being virtually inseparable. Once symbol is perceived in this way and a connection with the divine deemed to be made possible thereby, then the way is open for symbol to become a place of encounter, a place where unification can occur.

The Romantic view of symbol provides the entry point into their religious worldview. Such a *Weltanschauen* has not been without its critics. Paul Ricoeur makes the claim that the "masters of suspicion" of a theistic paradigm were Marx, Nietzsche, and Freud who, each from their different vantage points, offered a radical critique of religion. For Marx it was the opium of the people, for Nietzsche the maintenance of vested class interests, and for Freud, religion was nothing more than infantile neurosis. In what way, therefore, can Coleridge, who prefigured these three masters, address such accusations? Is Romantic symbol merely a cloak which hides the true reality of the world? Does symbol merely offer a fundamentally non-rational route towards knowledge? Coleridge, as a representative of the English Romantics, would have insisted, along with Schelling, that the image or symbol (*Bild-Vorstellung*) was not an infantile stage on the way towards *Begriff* but was an essential precondition for arriving at true knowledge. Such an assertion echoes the Platonic question of the nature of the relationship between *logos* and *mythos*.

The Coleridgean appeal to symbol rested on the assumption that rationality could be discovered within the apparently irrational; that the *logos* was contained within the *mythos*. Romantic notions of symbol were not therefore non-cognitive but sought to discover the cognitive within the experiential, and at times, mythic nature of world. Behind this quest was the belief that not all knowledge could be arrived at through a process of logical deduction. If the world is imbued with metaphysical meaning then some forms of knowledge can only be reached via the imaginative use of symbol. Coleridge, together with Schelling, rejected Kant's view of symbol as being simply representational without the capability of putting us in touch with noumenal reality. Whilst Kant had concluded that all our knowledge of God is "merely" symbol, Coleridge would have strongly objected to the word "merely."

Drama

Whilst Coleridge's project, articulated in his prose and philosophical writings, strove to construct a unified system of knowledge as an apologetic defense of orthodox Christianity, it is necessary to bear in mind that Coleridge was in the first instance a poet and dramatist as well as a philosopher and theologian. If this aspect of his complex personality is discounted our search to understand the convoluted contours of his thinking will remain truncated and inadequate. It has been asserted that the Romantics held a diminished view of drama as a form of artistic expression.[44] To what extent was this also true of Coleridge? Is it possible to assert, as Hamilton does, that drama was in reality the motor of Romanticism?[45] By this he does not refer to the theatre, which in the early nineteenth century had seen a significant decline in England, but rather to a dramatic mode of expression.

The English Romantic successors who followed in the wake of Kant were absorbed with the way in which human identity is constructed through a process of self-reflection and self-understanding. The matrix from which this new perception of identity is framed, however, is unavoidably linguistic and the Romantics were acutely aware that language never comes to us in a "pure" form but only ever within the context of communication. Such linguistic transactions are thus inherently dramatic and narrative in their expression. Yet Fichte's influence on post-Kantian idealism took him in a different direction. He laid the stress on the internal act of self-conscious reflection. It was by this inner process that humanity comes to a true understanding of the nature of the phenomenal and noumenal worlds. The resultant effect of weighting human interior self-consciousness in this way is the possibility that external communication with "the other" (*Nicht-Ich*) is rendered either unnecessary at best or

---

44. Hamilton, *Coleridge and German Philosophy*, 37.
45. Ibid., 37–43.

even redundant. Naturally this would issue forth in a denigration of the dramatic form.

Whilst Coleridge displays some structural affinities with Fichte as we have already observed, he departed radically form Fichte at this point. The *Biographia Literaria* was an attempt to show how the human mind is composed, which he attempted to achieve via the medium of his own autobiography. It was through the actual, real drama of his own life that Coleridge articulated his philosophical concerns. As Hamilton explains, "the drama of his life was not, it turns out, its presentation, but its substance."[46] The imagination was not solely an interior function but required external articulation if it was to achieve its synthetic potentiality. It was via the medium of poetry, and especially the poetry of William Wordsworth, that Coleridge encountered something inexplicably both divine and human. The poetry of both Coleridge and Wordsworth is intrinsically dramatic inviting its readers to step on stage and participate in the unfolding drama of the poem. It is no surprise, therefore, to note that in his *Biographia Literaria*, Coleridge expresses his deep admiration for Shakespeare. "I could not, I thought, do better, than keep before me the earliest work of the greatest genius, that perhaps human nature has ever produced, our myriad minded Shakespeare."[47] So wrote Coleridge at the beginning of the second volume of *Biographia Literaria*. But what was it about Shakespeare's genius that so inspired Coleridge to write such a eulogy?

After lengthy passages extolling the virtues of the great poet and playwright, Coleridge summarizes for his readers the source of Shakespeare's greatness. His poetry and dramatic prose is "a gift of the imagination; and this together with the power of reducing multitude into unity of effect, and modifying a series of thoughts by some one predominant thought or feeling, may be cultivated and improved, but can never be learnt. It is these that 'poeta nascitur non fit.'"[48]

Coleridge recognized an innate imaginative prowess in Shakespeare, which could only be attributed to "gift". This giftedness, in the mind of Coleridge, would naturally have been a God-given capacity, not merely a quirk of nature. It is pertinent to note the way in which Coleridge describes this Shakespearean gift, which possesses "the power of reducing multitude into unity of effect, and modifying a series of thoughts by some

---

46. Ibid., 48.
47. Coleridge, *BL* II, 19.
48. Ibid., 20.

one predominant thought of feeling."[49] Compare this to the definition of the secondary imagination articulated earlier. "It dissolves, diffuses, dissipates, in order to create; or where this process is rendered impossible, yet still at all events it struggles to idealize and to unify."[50] It is as if Coleridge is using Shakespeare as the embodiment *par excellence* of what the artistic, poetic, God-given human imagination looks like. Indeed, in his publication, *The Friend*, Coleridge comments that Shakespeare's characters enable the reader to commune "with the same human nature . . . that just proportion, that union and interpenetration of the universal and the particular that must ever pervade all works of decided genius."[51] If Shakespeare demonstrates what it means to deploy the imagination with the resultant extraordinary output of literary excellence achieving the interpenetration of the universal and the particular, then it is surely legitimate to argue that the Romantic imagination contained within it a strong dramatic motor.

49. Ibid., 20.
50. Ibid., 202.
51. Coleridge, *TF* I, 457.

Part 2

Imagination and the Playfulness of God

CHAPTER 5

Imagination and the Ontology of God

THE PRECEDING CHAPTERS HAVE been devoted to an exploration of the definition and function of the imagination in human knowing. In so doing the discussion has necessarily centered on questions of epistemology. Along this journey we have used Coleridge as a guide who has pointed to the environment from which the human imagination is derived, namely from within the very heart of God. As we have seen, Coleridge was adept at dissecting the nature of human experience, acutely observing the minutiae of humanity's engagement with creation whilst all the while maintaining a conversation with the key thinkers of his day. He has taken us to the edge of what it means to be an imaginative human being and has pointed us to another land where an imaginative God dwells. It is now necessary to explore that land too. In some respects Coleridge has already crossed this bridge for he developed a sophisticated Trinitarian theology which we will examine in the first section. This Trinitarianism attempted to address the way in which unity, his lifelong quest, is understood in relation to the many.

In other respects, however, his trail towards an ontological understanding of God's imagination goes cold and it will be our task to plot the trajectory of Coleridge's thinking, taking us into areas that Coleridge himself did not venture. This chapter explores three such areas:

1. Coleridge alludes to the imagination as possessing both passive and active qualities but tantalizingly does not appear to develop that line of thinking any further. What does this suggest about God's passive-active engagement with the world? This question will inform the substance of one section.

2. Coleridge's theological and philosophical system also rested, as we have already seen, upon a profound emphasis on the symbolic. If human imagination is a repetition of the imagination of the "I AM," as Coleridge claimed, then we must conclude that the "I AM" continually engages in creative, symbolic communication and interaction with creation. An exploration of what this might mean ontologically is undertaken.

3. Coleridge's emphasis on drama as "the motor of the romantic movement" raises the question of God's own dramatic identity and function. Is it legitimate to depict God as one who not only plots a narrative script but also steps on the stage and participates with humanity as an "actor" in his own right? This will issue will be explored.

Finally, we will consider the nature of Coleridge's "I AM," the God who eternally inhabits the present moment yet pulls us forward to a new future, and whose creative, redeeming, reconciling work is in an unfinished project.

This part of my book, therefore, will explore ways in which the concept of the "imagination" can be used as a paradigm through which to view a range of theological categories each of which contribute to a possible re-shaping of an understanding of the character of God. In so doing, we will be making a self-conscious move away from epistemological and hermeneutical issues and assessing whether the imagination can be deployed to answer questions of ontology. This is not so much a natural theology arguing from below to above without recourse to scriptural revelation. Coleridge was too astute a theologian to simply buy into *Naturphilosophie* uncritically. It is more a "conjectural" theology asking what might happen to our understanding of God if an imaginative filter is placed across our thinking and one adopts the paradigm of the imagination to address some of the thornier issues of theological discourse.

Unavoidably any discourse concerning the nature of God comes up against the limits of language. Language is often slippery, imprecise, and highly dependent upon context in order for meaning to be derived. The danger of using language in a theological context stems precisely from the tendency to take the normal human usage of words and apply them uncritically to the being of God. Barth was sensitive to this issue when he wrote,

> Does there exist a simple parity of content and meaning when we apply the same word to the creature on the one hand and

to God's revelation and God on the other? We are aware, or we think we are aware, of what being, spirit, sovereignty, creation, redemption, righteousness, wisdom, goodness, etc. mean when we use these terms to describe creatures. We are also aware, or think we are aware, what we are saying when in the sphere of the creature we say eye, ear, mouth, arm or hand, or love, wrath, mercy, patience and such-like. Does all this mean the same thing when we also say it about God?[1]

The way in which Barth has framed the question already implies the answer. For Barth, God is always the subject and never the object. One can therefore only begin with what is given to us as revelation. To speak of the "love" of God only carries any meaning with reference to the person and work of Jesus Christ and cannot be derived analogically from an observation of human love. Yet this is the approach taken for example, by Sally McFague,[2] who deploys the analogy of God as "lover" but cuts this metaphor loose from any scriptural moorings. As such she describes the human experience of God as "lover" but by starting from personal experience alone renders any conclusions about the real or actual nature of God's love impossible. McFague's approach, drawing on the actuality of human experience as a valid source of theological reflection, is not dissimilar to that of Schleiermacher in the nineteenth century. Schleiermacher's great achievement was to redefine religion by asserting that it was not primarily to be understood in moral terms nor in relation to belief. Rather, religion was to be understood as "an immediate self-consciousness or feeling of absolute dependence on God."[3] This kind of premise could invite the kind of criticism that is often associated with Feuerbach, namely that all theological statements are in fact nothing more than anthropological ones in religious disguise. One may ask therefore whether Coleridge too belongs to this theological tradition. If one concludes that he did concur with a purely experientially founded theological method then our exploration into the ontology of God using

---

1. Barth, *KD* 2/1, 253: "Besteht dann einfach Gleichheit des Inhalts und Sinnes, wenn wir ein Wort jetzt auf die Kreatur, jetzt auf Gottes Offenbarung hin, auf Gott anwenden? Wir wissen oder wir meinen zu wissen, was Sein, Geist, Herrschaft, Schöpfung, Erlösung, Gerechtigkeit, Weisheit, Güte usw. bedeutet, wenn wir mit diesen Begriffen Kreaturen bezeichnen. Wir wissen auch, oder meinen zu wissen, was wir sagen, wenn wir im Bereich der Kreatur Auge, Ohr, Mund, Arm oder Hand, wenn wir Liebe, Zorn, Barmherzigkeit, Geduld und dergl. sagen. Bedeutet das Alles dasselbe, wenn wir es nun auch von Gott sagen?"

2. McFague, *Models of God*, 13.

3. Ford, *The Modern Theologians*, 8.

Coleridge as our guide immediately runs aground. We can only conclude that Coleridge was an astute observer of the human condition but had nothing whatsoever to say about the ontology of God. So, does Coleridge belong with the theological tradition that begins from the raw data of human experience or with the theological tradition that came to be associated, over a century later, with Karl Barth?

To answer this question one must return to Barth's view of analogical theology. The analogical method, most commonly associated with Thomist theology, moves from observations of human engagement and discourse towards an attribution, by way of analogy, of those same human qualities to God. Barth unequivocally rejected such a method yet conceded that analogies were a factual necessity. It is by analogy that we are enabled to make sense of abstract concepts. Yet, whilst making this concession, Barth insisted that analogical metaphors can only be of God's making and choosing, not ours. Linguistic metaphors concerning the being of God are valid only in so far as they are offered to us and not constructed by us. In his *Kirchliche Dogmatik* 2/1 he writes:

> It is only possible where the analogy is understood as the work and proposition of revelation itself. Genuine proclamation must speak particularly and therefore restrictedly. It must be aware why it says this and does not say that; why it says this in one way and that in another. But its particularity must not be abandoned to an arbitrary philosophy, to the chances and changes of philosophies, and finally to the dictates of a teaching office. If it is going to be proclamation of God, it must rest on the choice made by God Himself.[4]

To reverse the order of priority is to risk making God in our own image.

Placing Coleridge within a distinct theological tradition is tricky and one can observe this most acutely by tracing his metamorphosis from a Unitarian in the mid-1790s to becoming a Trinitarian by 1810. As we have already observed, Coleridge considered that the notion of Trinitarianism was observable within nature itself. This did not stem from a crude and simplistic search for triadic relationships in the world around us but rather from his understanding of the human personality

---

4. Barth, *KD* 2/1, 262: "Sie ist nicht anders möglich als da, wo die Analogie als Werk und Setzung der Offenbarung selber verstanden wird. Echte Verkündigung muß bestimmt und also begrenzt reden. Sie muß wissen, warum sie dieses sagt und jenes nicht sagt, dieses so und jenes anders sagt. Diese ihre Bestimmtheit darf aber gerade keine willkürliche, sie darf nicht dem Zufall und dem Wechsel der Philosophien und schließlich dem Diktat eines «Lehramtes» ausgeliefert sein. Sie muß, soll sie Verkündigung Gottes sein, auf der von Gott selbst vollzogenen Auswahl beruhen."

as constituted in relationship with others. If to be human is to "be-in-communion," then this must be a hint or a trace of the true nature of the divine. In this regard Coleridge appears to argue from below yet this methodology possessed inherent limitations as Coleridge came to realize. A full understanding of the Trinity could not be derived simply from human analogy, and required the light of revelation for its fulfillment. The orthodoxy of his later Trinitarian position is evidence of his scriptural anchorage which would align him far more closely with Barth. By 1817 one can observe how far Coleridge had moved away from *Naturphilosophie*. In a letter written in September of that year, Coleridge comments that the arguments of the Natural philosophers (in which he included Schelling and Steffens) are "under the disadvantage of beginning with the lowest, per ascensum: whereas the only true point of view is that of Religion, namely descensum."[5] Here Coleridge sounds like a true Barthian!

To speak of the "being of God," or his "ontology" or his "attributes" is to enter a tangled web. Is it possible to talk of the "being of God" in an abstract way independently of the actions of God in history? To pose the dilemma in such a way is to highlight an ancient tension between that Christian tradition which emphasizes the attributes of God via a process of metaphysical abstraction and another tradition which stresses God's direct "action" in the world. The former tradition, associated with some strands of Greek philosophy places the stress on those qualities inherent in God's nature and being that allows humanity to recognize them as distinctively divine. Such attributes normally possess the prefix *omni,* to designate God's utter transcendence, his all-knowing, all-powerful, ever-present qualities. At the second pole lies a different Christian tradition where the emphasis is placed elsewhere, namely in God's immanent presence in the world. Within this far more Hebrew tradition, the rootedness of God in purposeful, intentional action in his created world is the ground of theological reflection. It is his agency that comes into view rather than his transcendence.

Both forms of discourse belong to the Christian tradition but appear to be at odds with one another. If, for example, one insists on asserting the "eternity" of God, existing entirely a-temporally, then it is problematic to simultaneously maintain that God acts within time.[6] Or one may cite the traditional view of God's immutability. If God is perfect in his essential being then any change would amount to a diminution of that perfection. Since any diminution within God is not conceivable then logically one

5. Coleridge, *CL* IV, 769.
6. Schwöbel, *God: Action and Revelation,* 52.

must deduce that God cannot change. And yet scriptural testimony bears frequent witness to apparent changeability of God in his engagement with humanity. If God possesses a freedom in his intentional interaction with creation then, by implication, there must be a mutability within God. The nature of God's aseity is not an attribute asserted independently of his actions in history. In the Hebrew world one always learns of the nature of God through narrative engagement. Once one asserts this approach there is an apparent antimony between those aspects of the Greek tradition which insist on a radical disjuncture between the divine sphere and the material world. How can such a dilemma be resolved?

Coleridge did not pretend to address all these ontological questions. Yet his emphasis on the unifying, creative, shaping function of the imagination, when applied to the being and agency of God, may offer some fresh insights. Coleridge was writing within the shadow of Enlightenment thinking, which sought a more engaging and subtle form of transcendence than it had inherited from previous generations. The Western theological tradition had bequeathed a concept of God that appeared monist, one who arbitrarily willed without due regard for the intrinsic integrity of creation. The search for a new transcendence was taken up by others, most notably Kant, who as we have already noted, concluded that any genuine divine transcendence was beyond the scope of human knowing. The result was that transcendence became relocated within the human mind and the objective reality of God was placed under threat, if not at times altogether eclipsed. The quest for a new open transcendence was all part of the late eighteenth- and early nineteenth-century obsession to find a reconciliation between the phenomenal and the noumenal, the One and the Many. Within these tangled skeins, Coleridge sought to find a way to assert both unity and relational diversity, transcendence and immanence, gift and reception. The natural arena within which to address such issues is within a Trinitarian frame of reference. It is to Coleridge's understanding of the Trinity that we must first turn.

A Playful Prologemena

There remains however one further task to address before plunging into a study of the imaginative ontology of God. That task is concerned with the question of prologemena. The issue of the correct starting point has long plagued theological discourse. Schleiermacher argued that the anchorage point for Christian theology lay in the human experience of "absolute dependence," a theme subsequently endorsed by others such as Tillich and Rahner. The Barthian approach by contrast eschewed such human foundations. To build upon the shifting sands of human experience was, for Barth, to make room for an external standard of verification by which God was to be judged rather than a simple adherence to the autonomous, self-authenticating nature of divine revelation. Barth averred that the first and most decisive place to begin, the prologemena, was a theology of the doctrine of the Word of God.

I suspect that such polarized positions would have been seen as unnecessarily divisive and unhelpfully antagonistic by Coleridge. Indeed one might argue that to stoutly claim that our starting point is the Word of God does not necessarily solve anything. If the Word of God, manifested supremely in the person and work of Christ, is offered to us without a framework for interpretation, it remains a mystery. All discourse, whether human or divine, verbal or symbolic, literal or metaphorical, demands a paradigm through which it is received and from which meaning is derived. The love of God revealed in the self-giving of the Son can only be understood *as* an act of love, if the notion of "lostness" is perceived as a defining theological marker. One requires a paradigm of what it means to be lost in order to view the self-offering of Christ as an expression of love that redeems the lost. Without such a paradigm, the revealing of the Son of God remains shrouded.

All theology therefore, begins from a reflection on the reception of the news of Jesus Christ in his death and resurrection. How are we to think about these events in such a way that the mission of the church in proclamation may continue in each generation? The story of God in Christ is given that it might be communicated and the appeal of that communication is that this historical narrative is profoundly and deeply very good news indeed. It is a story that contains a history yet is intrinsically proleptic, promising a new future to those who hear. Theological discourse is thus a secondary activity, in that it enables reflection on that which is primary, namely worship and proclamation. Theology is the grammar[7] of such activity, offering a structure within which hermeneutics can be conducted. Our task here to assess whether the speculative theological paradigm of "play" is both legitimate and valuable in portraying an ontology of God's being and action. Our study began with the playful story of Nathan and David which presents us with the possibility that "play" is indeed permissible when engaged in daring speech about God.

If we are to deploy the category of play as an obvious corollary of the imagination then the work of Johan Huizinga, *Homo Ludens,* is a natural place to begin. In this seminal work, Huizinga explores the nature and

---

7. Jenson, *Systematic Theology, Vol.* 1, 18.

significance of play as a cultural phenomena. In doing so he makes the bold claim that play is older than culture in so far as play is witnessed in both the animal and the human worlds.[8] It is because of the intrinsically instinctive quality of play that it must be understood as possessing a significance that is far more than the merely biological or psychological. Play is a foundational activity and constitutes an essential element in human culture yet despite its importance, it is profoundly irrational. To play is the predominant activity in the emotional and intellectual development of children without which healthy adult relationships and cognitive processing cannot adequately be formed. Play is in essence an aesthetic activity according to Huizinga which does not necessarily need to have a utilitarian purpose. It is quite simply "fun," giving pleasure and delight to all those involved.

Yet to describe play in these terms is to risk it being misunderstood as frivolous and unimportant. Play is the conscious and intentional relaxing of boundaries of what is normally considered possible yet contained within a framework of rules and conventions. It is in effect what Coleridge would have described as, "that willing suspension of disbelief for the moment, which constitutes poetic faith."[9] Huizinga offers the following definition of play: "Play is a voluntary activity or occupation executed within certain fixed limits of time and space, according to rules freely accepted but absolutely binding, having its aim in itself, accompanied by a feeling of tension, joy and the consciousness that it is different from ordinary life."[10]

The normal intellectual and emotional development of children requires an imaginative engagement in playful activities. As Huizinga's definition explains play takes place within its own agreed boundaries of permitted performance. Such boundaries provide a "safe space" within which new possibilities and combinations can be explored without fear. It is precisely this absence of anxiety that permits play to unfold for if certain of the "normal" rules of engagement are suspended this allows for fresh imaginative worlds to be explored. Whilst such play appears to the neutral observer to be "purposeless," for the child involved a "plastic" reality enables a repositioning of the co-ordinates of what is possible. Play is neither a waste of time nor is it something that humans necessarily need abandon with greater maturity. It engenders enhanced social relationships, creative energy and intrinsic joy.

---

8. Huizinga, *Homo Ludens*, 19.
9. Coleridge, *BL* I, 314.
10. Huizinga, *Homo Ludens*, 28.

Caution needs to be exercised however in applying Huizinga's definition of the human activity of play directly to God. God's "play" is not to be defined in terms of a restricted set of actions constrained within binding rules. Rather, a playful theological prologemena refers not to the conventions of play as commonly understood but to the essence of play as something that is fundamentally concerned with aesthetics. Play is about enjoyment, beauty, joy, and delight—aesthetic qualities that humankind may touch upon through the process of play. It is this aestheticism, with its deep and natural connection with the imagination that is in view when we deploy the paradigm of play in relation to the ontology of God. The playfulness of children too is about the same kind of aesthetics and whilst psychologists have rightly determined the immense fruitfulness of play in the healthy development of children, this is not at the forefront of a child's consciousness when engaged in play. The very heart of the coming kingdom of God announced by Christ is portrayed in terms that insist that we become like children. The eschatological images of the coming new world are drawn not from the battlefield or the world of work but from a re-engagement with childhood imagination. The activity of "play" was deeply revered by Plato, who deemed it to be a religious activity. And Schiller too, as we have already explored, was a great defender of play, claiming that it was neither irreverent nor frivolous. Fichte also could not escape the playful nature of his intellect. In his work *Die Bestimmung des Menschen,* Fichte observes that whilst the Will that humankind possesses is free and must eternally remain so yet there is a power that enables those free choices to be made.[11]

Coleridge's determination to address the legacy of Enlightenment thinking, which found expression in an oppressive mechanistic worldview, caused him to seek for alternatives in the realm of the imagination. This is precisely the arena in which Huizinga claims that play is able to function. He writes that, "play only becomes possible, thinkable and understandable when an influx of mind breaks down the absolute determinism of the cosmos."[12] A liberation from the restrictions of the supposedly possible allows for an exploration into what is yet to be. Yet in making this lofty claim for the power of play one risks missing the heart of the matter. Play is usually purposeless for engagement in playful activity is concerned with the joy and delight that it provides within an orderly convention-bound framework. In this regard play belongs to the realm of the aesthetic, an area which was an abiding interest of Kant and

11. Fichte, *Die Bestimmung des Menschen,* 74.
12. Huizinga, *Homo Ludens,* 3.

his successors. Huizinga comments on this relationship between the aesthetic categories of play and the establishment of order: "The profound affinity between play and order is perhaps the reason why play, as we noted in passing, seems to lie to such an extent in the field of aesthetics. Play has a tendency to be beautiful. It may be that this aesthetic factor is identical with the impulse to create orderly form, which animates play in all it aspects."[13]

We will return later to the notion of beauty in so far as it can be used as a form of speech about God. Suffice to say, at this stage of our investigation, that play has presented us with just that possibility. The paradox of play is that what begins as a purposeless activity intended merely to elicit pleasure can become profoundly purposeful in that it yields something that is both beautiful and creatively new. Beauty and the discovery of new possibilities are perhaps the unintended by-products of the "uselessness" of play.

One final note of caution needs to be injected at this point. It must not be assumed that the paradigm of play means the total absence of restraint or boundaried activity. Huizinga's definition quoted above makes it clear that all play takes place within a rule-bound framework. Within that scaffolding of agreed conventions, improvisation, and creativity can be free to roam. Play is held therefore in a careful balance of freedom and restraint. Our discussion of God's playfulness will proceed on this same basis that God is "constrained" as it were by his own character yet always remains in utter freedom to be himself. This understanding of play is a far cry therefore from any postmodern demand for the total removal of any form of restraint. Whilst Coleridge acutely critiqued the shortcomings of Enlightenment rationalism, he was not thereby opening the door to a theological and philosophical anarchy. The principle of imaginative play is only permissible within the framework of the Trinitarian relations.

God's Imaginative Search for Unification

Coleridge's emphasis on the intrinsic unity that lies behind and within all things was predicated upon a particular view of God. In his earlier years, as we have seen, Coleridge described his theology as Unitarian. By the early part of the nineteenth century this position had dramatically shifted towards a more orthodox Trinitarianism. Coleridge believed that the idea of a Trinitarian God could be deduced, albeit in a partial sense, by recourse to a process of logic, without the aid of scriptural revelation.

---

13. Ibid., 10.

The fullness of the Trinity could, of course, only be appreciated with biblical roots yet, for Coleridge, the translucency of the "Special" was so evident that the Trinity *could* be perceived if one but learned how to see and think aright.

Coleridge's understanding of the ontology of God emerged in a climate that was dominated by eighteenth-century rationalist views which portrayed God in either mechanistic or absentee terms. Coleridge sought for a God who was neither beholden to rationalistic demands of verifiability nor was aligned with Calvinist notions of absolute power. Coleridge's argument for a Trinitarian understanding of God proceeds from a discussion of the nature of human persons. By the early years of the nineteenth century there is an urgency about Coleridge's quest. Having discarded the Unitarianism of his youth he plots a course which attempts to establish a philosophical basis for the Trinity, an endeavor that would address the troublesome issues of pantheism raised by Schelling and Spinoza and would ground God's nature in an essentially personal, relational form.

Coleridge's Theological Anthropology

Influenced by Kant, Coleridge learned that humanity's predisposition towards personality lies in our capacity to respect the moral law as an incentive of the will. There is a moral agency, declares Kant, that distinguishes persons from "things."[14] Yet in his treatment of the moral imperative, Coleridge diverges from Kant in that he treats this essential aspect of personhood in relational rather than ethical terms. For Coleridge, relationality is a constitutive feature of being human for it resides at the very core of humanity. How is this expressed or known? One feature of relationality is the capacity for self-consciousness which distinguishes humankind from the animal world. This self-consciousness (*con-scire*) or inward conformity of the will to the moral law is, in his own words, "the root and precondition of all other consciousness."[15] Coleridge here is establishing the basis upon which he will later develop his Trinitarian theology. By placing the human will, the capacity to choose and to act, at the centre of what it means to be human, he is prefiguring his argumentation about the place of Absolute Will. Humanity is constituted in acts of the will. Alan Gregory sums up Coleridge's position in this way: "Personality is not a psychological given, an individual confluence of characteristics,

---

14. Kant, *Groundwork of the Metaphysical of Morals*, 95.
15. Coleridge, *OM*, 84.

but a vocation. We become persons and through our aggravated self-alienation from God, we diminish ourselves as persons."[16]

Coleridge's anthropology is located in the direction of moral choices and is thus intimately connected with sanctification. The concept of personality as "a vocation," as a direct derivative of "will," means that Coleridge is well placed to apply that term to God. Coleridge continues his argument about the place of self-consciousness in the architecture of humanity by insisting that this exercise of the will is not an individualistic venture. The self-conscious awareness of "I" requires a corresponding awareness of "thou." The "I-thou" relationship, in which he prefigures so much of the later work of Martin Buber, is essential to Coleridge's logic. Without a "thou" there can be no "I." It is a recognition both of difference and sameness, identification and differentiation. "Thou" is not the same as "I," but it is of the same nature, the same substance. We cannot, says Coleridge, exist in a vacuum, all alone. We are constituted as persons only in relation to one another as we make our moral choices by acts of the will. This understanding of human anthropology places humans in a kind of perichoretic relationship with one another. As Gunton has said, "there is no true freedom which does not also allow for the fact that we are passive as well as active in relation to others and the world: we are what we are in perichoretic reciprocity."[17]

The weight that Coleridge places upon the relationship between "I" and "thou" is highly significant; so much so that McFarland, in his introductory essay on the *Opus Maximum*, suggests that this is the "philosophical fulcrum" of Coleridge's whole project.[18] For Coleridge, the anthropological "I-thou" concept was not simply a question of relationship; it was also the foundation of human identity itself. Humanity is constituted in relationship with the "other." In this respect the relationship between "I" and "thou," pointing ultimately to our origin in divine creativity, is analogous to the claims that Coleridge makes in his definition of the human imagination as that which participates in the infinite imagination. Here is Coleridge in his own words: "But if the reader will place himself so far in the same state of Self-observation as the writer, he will discover that the consciousness expressed in the term 'thou' is only possible by an equation in which 'I' is taken as equal to but yet not the same as 'thou' and that this again is only possible by putting the 'I' and

---

16. Barbeau, *Coleridge's Assertion of Religion*, 192.
17. Gunton, *The One, the Three, and the Many*, 170.
18. Coleridge, *OM*, cxxxv.

'thou' in opposition to each other—in logical antithesis I mean—as correspondent opposites, as harmonies or correlatives."[19]

Self-consciousness is thus the action of recognizing the legitimacy of "thou" in relation to "I." The act of recognition is a dual one; "we negative the sameness in order to establish the equality."[20] On this point Coleridge radically departed from Fichte's view that the *Nicht-Ich* was essentially an adversary of the *Ich* with its need to be curtailed. Coleridge was writing at a time when the spirit of the age led inevitably, in his opinion, to a de-personalization of humanity. The atomizing tendencies of the Enlightenment reduced humankind to no more than the sum of individual parts with God a distant observer, the hypothetical watchmaker. By locating relational personality at the heart of what it means to be human with its corollary being the relational personality of God, Coleridge was attempting to restore to a central position an orthodox Trinitarianism with all the implications that this has for an understanding of human existence. If personality lies at the centre of human ontology it must therefore be a reflection of the divine personality, the "I AM" of God. Coleridge's definition of the primary imagination being a mirror of God's eternal I AM is a natural outworking of his theological anthropology.

Absolute Will

Given that Coleridge placed primary emphasis on the human will in choosing to perceive the unity of all things, it is hardly surprising that he defined God in such terms, by referring to God as "Absolute Will." The logic of this was grounded in the following line of reasoning. Firstly, the radical disjunction between subject and object, which Coleridge had perceived as a fatal flaw in the Kantian system, was removed. Rather than subject and object being seen as opposing forces, they were understood to be held in a kind of magnetic orbit around one another. Within the logic of human perception, the subject is given priority (following Kant) and so by a process of infinite regression there must be at some point an ultimate self-consciousness, an ultimate subject, not dependent on an object for its existence. This subject he referred to as "Absolute Will." "Our first position, therefore, is that in the order of necessary thought the Will must be conceived as anterior to all."[21]

---

19. Ibid., 75.
20. Ibid., 76.
21. Ibid., 194.

This may, at first glance, seem to be a strange formulation. How can there be a will before there is existence? Surely being is prior to willing? Not so for Coleridge. He insisted that whilst there may be antecedence in terms of priority this was not to be misunderstood as antecedence in terms of time. Willing and being belong eternally together and cannot be separated. Will suggests causality but when applied to God, cause and effect must be seen as contemporaneous. As John Barth has put it, "causality must therefore mean co-eternity."[22] This means that, for Coleridge, "Absolute Will" is causative of all reality and therefore of its own reality. "Will is the ground of the Trinity," states Reid, "but it has no existence other than its expression in the Trinity, nor is it to be equated with the Father."[23]

If this is so, how does Coleridge move from his understanding of "Absolute Will" to the nature of the Trinity? This is the second stage of Coleridge's logic. He does so by introducing his notion of personeity. By this he refers to the human desire for self-realization, which he defines as personality. It is essentially an openness to the "other." Coleridge struggled to arrive at this point and admitted as much in *Biographia Literaria*, when he wrote, "for a very long time indeed, I could not reconcile personality with infinity; my head was with Spinoza, but my whole heart remained with Paul and John."[24] So when he applied the notion of personal relatedness to God, Coleridge preferred to use a different term, personeity, rather than personality. He chose to do this in order to avoid any possible sense of limitation to God. It was a designation that described some kind of action or movement towards another reality than the Self. The concept of "Will" carries with it an implicit need for personality for only a person is capable of willing. In *Opus Maximum*, Coleridge writes in this way: "What remains to be communicated? It must in some high sense be other and yet it must be a Self. For there is not other than self . . . We must . . . proceed as if we substantiated Alterity itself . . . The Alterity must have some distinctive from the original absolute identity or how could it be contemplated as other, and yet this distinctive must be such as not to contradict the other co-essential term. It must remain in some sense the Self, through another Self."[25]

In order for God to be God he must be in relationship with the Other, yet that Other must also be intimately connected to the Absolute

---

22. Barth, *Coleridge and Christian Doctrine*, 88.
23. Reid, *Coleridge Form and Symbol*, 120.
24. Coleridge, *BL* I, 243.
25. Coleridge, *OM*, 217.

Will. Coleridge is attempting to demonstrate that the Trinity can be anticipated, if not fully understood, by a process of human reasoning. Coleridge's emphasis on God's being understood in terms of "Will" and therefore, by implication, as the God who acts, is significant in seeking a resolution between the so called "metaphysical" descriptions of God such as eternity and immutability, and the more dynamic engaged attributes of mercy and patience. Coleridge locates the beginning of his argument about God in intentional action, rather than in abstraction. It is by God's actions that God is revealed and known. These actions, however, are *personal* rather than abstract. This locates the heart of God in personhood rather than in being. The relationships that pertain within the Trinity constitute the essence of God being God. This correlates well with the conclusions of the Cappadocian Fathers who concluded that personhood in God is always prior to being. As Robert Jenson puts it, "God is not first divine and thereupon triune. He is triune and thereupon divine."[26]

Coleridge goes on to use the analogy of human thoughts and words, the one being the expression of the other yet not being identical. The thought *begets* the word just as the Father *begets* the Son. This act of begetting and its corresponding reciprocal response is a circular procession between the Father and Son. It is "the perichoresis of the primary, absolute, co-eternal inter-circulation of the Deity."[27] However, this is, as yet, an incomplete process. How, according to Coleridge, are the Father and Son connected? It is through the connecting bond of love that the Holy Spirit unites the Father and Son in perfect mutual harmony. Coleridge's debt to Augustine is plain to see. Coleridge's mature views on the nature of the Trinity were most clearly expressed in his "*Formula Fidei de Sanctissima Trinitate*" published towards the end of his life in 1830. Because his views on the ontology of God are central to our discussion here, it is worth quoting the entirety of his text. He writes of God in a fourfold manner:

<u>The Identity</u>

The absolute subjectivity, whose only attribute is the Good; whose only definition is—that which is essentially causative of all possible true being; the ground; the absolute will; . . . which whatever is assumed as the first, must be presumed as its antecedent . . . But that which is essentially causative of all being must be causative of its own—*causa sui* . . . Thence,

---

26. Jenson, *Systematic Theology, Vol.* 2, 96.
27. Barth, *Coleridge and Christian Doctrine*, 91.

The Ipseity

The eternally self-affirmant, self-affirmed; "the I am in that I am," of the "I shall be that I will to be;" the Father; the relatively subjective, whose attribute is, the Holy One; whose definition is, the essential finific in the form of the infinite; *dat sibi fines*. But the absolute will, the absolute good, in the eternal act of self-affirmation, the Good as the Holy One, co-eternally begets,

The Alterity

The Supreme being . . . the supreme reason; the Jehovah; the Son; the Word; whose attribute is the True (the truth, the light, the fiat); and whose definition is the *pleroma* of being, whose essential poles are unity and distinctity, or the essential infinite in the form of the finite; lastly the relatively objective, *deitas objectiva* in relation to the I AM as the *deitas subjective*; the divine objectivity . . . But with the relatively subjective and the relatively objective, the great idea needs only for its completion a co-eternal which is both, that is, relatively objective to the subjective and relatively subjective to the objective. Hence,

The Community

The eternal life, which is love; the Spirit; relatively to the Father, the Spirit of holiness, the Holy Spirit; relatively to the Son, the Spirit of truth, whose attribute is Wisdom, *Sanctus sophia*; the Good in the reality of the True, in the form of actual Life.[28]

Coleridge articulated a similar formula in his book *Table Talk*, where he proposed a Prothesis (the Absolute Will or Identity), Thesis (the Father), Antithesis (the Son), and Synthesis (the Spirit).[29] Some Coleridge commentators have argued that this philosophical construction of the nature of the Trinity bears the hallmarks of a latent modalism. It suggests that, for Coleridge, there lay an antecedent power of absolute Will or the Logos or indeed the principle of diversity-within-unity which lay "behind" the Trinity, which in effect was an expression of that antecedence. It hints at a departure from the classic orthodox understanding of the Trinity as a self-complete being and opens the door for the Trinity as a being in the process of development.

Coleridge would have strenuously denied such claims. In the *Opus Maximum* he states quite explicitly that he believes that God is self-caused *(causa sui)* and that this is his starting point. "The will, the absolute will,

---

28. Ibid., 94.
29. Coleridge, *TT* 1, 77.

is that which is essentially causative of all reality, essentially and absolutely, that is boundless from without and from within. This is our first principle."[30] The concept of self-causation is in itself problematic. If something is the cause of its own being it suggests a distinction between cause and that which is caused. *Causa sui* was thus unintelligible for Kant. For pantheists, like the influential Spinoza, however, auto constitution of the Divine at the same time as the creation of the Cosmos was less troublesome. *Deus ipse se facit!* Coleridge, however, was at pains to distance himself from such Neo-Platonic ideas of self-generation. Yet, as we have already noted, Coleridge was influenced greatly by Plotinus who was one of the first of the Greek philosophers to identify "The Good" in terms of "Will." How does Coleridge escape the charge of following in the footsteps of Plotinus and adopting an emanationist view of God and how does he avoid falling under the pantheistic spell of Spinoza?

Coleridge believed that in order to avoid the logic of infinite regress an Absolute must be postulated. He writes in *Biographia Literaria*, "we must break off the series arbitrarily and affirm an absolute something that is in and of itself at once cause and effect, (*causa sui*), subject and object, or rather the absolute identity of both."[31] For Coleridge the Trinity must be grounded in something. It could not be grounded in the Father for that would open the way to Subordinationism. It had therefore to be grounded in "the One" or "Monad" or "Prothesis," which is expressed eternally in the triad of Father (Ipseity), Son (Alterity), and Spirit (Copula). The three persons are one and the absolute Divine subjectivity (the great I AM) is constituted as a relation between the hypostases of Father, Son and Spirit. Whilst Coleridge was anxious to avoid pantheism, emanationism, tritheism, and subordinationism, it is still not entirely clear to some scholars[32] that he has avoided Sabellianism. Perkins, for example, claims that Coleridge rejects the *trias*[33] as a symbolic expression of reality in favor of a *tetractys*. This *tetractys* is not a synthesis, but a prothesis and is prior to Reason. Perkins however appears to present Coleridge's notion of "priority" as one which is related to chronology, and thus, by extension, to importance. Other Coleridge scholars however, (e.g., Hardy, Gregory, and Hedley) take a different position.

Their argument is that in some respects Coleridge's work on the Trinity follows in the footsteps of Augustine in his work *De Trinitate*.

30. Coleridge, *OM*, 220.
31. Coleridge, *BL* I, 285.
32. For example, Barth, *Coleridge and Christian Doctrine*, 1969.
33. Perkins, *Coleridge's Philosophy, the Logos as Unifying Principle*, 349.

Augustine explored the relationship between the deity of God and the Tri-unity of God. Eastern Trinitarianism identifies the Father with God's deity and the Son and the Spirit receiving their deity and substance from the Father. Augustine proposed that the Father, Son, and Spirit each possessed intrinsically a divine "substance" or ground of being. This formulation is, of course, fraught with theologically dangerous implications. Is it possible, for example, to consider the "essence" of God independently of the persons of the Trinity? Does one "need" the Trinity at all if there is a prior ground? Does this not open the doors towards a latent atheism?

Yet for Coleridge the position of the Father is related not to substance but to relations. The substance (*homoousios*) of the deity is common to all three persons. This "substance" Coleridge names as the Absolute Will or Prothesis. The Trinity does not *emanate from* this but rather is *constituted by* it. The Absolute Will is not an impersonal substance but is intrinsically relational in that Will and Being are ontologically synonymous. Coleridge is attempting to secure the absolute freedom of God by establishing the principle of *causa sui* which is expressed in the mutual giving and receiving of the three Persons who recognize in one another both sameness and difference. In his *Opus Maximum* Coleridge writes about this "ground" in this way, "the ground is not to be called God, much less God the Father; it is the abysmal depth of the eternal act by which God as the alone *causa sui* affirmeth."[34]

The gift of God to humanity and to creation is thus to share in the same freedom that God enjoys whereby distinctiveness and inter-connectedness are held together. It is my contention that Coleridge does not thereby fall into the trap of Sabellianism. Hedley summarizes Coleridge's position in this way: "The unity of God, then, is not prior to the 'persons' but realized in their relations. Far from relativizing the Trinity through a prior undifferentiated unity, the Tetrad opens the possibility of seeing the unity of God as the uniting of persons."[35]

Coleridge is thereby strenuously trying to preserve the *trias*, rather than reject it as Perkins has asserted, but in order to do so he uses the tetractys as a model. He is using the four as a way of showing how the three can be one. It is admittedly speculative theology, endeavoring to maintain the eternal *perichoresis* of the three whilst avoiding the perceived subordinationist tendencies of eastern theology.

---

34. Coleridge, *OM*, 232–33.
35. Barbeau, *Coleridge's Assertion of Religion*, 207.

Imaginative Engagement

Having outlined Coleridge's own understanding of the Trinity we are now in a position to consider how such an imaginative, Trinitarian God "acts" and "interacts" with creation. Schwöbel has outlined the scope of such an enterprise: "If metaphysical attributes, based on the enterprise of philosophical theology of making the existence and intelligibility of the world plausible in the framework of a conception of God, and personal attributes, based on the model of divine action understood in terms of personal agency, are seen as related through mutual qualification, some of the pitfalls of each respective approach can be avoided."[36]

Schwöbel here posits the necessity of maintaining the mutual compatibility and complementarity of the metaphysical and personal attributes of God. To hold them together through "mutual qualification" ensures a modulating, balancing appropriateness in our depiction of the God who is. Neither the transcendent nor the immanent attributes of God are swallowed up by each other. How is such a mutual qualification effected? By what means are the eternal, transcendent properties of God and the personal, immanent attributes interpenetrated? To begin to formulate an answer to such a question, I propose to take the Coleridgean notion of the imagination and place it alongside the work of Karl Barth in his major work, *Die Kirchliche Dogmatik* (2/1). An engagement with Barth's use of the notion of the "perfections" of God may provide a helpful link between divine action and metaphysical characterization. The perfections of God are seen in his interaction with creation thereby demonstrating that there is a positive engagement with the world. To abstract God's attributes, placing them at a distance from creation, possessing an independent existence is in effect to propose a negative theology in which God is understood primarily in terms of his "otherness" rather than his inter-relatedness. So how does the imaginative freedom of God manifest itself?

Barth's work is predicated on the truth that God is both fully revealed and fully concealed in his own self-disclosure. This distinction flows from his assertion that God is the one who loves us and thus is completely knowable to us and yet this love is an expression of his freedom. God remains sovereignly free and thus is also, in some senses, completely unknowable. Barth strives to hold together both the perfection of the divine love and the perfection of the divine freedom. He states, "The divinity of the love of God consists and confirms itself in the fact that in

---

36. Schwöbel, *God: Action and Revelation*, 61.

Himself and in all His works God is gracious, merciful and patient, and at the same time holy, righteous and wise."[37]

A further classification follows: "The divinity of the freedom of God consists and confirms itself in the fact that in Himself and in all His works God is One, constant and eternal, and therewith also omnipresent, omnipotent and glorious."[38] Thus Barth presents us with a tightly structured list of attributes. When depicting God's love, Barth uses six adjectives. God is described as gracious, merciful, patient, holy, righteous, and wise. When describing the freedom of God, Barth states that God is one, constant, eternal, omnipresent, omnipotent, and glorious. There would appear to be little room for a further category, imagination, in such a symmetrical and tidy ordering. Indeed the category of imagination with its definition open to multiple interpretations and its operation seemingly applicable in each and every context, may at first sight seem to add only a further layer of unnecessary confusion. So how can the category of the imagination beneficially enrich our understanding of God's perfections?

The twin lists of perfections that Barth enumerates significantly do not include the term "love." This apparent omission only serves to emphasize Barth's fundamental view that all of God's perfections are a manifestation of his love and that the being of God is the one who loves in perfect freedom. In *Die Kirchliche Dogmatik* 2/1, Barth asserts that God's love consists of seeking and creating fellowship with the unworthy. In extending love to humanity God does so in perfect freedom, not constrained or conditioned by any human attribute or external compulsion. So when Christ enters into dialogue with Zacchaeus (Luke 19), it is not because of any endearing charm that Zacchaeus possessed neither is it due to the neediness of his condition. Jesus is not compelled by external necessity to engage with Zacchaeus. Instead he freely chooses to extend himself towards him in an act of mercy.

How does Christ then enter into Zacchaeus' world and effect transformation? Barth uses a range of metaphorical devices to describe such an encounter: "The love of God always throws a bridge over a crevasse. It is always the light shining out of darkness. In His revelation it seeks and creates fellowship where there is no fellowship and no capacity for it . . . That He throws a bridge out from Himself to this abandoned one, that

---

37. Barth, *KD*, 2/1 394.

38. Ibid., 495: "Die Göttlichkeit der Liebe Gottes besteht und bewährt sich darin, dass Gott in sich selber in allen seinen Werken, gnädig, barmherzig und geduldig und eben damit auch heilig, gerecht und weise ist."

He is light in the darkness, is the miracle of the almighty love of God."[39] This is highly evocative, imaginative language that Barth is using. He speaks of God constructing a bridge over a crevasse and shining a light into dark places. It is a picture of God on the move, seeking, searching, extending himself, to seek and to redeem the lost. When God acts in this way in Christ, he makes himself immanent towards humanity, he draws close in order to empathize, to understand, to sit exactly where humanity sits in all its frailty and woundedness. This deeply personal action on the part of God is made without insisting on a reciprocal and corresponding response. A human response is invited but cannot be coerced. "The mercy of God," writes Barth, "lies in His readiness to share in sympathy the distress of another, a readiness which springs from His inmost nature and stamps all His being and doing."[40] Such a move is made without God losing any of his transcendence at the moment of closest immanence. God's projection of himself into the state of the other who is a sinner is a profoundly imaginative activity, based on his deep understanding and empathy for the person standing before him. In this imaginative penetration, God does not lose any of himself nor does he become the other. He remains distinct and transcendent yet displays all of his attributes within an imaginative engagement. "But the personal God," writes Barth, "has a heart. He can feel, and be affected. He is not impassible"[41]

When Barth writes of God's perfections in this way, he is, in effect, describing the actions of penetration, empathy, and recognition of the distress of the other, as those which demand a high degree of imaginative processing. Patience is illustrative of this and Barth describes the patience of God as an enrichment, clarification and intensification of the idea of mercy. God takes the plight of human beings into his heart without at any time diminishing their independence. Here is sensitivity of the highest order involving no violation of the integrity of persons. The copula therefore between God's transcendent qualities and his personal agency is God's own imaginative engagement. Such an engagement permits no

---

39. Ibid., 312: "Die Liebe Gottes schlägt immer eine Brücke über einen Abgrund. Sie ist immer das aus der Finsternis leuchtende Licht. Sie sucht und schafft in seiner Offenbarung Gemeinschaft und an sich auch keine Fähigkeit dazu vorhanden ist . . . Daß er von sich selbst zu diesem Preisgegebenen die Brücke schlägt, daß er in der Finsternis Licht ist."

40. Ibid., 369: "Die Barmherzigkeit Gottes ist seine in seinem Wesen liegende, sein Sein und Tun konstituierende Beteiligung am Elend eines Andern und damit sein in seinem Wesen liegender."

41. Ibid., 416: "Der persönlicher Gott aber hat ein Herz. Er kann fühlen, empfinden, affiziert sein. Er ist nicht unberührbar."

diminution of God's "otherness," yet allows for the particularity of his dealings with humanity in space and time. It further preserves the dignity and freedom of humanity to "be itself" without being overwhelmed by divine occupancy of temporal space. This imaginative copula bears resemblance to Schiller's *Spieltrieb* which had exerted such a powerful shaping influence upon Coleridge. It brings together both subject (humanity) and object (God) without disparaging the integrity of either.

From this brief excursus into Barth's *Dogmatics* I have asserted that it is possible to perceive the imagination of God as a direct derivative of his love in that it is the medium, the conduit, by which God's love penetrates the world of the sinner and is the ground of his immanence ensuring no loss of his transcendence. I have proposed that the imagination is not to be viewed as a further attribute to be added to Barth's already existing list but rather that the imagination is to be understood as the manner or mode of the expression of God's perfections.

The Nature of the Unity between God and Creation

We have already considered that Coleridge's definition of the primary imagination, articulated in chapter 13 of *Biographia Literaria*, makes the claim that the human imagination both reflects and participates in the creative imaginative activity of God. It is, "a repetition in the finite mind of the eternal act of creation in the infinite I AM." The rich phrase that Coleridge uses, "the eternal act of creation in the infinite I AM," implies that God's engagement with creation is continual and eternal. It is an engagement that, to borrow phrases from Coleridge's definition of the secondary imagination, "dissolves, diffuses, dissipates, creates; idealizes and unifies." Coleridge maintains here that God is continually engaged in the process of dismantling, separating, reforming, reshaping with the intention of bringing about a unity. This is how the activity of God is perceived, almost as a sculptor working and re-working his raw material into the desired form. Our task as humankind is to learn to perceive this process through the God-given power of our imagination.

How does this faculty develop? In an earlier chapter on symbol we have alluded to Coleridge's approach to the physicality of the material world. It is now appropriate to return to this topic to explore it more fully. Coleridge's views on the consubstantiality of symbol and the divine drew heavily on the Nicene Trinitarian formulation. The Nicene Creed was a carefully formulated document intended to counter, amongst other concerns, a perceived Arian threat to Christian orthodoxy. The assertion of the identity of the Father and Son in substance if not in form was a hard fought battle. For Coleridge to appropriate the term consubstantial for his own purposes of developing a theory of symbol was a bold move. In doing so he risked collapsing the distinction between *generation ex Deo* and *creatio ex nihilo*. By identifying the symbolic nature of the world so completely with the divine, Coleridge appeared to disparage the inherent creatureliness of creation. Halmi asserts that Coleridge was in agreement with Schelling on this point in denying the reality of matter.[42] Coleridge, in effect, conflated the eternal self-generation of the Trinitarian Godhead with creation itself such that it is not possible to distinguish the two. Naturally this raises significant questions as to whether Coleridge's theory of symbol, and therefore his understanding of matter, was compatible with his Christology. If the cosmos and God are consubstantial then how does the incarnation have any real import? Halmi claims that Coleridge's theory of the symbol displaces the Son and replaces him with the universe.[43]

Halmi's view is supported by other Coleridge scholars, most notably Cutsinger in his work entitled "The Form of Transformed Vision. Coleridge and the Knowledge of God."[44] Cutsinger asserts that the great challenge that Coleridge poses for contemporary society is to learn to perceive, through the imagination, that the boundaries and limits of the material world are in effect illusory and only serve to inhibit our capacity for seeing the unity within all things. In support of his position Cutsinger cites the observations that Coleridge makes in his work *Aids to Reflections* where he addresses the question of materialism. Coleridge describes materialism as being of ill-repute for it claims for itself the capacity to determine what is material and what is not. In their analysis of subject object relations, Coleridge claims that materialists assert somewhat crudely that Mind (that which belongs to the subject) is immaterial, and Matter (that which pertains to the object), clearly possesses quite different attributes. Matter is about the real, the tangible, the substantial, the solid, that which has a surface and an edge and can be identified without ambiguity or any hint of indeterminacy.[45] Cutsinger argues that we need to learn to see as Coleridge did; a process that demands a radical rethinking of our approach to the material world. He asserts that the Enlightenment legacy is a deadly one, concerned with surfaces, edges, boundaries, with the actual physicality of the sensual world. Once we remain tied to materialism in

42. Halmi, *The Genealogy of Romantic Symbol*, 117.
43. Ibid., 121.
44. Cutsinger, *The Form of Transformed Vision*, 1987.
45. Coleridge, AR, 394.

all its many guises we will fail to perceive the translucency of the divine. Cutsinger cites Coleridge's remarks in *Aids to Reflection* in support of his argument: "Mechanico-corpuscular philosophy, with both its twins, Materialism on the One hand and Idealism, rightly named Idolism, on the other: the one obtruding on us a world of specters and apparitions, the other a mazy dream."[46] Materialism for Coleridge is here described as a world of "specters and apparitions." Once we remain wedded to such a view of the physical world we will always fail to perceive the divine. This view of the material world is a direct derivation of his concept of space and time. Materialism, according to Coleridge, was a false system precisely because it considered these two properties as being fixed and linear. God could not be bounded by such limitations. In his *Notebooks*, Coleridge writes, "Is God then confined to a Place? Or is not rather Place the Phantom, which our limited facilities create, as the picture, the word, of our own state of being. Is it not the dream of one who in full sun shine has bricked himself up, or excluded thought by voluntary Blindness?"[47]

Cutsinger's argument rests upon these citations from Coleridge's remarks about the evils of materialism. From these he draws the conclusion that the Coleridgean view of God is ultimately a panentheistic one.[48] Panentheism is an ill-defined theological term providing an umbrella under which a range of views find shelter. Cutsinger's position is that Coleridge's panentheism is one in which the material world, in the very physicality of its existence, is deemed to be illusory. There is but one unified reality, the complete unity of subject and object with no place for boundary or limit. It is only when we come to this "new" perception claims Cutisnger, that we will be able to appreciate the true significance of Coleridge's theological imagination.

Such an assertion is loaded with huge theological implications. It implies that the distinction between the One and the Many is collapsed. In an anti-materialist view there is only the One and the principle of unity-with-diversity is rendered impossible. Furthermore it demands a major shift in Coleridge's Christology away from the traditional formulation of Christian doctrine. If the material world is composed of boundary-less entities which are merely part of a hidden divine unity, then the incarnation of Christ becomes a nonsense.

It is my contention therefore that Cutsinger has fundamentally misconstrued Coleridge's polemic against materialism which has inevitably

---

46. Ibid., 344.
47. Coleridge, *CN* III, 4341.
48. Cutsinger, *The Form of Transformed Vision*, 113.

caused him to draw conclusions about Coleridge's views on the natural world which are at variance with other parts of his philosophical theology.

To appreciate what Coleridge meant by his denigrating comments on "the Corpuscular School," one needs to return to his earlier obsession with the associationism of Hartley. In Coleridge's more mature years, as we have already noted, he viewed associationism as inherently deficient in that it was solely concerned with mechanical configurations of sensible data. His move away from this school of thought stemmed from its perceived inability to address the deeper, more profound questions of meaning, and the place of ideas and reason. In so doing, Coleridge was not railing against the material world *per se,* but rather against the claims that the materialists were making about their philosophical stance. To confuse Coleridge's view of the natural world with the philosophical system, known as materialism, is thus to do Coleridge a disservice.

In order to make sense of his attitude to nature one needs to return to his theological anthropology and the Trinitarian conclusions that flowed from that. Coleridge's musings on human personality centered on the concept of the self, the "I," which was constituted only in its relation to the "other" or to the "thou." The I-thou relationship which recognized both similarity and difference simultaneously was central to Coleridge's understanding of what it meant to be human. This relational understanding of humanity was for him a mirror, a derivative, of the divine nature. If humanity is constituted relationally, it is merely because God is likewise intrinsically relational. Naturally this points to a Trinitarian conclusion concerning the ontology of God within which there is both unity and diversity. Indeed, Colin Gunton has stated that Coleridge was "the first to have developed both a Trinitarian understanding of God and a relational view of the human person."[49] A relational anthropology and theology possesses the advantage of maintaining respect for the dignity and validity of "the other" whilst also affirming the One. There is the recognition of both particularity and unity. Once this principle, which flows like an underground stream through all of Coleridge's writings is apprehended, it becomes clear that he could never have assumed an attitude to creation which dissolved the differences between objects subsumed under a generalized whole. It was by insisting on an ontology of God that was grounded in relationality that Coleridge was able to steer a course away from the pantheism of Schelling and Spinoza whilst also avoiding an undifferentiated panentheism. Whilst Coleridge firmly advocated that God could be encountered in and through nature, his position is not

49. Gunton, *The Promise of Trinitarian Theology,* 97.

to be equated with pantheism. He was too well acquainted with both Greek and Hebrew poetic forms not to appreciate their distinctiveness. For Coleridge, Greek writers were "poets of fancy, whereas Hebrew poets wrote of the power of the imagination."[50] Coleridge himself wrote of this distinction in one of his letters. "In the Hebrew Poets each thing has a life of its own, and yet they are all one Life. In God they move and live and have their being—not *had*, as the cold system of Newtonian Theology represents—but have."[51]

The biblical canon thus provided the basis for Coleridge's assertion that there is an ontological connection between distinction and plurality. Alan Gregory has summarized the position of Coleridge in this way: "Distinction and plurality are ontologically fundamental. In the eternal act by which the Son 'becomes,' is distinguished from the Father, all God's creative possibilities are established as finite expressions of the eternal distinction and self referral of the Son from and to the Father."[52]

A consideration of the kind of relationship that pertains between God and the created order necessarily demands a discussion of the interface between science and faith. The philosopher of history, R. G. Collingwood, argues in his book *The Idea of History*,[53] that there have been three eras in reflective thinking about the nature of the created order. The ancient Greeks and their mediaeval successors conceived of the world as an organism in which the world of nature is saturated or permeated by mind. In the second era, which encompassed the Renaissance period and the birth of modern science, nature was thought of much more in terms of a machine that operated according to fixed unchanging laws like clockwork. In the modern period of the last two hundred years, the third era, nature has been understood in terms of an unfolding process, part of the flow of history. Although this somewhat crude classification lacks any nuanced finesse, it does provide a broad framework within which to explore how God is perceived to relate to the created order.

If, for example, creation is depicted organically, the metaphysical and theological problems this produces are considerable. Within such a pantheistic schema God is bound so closely to creation as to be virtually indistinguishable from it making divine existence coextensive with that of the universe. If God began with the Big Bang, then he will die with the final Big Crunch. Such a total identification of God with creation

---

50. Brett, *Fancy & Imagination*, 41.
51. Coleridge, *CL* II 1, 866.
52. Barbeau, *Coleridge's Assertion of Religion*, 209.
53. Collingwood, *The Idea of History*, 1983.

places God effectively under the dominion of creation in which the history of creation is synonymous with the "history" of God. A different set of theological problems arise when considering the Renaissance concept of a mechanistic nature. If the world is a mechanism then it would be natural to think of God as a Celestial Engineer, with divine action being limited to the initial construction phase. The rise of deism as a theological category is closely allied to this view of nature. If God is relegated to the role of the cosmic clockmaker then after the work has been completed his role becomes redundant altogether. A deistic universe accommodates no place for prayer or providence. The way is paved then for an atheistic universe where everything is reducible to the laws of physics.

Ironically, in recent decades, it has been through the advancement of mathematical theories of the universe that a far greater indeterminacy and uncertainty has arisen. The twentieth-century discoveries of quantum and chaos theory have introduced an intrinsic unpredictability showing that the physical world is not something that is mechanical, predictable, and controllable but is in fact far subtler and indeed more supple than we have hitherto imagined. What is increasingly being noted within the scientific community is the perichoretic nature of the universe itself. Everything in the universe only finds its true being by virtue of the fact that it is in intimately interwoven relationship with everything else. The wings of the African butterfly affect the jet streams over Asia. This dynamic interconnectedness suggests that the created order is still in the process of being formed, the continuing and ongoing product of historical forces. If creation is an uncompleted act then it is necessary to reconstitute an understanding of how God relates to it. Polkinghorne writes lucidly on this point: "If the world is an evolving process, in via, then God may be expected to be in interactive relationship with its unfolding history. There is no need, however for the Creator to be Cosmic Tyrant, in total control of all that is happening. Indeed the play of creation, as we perceive it has more the appearance of an improvisation than the appearance of the performance of a predetermined script."[54]

The intention here is to maintain a metaphysical distinction between God's providential agency and creaturely intentionality. Perhaps the key to understanding this distinction is to assert the kenotic nature of God's creative acts. In allowing creation to "be itself" God voluntarily chooses, by an act of self-limitation, to permit a freedom and indeterminate outcome to the unfolding of cosmic history. It is only by such an act of kenosis that God's love can be manifested for by acting in this

54. Polkinghorne, *Faith, Science and Understanding*, 110–11.

way God respects the integrity of creation. This very kenosis means that God's interaction with creation is neither a heavy-handed control, nor a hands-off distancing but rather an involved improvisation whereby God allows a degree of free play in the creative process. In Barthian terms this is described as an aspect of God's patience.

> Patience exists where space and time are given with a definite intention, where freedom is allowed in expectation of a response. God acts in this way. He makes this purposeful concession of space and time. He allows this freedom of expectancy. That He does so lies in His very being. Indeed, it is His being. Everything that God is, is implied and included in the statement that He is patient. But this is no more self-evident than our previous considerations. It cannot in any sense result from a simple development of ideas.[55]

The One and the Many

As with all theological speculation, Coleridge's Trinitarianism emerged as a result of his engagement with a panoply of competing voices. Gunton[56] has argued persuasively that the question that lies at the root of any doctrine of God is the choice between Heraclitus and Parmenides. The disagreement between these two pre-Socratic philosophers turned around the question of the One and the Many. Heraclitus, being the philosopher of the Many, argued that plurality is prior to unity, that diversity, and by implication instability, is the essential nature of the cosmos. Parmenides, by contrast, took entirely the opposite view. Behind the appearance of chaotic diversity there is a prior unity. There is no plurality within reality and thus plurality is merely an epiphenomenon, a mirage, that bears no correspondence with the true nature of being. Reality is timelessly uniform and stable. Parmenides was the pre-eminent philosopher of the One. Although this was an ancient dispute, its intellectual descendants are alive and well today as they were in Coleridge's time. The Parmenidian position, being at heart profoundly dismissive and suspicious of the many,

---

55. Barth, *KD*, 2/1, 459: "Geduld ist da, wo Einer einem Anderen in bestimmter Absicht Raum und Zeit gibt, wo Einer einen Anderen auf ihn wartend gewähren läßt. Daß Gott dies tut, ja, daß solch planvolles Raum- und Zeitlassen, solches wartende Gewährenlassen in Gottes Wesen liegt, ja selber ganz und gar Gottes Wesen ist—daß Alles, was Gott ist, auch darin beschlossen, damit gesagt ist, daß er geduldig ist, das versteht sich wirklich so wenig von selbst wie alles Frühere; auch das ergibt sich keineswegs aus einer einfachen Begriffsentwicklung."

56. Gunton, *The One, the Three, and the Many*, 17ff.

could not fail to denigrate the intrinsic value and dignity of the material world. The diversity and particularity of creation was inherently inferior to the unchanging stability of the One.

The elevation of the One over and against the Many typifies much of the theology of the Origen/Augustin tradition giving it a strongly monist orientation. When God is conceived of in static, timeless terms the resulting stress is on the oneness and arbitrariness of the divine will at the expense of the integrity of the created world. Coleridge's position at this point is apparently paradoxical. One aspect of Coleridge's worldview, which has already been explored, is the "*Logosophic*" principle, namely the quest to unearth the inherent underlying unity behind all things. Coleridge draws both from his Neo-Platonic sources and, increasingly in later life, from the Johannine tradition to support this view. One might expect, therefore, that Coleridge would instinctively be pulled towards at Parmenidian position. Yet another aspect of Coleridge's life was his profound appreciation of the particular; the individual flower, the raindrop or the frost on the window pane. These examples of particularity could never be dismissed with a Parmenidian wave of the hand. Furthermore, Coleridge's appreciation of the arts and all things aesthetic meant that he required a philosophical and theological framework within which both the unity of Parmenides and the many of Heraclitus could be held together without tension or opposition.

The issues at stake are manifold. To take the Parmenidian position too strongly leads, in effect, to the eclipse of both human diversity and human freedom. "The elevation of God," states Gunton when discussing a Marxist critique of Parmenidian views of God, "necessarily diminishes the worshipper."[57] A unitary God can, and often does, lead to a unitary society, intolerant of diversity and individual choice. The visible expression of this view may produce an oppressive totalitarianism which denies the possibility and beauty of difference. The Heraclitan position is no less troublesome. The exaltation of diversity at the expense of any underlying unity can only lead to chaos and moral anarchy.

Coleridge was instinctively attracted to the Many of Heraclitus as this position offered a basis upon which to affirm a dynamism to God who created space for existence of "otherness." Yet Coleridge also wished to maintain the essential unity of the cosmos—a far more Parmenidian view—and thus he sought a way to hold the One and the Many together within a single, yet diverse, divine being. Germane to this discussion is the Coleridgean notion of an "idea" to which reference has already been

---

57. Ibid., 26.

made. An idea, belonging to the realm of reason, possesses the capacity to both contemplate the particular within the universal and universal within the particular. It is this interaction of the many within the one and the one within the many that Coleridge sought for without either pole being given pre-eminence. An idea, in the Coleridgean sense, is not a Platonic abstraction, nor is it fixed and static but rather possesses a dynamic, constitutive, ontological quality. Colin Gunton defines the Coleridgean concept of an idea in this way: They are, "fathomless concepts by which the mind and the deep things of existence come into relation."[58] An idea does not embody the universal mark of being yet ideas may give rise to transcendentals which do possess such marks. Ideas point towards transcendentals and it is from transcendentals that ideas owe their origin. So, for example, relationality, freedom, spirit, truth, beauty, goodness are all, according to the Coleridgean framework, ideas that resist easy definition and are open to multiple expressions of form. Thus an idea contains within it something that is universal in that it is not limited by geography or time yet it is also particular in that ideas find myriad ways of individual manifestation. For Coleridge the ultimate idea of all ideas was, of course, the Trinity. In his notebooks, he writes, "The Trinity is indeed the primary Idea, out of which all other Ideas evolved."[59]

The interpenetration of the universal and the particular, which is the abiding hallmark of an idea, speaks of its *perichoretic* nature. This draws us inexorably towards Trinitarian perichoresis as the source and fountain of all other perichoretic relations. The perichoresis of the Trinity is not a co-habitation of the three together but a form of inter-relating in which each member of the Trinity is constituted and shaped by being in communion with the other. "It implies that the three persons of the Trinity exist only in reciprocal eternal relatedness," explains Colin Gunton.[60] Coleridge was keen to emphasize the essentially constitutive nature of Trinitarian relationships. They were, according to Perkins, "an ineffable cycle of Being, Intelligence and communicative Life, Love and Action."[61]

To describe the Trinity in such terms has profound implications in addressing a range of questions. A Trinity which is constituted in dynamic terms of endless possibilities is very different from the more static monistic portrayals of God found in much of the western tradition. The Coleridgean Trinity, as the ultimate source of all "ideas," has the advan-

---

58. Ibid., 161.
59. Coleridge, *CN* IV, 5294.
60. Gunton, *The One, the Three, and the Many*, 164.
61. Perkins, "Logic and Logos," 195.

tage of preserving the transcendent otherness of God and in this respect remains firmly within the Augustinian/Barthian tradition. God remains utterly distinct from the world and separate from it within a boundaried integrity. This distancing is vital if one is to avoid collapsing God into the world with a resultant form of Process theology. Yet because the Trinity is essentially dynamic, marked by a mutual giving and receiving within the Godhead, then this permits a far greater fluidity and imaginative possibility when considering God's engagement with the world.

Reconciliation in God

No discussion about the search for unity would be complete, however, without a further exploration into a theology of reconciliation. Whilst Coleridge used the term "unification" with reference to the Logos (whom he identified as Christ), what he had in view was nothing other than the concept of reconciliation. The task of reconciliation is summarized in the drama of salvation, conceived and accomplished through Trinitarian relationships and Trinitarian action. That this can be described as "drama" is self evident given the narrative and historical nature of the divine human encounter. A later chapter will explore how this dramatic engagement is manifested in the biblical corpus. This chapter poses the question as to whether there is anything *in* God that enables us to witness the originating source of reconciliatory drama?

Robert Jenson[62] has explored this very possibility beginning with two texts which elicit an exchange between the three persons of the Trinity; the story enacted in the garden of Gethsemane, and the baptism of Jesus. In Gethsemane we read of the struggle to reconcile the will of the Son with the will of the Father. It cannot be supposed that this is a description of conflict between the Father and Son for the biblical witness, particularly in the Johannine Gospel, affirms that the Father and Son are eternally and indivisibly united. Yet the text does portray the desperate cry of Jesus for a uniting of wills at this crucial moment of decision. "Abba, Father, he said, everything is possible for you. Take this cup from me. Yet not what I will, but what you will."[63] Whilst this is not the speech of reconciled warring parties it is nevertheless the language of reconciliation. Even though the Holy Spirit is not specifically mentioned here, the words on the lips of Jesus, *Abba, Father,* are the same as those attributed to the work of the Spirit in Rom 8:15: "for you did not receive a spirit that makes you a slave

---

62. Gunton, *The Theology of Reconciliation*, 159–69.
63. Mark 14:32.

again to fear, but you received the Spirit of sonship. And by him we cry, Abba, Father." The Augustinian theological tradition names the Spirit as the *vinculum amoris,* and it is precisely this bond of reconciling love that the tussle in Gethsemane points us towards.

The second text under consideration is the baptism of Christ in the Jordan. This story, used by the early church fathers in their Trinitarian formulations, exhibits the three persons in partnership. The partnership, however, is one in which the Spirit mediates between the Son and the Father and then drives the Son into the desert where he is tempted. The bond of love between the Father and Son is maintained and sustained by the active work of the Spirit. Whilst the intra-trinitarian relationships are never finally ruptured, the work of reconciliation within God is perhaps the fountain from which all other acts of reconciling love flow. The form of this imaginative engagement will be the subject of the next three sections.

The Passive-active Imagination of God

The Question of Language

To assert that the human imagination functions both actively and passively, as Coleridge observed, is to state what is perhaps obvious, certainly to those whose work demands any degree of creativity. To claim that this imaginative process is a participation in God's own imaginative speech and action is a far more provocative statement to make. It is also rich in theological imagery and this section will begin to make an exploration of that potential. Before doing so, some preliminary observations need to be made. When deploying the term "the passive-active imagination of God," we are operating at the very edge of what language is capable of articulating and care needs to be taken to define terms. When Coleridge made his famous observations of the water skater insect and the failure to recall the name of "Daniel," to which reference has already been made, what he clearly had in mind was the way in which the human unconscious worked. In his day the science of human psychology was relatively undeveloped and Coleridge did not have a rich store of academic research from which to draw inspiration. Yet his tacit acknowledgment of the role that the unconscious could play foreshadowed the much later work of Freud. Coleridge observed that the human mind is still active in an unconscious or even subconscious way even when apparently passive. This passive mode of being could indeed be profoundly creative and the source of much that is intuitive and spontaneous. To apply the notion of the "unconscious passivity" to the being God is perhaps to take a linguistic step too far. Yet the human experience of God being apparently passive was a common one for the Psalmists. It is not uncommon to find in the Psalms of Lament, a heartfelt cry of despair at the sense of abandonment by God precisely at the moment of greatest stress and harassment. Witness the anguish in Ps 22. "My God, my God, why have you forsaken me? Why are you so far from saving me, so far from the words of my groaning? O my God, I cry out by day, but you do not answer, by night, and am not silent."

For David it appeared that at that particular moment God was indeed inactive, absent, and apparently unconcerned about his plight. His cry of dereliction was taken up by Christ himself on the cross, which suggests a similar experience of abandonment. Our discussion concerning the ontology of God however requires us to view the question of activity and passivity not primarily from the perspective of the human perception of God but from within the very heart of the Trinity. Is there a way in which the paradigm of activity and passivity is a useful one with which to engage when exploring Trinitarian questions? Its usefulness may become more evident if a different linguistic tone is used. The problem of using the word "passivity" in relation to God is it that implies that God, at certain times in history, actually does nothing and indeed is the object of action rather than its subject. To go further down this road is to invite a conflation of God with creation and, potentially at least, to impose an external force upon God that ultimately removes any divine freedom. Yet this is perhaps merely a trick of language, a linguistic sleight of hand, and one may legitimately use alternative forms of speech with which to explore this theme which are not so theologically loaded.

The language of "activity and passivity" resonates immediately with the alternative language of "gift and reception." In the making of a gift one is, of necessity, active. In the reception of a gift one is likewise required to be passive. When we apply the terms "gift" and "reception" to our understanding of Trinitarian relationships then a rich world of possibilities opens up. It was this idea of a Trinitarian framework of divine relationships within which there is both gift and reception that, I believe, Coleridge was attempting to articulate in his definition of the structure of the tetractys. His description of the Christ as The Alterity is an intriguing one. Coleridge places Christ as "the significant other" (to use a Ricoeurian phrase[64]) who relates to the Father, the Ipseity, in

---

64. In his book entitled *Oneself as Another*, Paul Ricoeur explores the notion of selfhood. He writes that, "the selfhood of oneself implies otherness to such an intimate degree that one cannot be thought of without the other." Ricoeur, *Oneself as Another*, 3.

perfect reciprocal mutuality. In like manner his description of the Holy Spirit as "The Community," defines the heart of the being and action of the Spirit in relational terms. Coleridge struggles to communicate the way in which the persons of the Trinity are intimately interwoven. We have already made reference to his definition of Christ and it is worth repeating here. "The Alterity . . . the relatively objective, *deitas objectiva* in relation to the I AM as the *deitas subjective*; the divine objectivity . . . But with the relatively subjective and the relatively objective, the great idea needs only for its completion a co-eternal which is both, that is, relatively objective to the subjective and relatively subjective to the objective." And with reference to the Spirit he writes, "The eternal life, which is love; the Spirit; relatively to the Father, the Spirit of holiness, the Holy Spirit; relatively to the Son."[65]

Coleridge's understanding of Trinitarian relationships is one in which there is mutual interchange between subject and object. However dense his definitions are, they are at least an attempt to articulate the Trinity in terms of gift and reception between the three persons. This theological anchorage point builds on the Coleridgean understanding of both human personality and divine personeity which we have already explored. Coleridge insisted on the central priority of the "I-Thou" relationship in his construction not only of a human anthropology but also his Trinitarian explorations. The mutuality that is inherent in this formulation is a reflection not only of the mutual giving and receiving evident in intra-Trinitarian relationships but also in the way in which God interacts with humankind. If one asserts that in the very heart of God there lies a mutual giving and receiving between the Father and Son, bound within the love of the Spirit, then one must equally claim that this is the way in which God manifests his being towards creation. God cannot be one kind of person within himself internally and then display an utterly different character towards humankind, one that is perhaps couched in terms of a uni-directional dominance.[66] If God is intrinsically reciprocal in relational terms then this must be expressed too in his dealings with humankind. This is the point that Karl Barth is anxious to stress in his *Kirchliche Dogmatik* 2/1: "God is who He is in His works. He is the same even in Himself, even before and after and over His works, and without them. They are bound to Him, but He is not bound to them. They are nothing without Him. But He is who He is without them. He is not,

---

65. Barth, *Coleridge and Christian Doctrine*, 94.

66. My use of gender specific language here it not intended to carry with it any gender specific definitions of God.

therefore, who He is only in His works. Yet in Himself He is not another than He is in His works."[67]

Improvisation and the Present Moment

What however does this way of reciprocal relating look like? The mutual interaction that the category of gift and reception requires, points us in the direction of improvisation and to the suggestion made at the outset of this project that this notion of improvisation, hinted at in the story of Nathan and David, is a valid theological category in itself. A number of authors have explored the epistemological fruits of improvisation, most notably Jeremy Begbie in his work on musical improvisation. Others, such as Stanley Hauerwas and Sam Wells, have applied the concept to ethics. It is our task here to assess the way in which we can construct an ontology of God that makes space for improvisation in a context of active and passive participation. In what way do God's actions and revelation bear the distinctive traits of one who improvises?

The picture of a God who improvises must be placed beside the traditional teaching of the church that there is a constancy and immutability in God expressed perhaps mostly forcibly the words of the prophet Mal 3:6 "I the LORD do not change." The notion of God's constancy need not mean that at all times and in all places God's actions are always entirely predictable and exactly uniform. To assert that is to turn the constancy of God into something that is mechanical and subject to hidden mathematical formulations. It is also to deny the very life of God; a person who is alive and therefore profoundly responsive to that which is new and contingent. In the biblical corpus the immutability of God is manifested in a "mobility and elasticity" ("eine Beweglichkeit, eine Elastizität")[68] in which divine perseverance and trustworthiness is assured. It is God's faithfulness and love which never change and are the ground of faith. Yet this faithfulness and love can only be manifested within the particularity of each new contingent event. The "mobility and elasticity" that Karl Barth describes in his discussion concerning the perfections of God is simply another way of articulating the notion of improvisation.

---

67. Barth, *KD*, 2/1, 291: "Gott ist, der er ist, in seinen Werken. Er ist derselbe auch in sich selber, auch vor und nach und über seinen Werken, auch ohne sie. Sie sind an ihn, aber er ist nicht an sie gebunden. Sie sind nichts ohne ihn. Er aber ist, der er ist, auch ohne sie. Er ist also, der er ist, nicht nur in seinen Werken. Er ist aber auch in sich selber kein Anderer als eben der, der er in seinen Werken ist."

68. Ibid., 558.

The Coleridgean definition of the imagination rests upon the self-designation of God in Exod 3, "I AM who I AM." Coleridge makes the bold claim here that the paradigm of all human artistic endeavor, all imaginative productive creativity, indeed the very capacity to imaginatively perceive God, lies in the creativity of the divine "I AM." If human identity is lodged within the reciprocal relationship of the "I AM" then it is necessary now to turn to this enigmatic phrase in search of clarity. To what does Coleridge refer when he describes God in this way? The creation to which Coleridge alludes in the citation above is not the eternal on-going emanation of the cosmos in some kind of Neo-Platonic, Plotinian sense. Coleridge is referring to the infinite yet self-conscious, self-referential, Creator,[69] the self-generation of the Tetractys.

The phrase "I AM who I AM," formed in the imperfect tense in the original Hebrew, is normally used to indicate an uncompleted action. As such the term can equally well be rendered "I will be who I will be," as the Hebrew makes no radical grammatical distinction between present and future temporal forms. This suggests that the self-disclosure of God is to be understood as ongoing, being continually renewed and refreshed. The God who calls to Moses from within the burning bush is the One whose character and being is framed in perfect freedom, self-authenticating and self-referential. This divine revelation is uncompleted in the sense that at each moment of immanent encounter there is a fresh exposition of his ontology expressed in his agency. The sense of the overwhelming significance of the present moment is intense and refers perhaps to an attentive engagement with the very "now-ness" of existence.

Walter Brueggemann makes the point that this enigmatic and puzzling expression belongs to a tradition of divine self-disclosure in which there is either a tendency to state Yahweh's *relationship* to Israel or a tendency to attest to Yahweh's *being or character*.[70] In this text both forms of disclosure are in purview. Initially the divine declaration appears to be a simple statement of character or being. It is contained within its own linguistic circle of reference and does not touch upon divine agency or action. Yet the context of the narrative in Exod 3 reveals a different layer of meaning. Prior to the answer given to Moses about the "naming" of God, the text declares, "Then he said, I am the God of your father, the God of Abraham, the God of Isaac and the God of Jacob."[71] The intention is clear. The dialogue refers Moses to a redemptive narrative in which the

---

69. Coleridge, *BL* I, 203.
70. Brueggemann, *Theology of the Old Testament*, 124.
71. Exod 3:6.

key player, God, has engaged intimately and powerfully within Moses' ancestral history. This is a form of discourse that is framed in terms of relationship to Israel and not simply a portrayal of Yahweh's being or character. It is because of the configuration of the meaning of this narrative that Moses can draw strength and encouragement to engage in future leadership exploits. The naming of Yahweh as "I AM who I AM" thus possesses a dual reference, both to the actions of Yahweh in history (and therefore, logically, also in the future) and to the eternal self-referential definition of God which is independent of historical or geographical particularity.

The "now-ness" of God is pregnant with theological potential. That this is so is evident through its repeated use by the writer of the book of Hebrews, who insists that, "today, if you hear his voice, do not harden your hearts."[72] Whilst such injunctions have in mind the human response to the call of God, the critical importance of the present moment in the economy of God is also in view. What does this suggest? The present moment, the "now" of God, carries with it an implicit reference to time. In what way does God inhabit both an eternal "timeless" space yet also engage with creation within the "constraints" that time affords?

An exploration into the relationship between God and time naturally leads our journey towards the realm of music for it is in this artistic arena above all that time is of critical importance. It is at this point that a musical analogy may be pertinent.[73] Coleridge was not unaware of the relationship between music and the imagination. In his *Biographia,* he astutely observes, "the sense of musical delight, with the power of producing it, is a gift of the imagination; and this together with the power of reducing multitude into unity of effect, and modifying a series of thoughts by some one predominant thought or feeling, may be cultivated and improved, but can never be learnt. It is in these that '*poeta nascitur non fit.*'"[74]

The craft of the musician was, for Coleridge, an innate God-given ability, a reflection of the musical imagination of the Creator. It can be harnessed and developed but its source and wellspring come not from within but from without. Coleridge was persuaded that there was an analogous relationship between art and faith due entirely to the unavoidable role of the imagination. If it is legitimate therefore to place faith and

---

72. Heb 3:7.

73. Jeremy Begbie has demonstrated the significant value of using the arts, and in particular musical resonance, as a route to a greater depth of theological perception, particularly in *Theology, Music, and Time.*

74. Coleridge, *BL* II, 20.

music within the same frame of reference, how then may one characterize the musical qualities of God? May one liken God to a musician, or to a composer or to a conductor? Let us explore here briefly the function of the latter.

The conductor of an orchestra may choose to produce music by exerting a firm influence over the performances of each musician. Such a conductor is fully in control and determines the precise shape, timbre and feel of the music; the task of the musicians being primarily one of artistic obedience. Arturo Toscanini would be a good example of such an approach. Norman Lebrecht, the well-known music critic, describes Toscanini as someone for whom "interpretative notions that enabled music to be played in subjective, variable manner . . . were anathema to him."[75] Alternatively, a conductor may choose to relinquish some control, to permit a little contingency as it were, and allow each musician a degree of artistic freedom. Wilhelm Furtwängler could well be cited to stand in this tradition. For him each performance was a new act of creation; the conductor was not the servant of the work, but rather its master. Furtwängler saw his function as more passive, even "female," in that he was the receptacle of the composer's spirit. It was because of this radically controversial philosophy of conducting that he would say to his singers, "You are waiting for me to give you cues. I am not giving you cues. You are to come in, and I come to you. I want you to take over!"[76] Such a style involves greater risk but also affords the possibility of greater individual creativity. As a result of this approach to conducting, Furtwängler's music was often received as being "opaque, tremulous, pregnant with manifold possibilities."[77]

To maintain a balance between relinquishment and control, freedom and constraint, the present and the future, activity and passivity, requires great delicacy and the ability to stay focused on the present moment in order to facilitate musical beauty. To stay in the "now-ness" of such an ephemeral artistic medium as music is a profound skill. It demands that the conductor incorporates into the complete piece of music the particularity of expression that each musician brings. It suggests a respect for individuality without losing sight of the greater unity. It joins together both diversity and unity in one present moment and it is this very capability that can produce something that is truly sublime. The Kantian project faltered when it encountered the sublime realizing that *a*

75. Lebrecht, *The Maestro Myth*, 74.
76. Ibid., 85.
77. Ibid., 84.

priori judgments were not capable of making sense of the response of awe that the sublime elicited. Coleridge, fascinated by the sublime, connected it with the creative imaginative genius of the great I AM. The analogy of God as exuberant conductor making space for individuality and creativity of each player, both actively engaging and "passively" receiving may shed some light on the true nature of the divine habitation of "now." To dwell in the present moment, blending together the particular into the universal in order to reach the divine *Ziel,* is perhaps part of the improvisatory nature of the "I AM."

C. S. Lewis uses a similar analogy in his book, *The Screwtape Letters*, an imaginary series of written exchanges between Satan and his lesser devils. He writes,

> Music and silence—how I detest them both! How thankful we should be that ever since our Father entered Hell . . . no square inch of infernal space and no moment of internal space and no moment of infernal time has been surrendered to either of those abominable forces, but all has been occupied by Noise—Noise, that grand dynamism, the audible expression of all that is exultant ruthless and virile—Noise which alone defends us from silly qualms, despairing scruples and impossible desires. We will make the whole universe a noise in the end. We have already made great strides in this direction as regards the Earth. The melodies and silences of Heaven will be shouted down in the end. But I admit we are not yet loud enough, or anything like it.[78]

C. S. Lewis here suggests that the "music" of creation itself is a place of great beauty. Music, in its very essence, is the result of the interplay between sound and silence, the active playing of notes with careful attention given to the silence between the notes. Continuous musical activity merely results in devilish noise; no activity at all however produces only silence. Music needs the subtle inter-penetration of activity and passivity in order for beauty to result. Could it be, therefore, that God's improvisation is framed within the way that Coleridge described the water skater insect, with a divine combining of action and rest, giving and receiving, activity and passivity?

It is necessary here to inject a note of caution when applying the analogy of musical improvisation to the ontology of God. Improvisation is suggestive of the complete absence of constraint, the perfect freedom to create music in spontaneous fashion without reference to any external structures. In reality improvisation in the musical arena is contained

---

78. Lewis, *The Screwtape Letters*, 102–3.

within a delicate balance of contingency and constraint. The constraints imposed by key signature, tempo, and rhythm, for example, permit the musician to perform or compose within certain norms of expectation. Yet within this framework there are always opportunities for the contingent, for multiple ways of expression. This sets up the possibility of surprise and the arousal of strong expectation. The attraction of jazz as a musical medium is precisely this blending of the contingent and the non-negotiable and the degree to which each is mutually enhanced by the other.[79]

Our discussion of the theological analogy of jazz raises questions about the nature of the interaction between God's perfect freedom to act and the God-given gift of freedom to humanity. These two freedoms require a balanced blending such that neither one extinguishes the other. To insist on the absolute freedom of God at the expense of human response is to place human integrity in jeopardy. To insist on the absolute unbridled necessity of human freedom and choice is to place God in a constraint that denies a core quality of God's own perfections. To hold the two together points in the direction of divine improvisation.

A biblical example of such improvisation may be drawn from the events of the day of Pentecost as described in Acts 2. This discussion necessitates a consideration of the interface between both the general and the particular functioning of the Spirit and the relationship between constraint and freedom. In the economy of God this moment in history was to be pivotal in the continuing expansion of the coming kingdom, inaugurated during the earthly ministry of Christ and continuing now in fuller measure in the aftermath of the resurrection. The freedom of the love of God is evident in the broadening of the compass of grace to include those both near and far. Yet the constraints in operation on this day were manifest in the limited horizons of those people present. Jeremy Begbie, in his book exploring the relationship between music and theology, refers to this event as "improvisation in advance." To explain this phrase Begbie describes the way in which some forms of musical improvisation introduce a new theme before an earlier theme has found its musical resolution. In the 1960s, the musician Derek Bailey experimented with improvising, not on the current chord being played but on the chord that was about to be introduced. The resultant discordance was both disturbing yet compelling.[80] In a similar way, Beethoven was known to introduce a new beginning before a true ending had been resolved.

79. Begbie, *Theology, Music and Time*, 185.
80. Begbie, *Theology, Music and Time*, 221.

Such improvisation techniques introduce an element of instability yet simultaneously cannot fail to awaken interest. Begbie claims that this is precisely what the Holy Spirit does on the day of Pentecost. "The Spirit is improvising on music the crowd have yet to hear from Peter, and moreover, in a manner which explores the particularities of the occasion . . . The crowd ask, 'what does this mean?' Peter directs them to the harmony and theme which has produced the improvisation, the story of Jesus. The remarkable togetherness they have heard through their ears is what the Spirit has improvised out of what has happened in Jesus Christ and in such a way that their particularity flourishes."[81]

The manifestations of the giving of the Holy Spirit on the day of Pentecost both disturbed and attracted at the same time. They were the harbinger of a radically new theme played over the existing familiar music, namely the celebration of the day of Pentecost. This music was uncompleted for the festival was still "in process" and had not come to completion, yet something new was being introduced. There is here both the ending of one "musical phrase," theologically speaking, and the introduction of radical newness. The Spirit takes the particularity of this occasion with a multiplicity of ethnic groups gathered in one geographical place and improvises in such a way that each person is able to access this gift of God. The resultant story has universal significance despite being conceived in its own particularity.

The relationship between freedom and constraint in the musical sphere has highlighted the delicate interplay between the two. The notion of any kind of limitation on human self-determination and self-expression as being inimical to freedom needs to be questioned. It betrays an assumption that freedom, by its very definition, permits no restraint whatsoever. Yet the freedom of jazz improvisation is only made possible because of the very constraints that give the music shape in the first place. In this context constraint does not refer to confinement or diminution but to the provision of identity within boundaries providing definition. The theological sensitivity that surrounds the notion of constraint when applied to God is understandable for to constrain God is to diminish God's own divinity. Yet such concerns are perhaps more linguistic than theological. When constraint is understood as that which provides shape rather that which negates, then God's own improvisatory engagement in the human arena is made not only possible but is profoundly necessary.

The trouble with the word "improvisation" is that it does not sound serious enough. It suggests that God simply makes up the divine story

---

81. Ibid., 222.

as it unfolds and that divine agency appears suspiciously like some kind of joke or artifice. Yet the Christian narrative is full of joy and surprise, with twists and turns of failure and success. Sam Wells argues that the task of the church is to interpret and perform the Christian story afresh in each generation, improvising in the space between culture and revelation. He writes, "taking time for the trivial is therefore a sign of faith not foolishness. The church can afford to take the risk of the humorous and ephemeral, because the joke is God's and the laughter divine."[82] The notion of improvisation that we have been exploring via a musical medium carries natural resonances with activity of "play." Is there a connection between imagination, improvisation, and play and can we legitimately apply such categories to God?

"Purposeless" Play

At the outset of this investigation reference was made to the story of creation in which we read of the tender description of the creation of Adam. The text of Gen 2 is couched in playful language. A picture is constructed by the storyteller of God taking the dust of the ground, much as a potter or a child would take a lump of modeling clay, and breathing into the human form that had just been shaped. It is the language of the kindergarten yet it is profoundly serious in its intent. The first Adam is taken from the red earth itself and given the gift of life via the very breath of God. But to what end is this divine shaping and forming? This is the question posed by Jürgen Moltmann in his book "*Die Ersten Freigellasen der Schöpfung.*"[83] He proposes three possible answers.

The first is that there was some kind of compulsion, either external or internal, that drove God to create the world. Moltmann rebuffs this notion by asserting that if there is such an external necessity pressing upon God then God would cease to be truly free and would effectively be beholden to a more powerful "other." Moltmann finds such a conception of God to be utterly inadmissible. The second option is that God created the world capriciously, merely on a whim, without any serious loving intent. The ramifications of this option lead to a depiction of God who bears the fickle character traits of fallen humanity. The only remaining option, according to Moltmann, is that God created out of sheer delight and good pleasure thereby placing joy at the heart of creation. If God exhibits within himself the extravagant exuberance that one witnesses in creation

---

82. Wells, *Improvisation*, 69.
83. Moltmann, *Die ersten Freigelassenen der Schöpfung*, 1–6.

itself then God becomes the playful creator. This is an entirely non-utilitarian view of creation, that it serves no useful or functional purpose. "Why does the world exist? . . . the answer is . . . for no reason at all. The uselessness of God implies the uselessness of creation. Creation exists only because God takes pleasure in it."[84] So writes the Dutch theologian Jean Jacque Suurmond, taking up Moltmann's thesis. This lack of functionality strikes at the very heart of the Kantian view of religion. Whilst Kant insisted that nothing of God could ever be truly known, the notion of God served a useful purpose in instilling some kind of moral rigor into society. Yet if Christianity is merely "useful" as a foundation for moral imperatives then this effectively makes God the servant of morality. Schleiermacher in Germany and Coleridge in England both rebelled against such reductionism. Suurmond argues that the culmination of creation is not humanity but the Sabbath, the point at which God rests from activity and enjoys his own handiwork. Indeed this concessive relationship between God and creation can be described as joyful "play." The story of the Garden of Eden is filled with such playful images. We read about a garden where things are not what they appear to be, a place of gold and chrysophrase. The man and woman give names to the animals and run around naked and unashamed. At the culmination of each "week" they cease from such "labors" and enter into the same rest that God enjoys by observing that the world is indeed a "good" place.

Yet Moltmann's view of creation arising from the purposeless delight of the playful creator is at odds with other theological possibilities which demand that an alternative reading of the creation story be heard. Key amongst these options is the Barthian view that the work of creation is intensely purposeful and can only be conceived of from a Trinitarian position. Barth strenuously insisted that the work of the Son in redemption must never be viewed as an expedient solution to the problem of the Fall.[85] If one asserts that the crucifixion and resurrection only became necessary through the failure of God's original intention in creation then a hornet's nest of theological problems open up. The work of the Son in redemption and reconciliation loses its centrality in relation to his identity as it is reduced to mere expediency. The Barthian position would appear to take seriously texts such as Rev 13:8 which states that "the Lamb . . . was slain from the creation of the world."[86] The notion of purposeless play as divine motive for creation sits uneasily with this assertion. This

---

84. Suurmond, *Word and Spirit at Play*, 31.

85. Barth, *KD*, 4/1, 68.

86. New International Version.

text however is notoriously problematic to translate. The New American Standard Version offers this rendering. "All who dwell on the earth will worship him, everyone whose name has not been written from the foundation of the world in the book of life of the Lamb who has been slain." Here the emphasis is placed not on the time when the Lamb was slain but on the fact that some names have been omitted from the book of life from the foundation of the world. The key exegetical issue is what the phrase "from the foundation of the world" refers to. In this particular context it can legitimately refer to either the Lamb or to the people. Yet there is a further factor to consider which concerns the way in which the concept of time is handled in the book of Revelation. The entire drama appears to be located outside of the normal parameters of time as we know them, such that past, present, and future are seemingly conflated or distorted in ways that are hard to conceive. The difficulties inherent in translating this text therefore should produce a degree of caution in building a theological edifice upon it.

Barth claimed that the creation was the work of the Trinity and provided that stage upon which the drama of reconciliation could be made manifest. "The actual world," writes Robert Jenson building on Barth's view, "is the God commanded stage and supporting players to this drama; we should not be surprised to find it glorious but painful and even self conflicted."[87] The intention of creation therefore, according to Barth, is to accommodate and include humanity within the orbit of Trinitarian relations. Creation provides the arena within which such reconciliation is made possible. The formula that Barth summarized his position was, "weil servatio, darum creatio."[88] It is because of the servanthood of the Son in relation to the will of the Father for the completion of the task of redemption that creation came into being.

Whilst this position has much merit, not least of which is the Trinitarian foundation of the act of creation, it risks several dangers. The first of these is the relegation of creation itself into the role of mere narrative backdrop, the curtains and lighting as it were, (to pursue the dramatic metaphor), thereby diminishing its intrinsic value. Secondly, we are forced to conclude that the crucifixion is an "intermediate good."[89] If the identity of the Son is intimately bound up with his work then the death of Christ for sin demands that sin also be understood as an intermediate good and thus part of the "purposefulness" of creation. Conceptually and

87. Jenson, *Systematic Theology Vol. 2*, 23.
88. Barth, *KD*, 3/3 91.
89. Jenson, *Systematic Theology Vol. 2*, 20.

morally such a conclusion is hard to imagine. Thirdly, the formulation carries with it the implied necessity for creation to be, in order that the task of redemption can be fulfilled. The note of compulsion driven by the requirement for an arena for the Son to do his work could be construed as a constraint upon the absolute freedom of God. Lastly all theological reflection has to be grounded in reliable exegesis of the sacred texts. The question being addressed here, stated baldly, is this: "with what motive did God create the world"? It is therefore a "why?" question addressed to the Creator. The book of Job is consumed with the story of individuals who demand an answer from God to just this kind of question and no answer is given that satisfies any kind of philosophical, theological or moral curiosity. God merely declares at the conclusion of the narrative that he is the Creator. In similar fashion when the disciples of Jesus asked him why a tower collapsed killing eighteen unfortunate inhabitants, he likewise offered no explanation.[90] The search for a theologically satisfying answer to the question of divine intention or motive for creation is perhaps to move beyond the remit of biblical warrant.

However the dichotomy between Moltmann's view that creation is purposeless and the Barthian view that it is highly intentional may prove to be more apparent than real. It is precisely here that the paradigm of "play" offers a way to unpick some of these Gordian knots. The story of creation in Gen 1 includes the declaration by YHWH at the conclusion of each day that what he saw was "good" *(tob)*. The Hebrew word, *tob*, also means "pleasant" and so the storyteller invites his hearers to imagine God deriving pleasure from the execution of the creative fiat. The response of God to what he had created was that it gave him pleasure to behold. The theological intention of the writer of this account was not to offer a divine motive but rather to declare to a chosen people that creation itself is blessed and filled with divine "goodness." God's movement towards creation is one of unending generosity and the reciprocal response of creation to the creator is doxology.[91] As Walter Brueggemann has stated, "Delight is here understood as structured into the character of reality."[92] The language of the story of creation is located in the playroom rather than the workshop. It is the very intrinsic joy that is built into the very fabric of creation that elicits the response of joyful adoration from creation to the creator. The lack of intentionality is the foundation of the subsequent doxology.

90. Luke 13:4
91. Job 38:7 and Ps 19:1.
92. Brueggemann, *Genesis*, 27.

Yet, as we have already observed from the writings of Huizinga, it is precisely because play is non-utilitarian that makes it so productive. The divine play between the Father, Son, and Spirit in the act of creation is inherently centrifugal. The "otherness" of the Son in relation to the Father allows for and permits the inclusion of "othernesss" elsewhere. The Trinitrian bond of love always moves outwards in hospitality towards the other and others are invited to be included in the playfulness of God's creative purposes. This suggests that the inclusion of humankind in the orbit of Trintarian love is the inevitable result of creation even if it may not have been the foundational motive. Divine hospitality and the inclusion of humanity into the heart of the Godhead is, however, a risky business. To choose to include others as an act of love is to permit contingency and thus to make space for the possibility of estrangement and damage. The generous hospitality of God is not to be conceived of as something cozy and warm; it is nothing other than the costly grace that Bonhöffer described with reference to the events of Good Friday. The paradigm of play however, permits the non-necessity of creation whilst simultaneously granting the utter appropriateness of redemption. Robert Jenson articulates the character of creation in this way: "God does not become active and relational when he creates; just so creating is both appropriate and unnecessary for him."[93]

We have delayed on this point for good reason. Coleridge located the fountainhead of the imagination in the creative activity of God. It is highly germane to this discussion therefore, to inquire as to the theological DNA of creation. Is it found in divine law with a reciprocal demand for adherence? Much of Protestant theology in the Western tradition has placed the foundational theological co-ordinates precisely here in the juridical dominion of God with a corresponding demand placed upon humanity for an obedient response. It is the language of lord and servant or master and slave. The outcome of this starting point has been to place ethics at the heart of what it means to be human with the originating reference point being legal decree rather than the divine creative Word. This appears to be at odds with the Pauline insistence on the freedom of humanity brought about by the work of Christ. This freedom is always couched in expressive, joyful, exuberant terms, human attributes that mirror the playful delight of God himself. The imaginative, playful engagement of God with creation necessitates a fundamental shift in the locus of Christian worship. That shift points us towards the ancient literature of wisdom which revels in the story of creation.

---

93. Jenson, *Systematic Theology, Vol.* 2, 28.

The Sapiential Tradition

The change of focus that the paradigm of play demands, locates the discussion of the imaginative, creative, shaping activity of God within sapiential tradition. The wisdom genre of biblical literature is replete with examples of poetic imagery, metaphor, and the personification of abstract concepts. Huizinga claims that such language usage is born as an act of the imagination and is thoroughly playful. He goes on to assert that, "holiness and play always tend to overlap. So do poetic faith and imagination."[94] One may cite an extra-biblical example of St. Francis of Assisi who revered his bride, Poverty. What was he doing in making such an apparently absurd remark? On the one hand he was making a statement of the utmost seriousness that poverty was his chosen vocation. Yet he was also "playing" with the figure of poverty, drawing upon his poetic imagination and demanding from his hearers a reciprocal response. In similar fashion the poet submits his words to the demand for rhythm and cadence and a vehicle to express emotion. This poetic craft is, according to Huizinga, a play function. "All the qualities of poetry which come to be recognized as specific of it, i.e. beauty, sacredness . . . are originally embraced in the primary play-quality."[95]

The sapiential tradition exhibits just these characteristics as it explores the value of wisdom and necessity of embracing mystery. This is the import of the Pauline utterances in Col 2: 2–3 where he explains in this pastoral letter that, "My purpose is that they may be encouraged in heart and united in love, so that they may have the full riches of complete understanding, in order that they may know the mystery of God, namely, Christ, in whom are hidden all the treasures of wisdom and knowledge." Paul is attempting to explicate the narrative of the gospel but acknowledges here, as he does in Rom 11:33, that the purposes of God in Christ are indeed profoundly mysterious and beyond full comprehension. This mystery, he asserts, is an expression of the wisdom of God—a clear allusion to passages such as Prov 8 which exalt the place of wisdom. In commenting on this passage Brueggemann writes, "Proverbs 8 imagines and articulates a way of God with the world that is not intrusive and occasional, but that is constant in its nurturing sustaining propensity. It does indeed do the God-talk in a different tone, which witnesses to the mystery that can only be expressed as intuitive, playful, suggestive,

---

94. Huizinga, *Homo Ludens*, 163.

95. Ibid., 165.

doxological language, and which opens the way for speculation about the precise relationship between the world and God."[96]

The language of Prov 8 is indeed playful poetry. The opening verses depict wisdom in distinctly dramatic terms, "does not wisdom call out? Does not understanding raise her voice? On the heights along the way, where the paths meet, she takes her stand." This text invites the reader to imagine the scene. It is as if a stage has been erected at the well-worn crossroads where travelers often journey. Just at this junction "wisdom" waits to issue her call to all who will listen, much as a town crier would proclaim the latest news in the market places. It is highly theatrical in its presentation and challenges the hearer to stop and pay attention. This is playful drama of the most colorful kind but notwithstanding the light-hearted form of communication, the seriousness of intent is not to be missed. Without the acquisition of wisdom all is lost and humanity becomes foolish.

Later in the same chapter we see wisdom personified once more, standing by God's side at the moment of creation bringing all that there is into life and being. "Then I was the craftsman at his side. I was filled with delight day after day, rejoicing always in his presence, rejoicing in his whole world and delighting in humankind," claims the sacred author. The word translated as "rejoicing" here stems from the Hebrew *sahaq*, which can also be translated as "to frolic," as in Ps 104:26: "There the ships go to and fro and the leviathan, which you formed to *frolic* there." This translation from the New International Version does not adequately bring out the witness of this Psalm to the true character of God that the Psalmist wishes to convey. The Hebrew text uses the verbal form containing a significant suffix which carries the sense of Yahweh "playing with" the Leviathan. For the Jewish community the Leviathan was a huge mythical sea creature greatly to be feared. Yet the Psalmist declares that not only has Yahweh formed this creature but that Yahweh also takes delight in "playing with" it. The Psalmist deals with the question of Yahweh's faithful trustworthiness by pointing to the divine capacity to play with the most feared creature on earth. The testimony of the wisdom tradition to the character of God is that whilst God's wisdom is often mysterious, essential and inscrutable, yet it is also marked by this joyful, childlike playfulness.

The text of Prov 8 bears witness to a distinct tradition in the history of Israel's testimony to the true nature of Yahweh. Here we read of the manner in which the world was brought into being, via the agency of wis-

---

96. Brueggemann, *Genesis*, 346.

dom. When God created the world, wisdom was by his side as the architect, the master craftsman, even the nursemaid of this creative process.[97] The prevailing characteristic of this wisdom is described as his source of delight (*sha'shua'*) and playfulness (*sachaq*). Wisdom plays before the face of or in the presence of Yahweh, a highly suggestive theatrical image with wisdom as the actor playing for and delighting in Yahweh who enjoys the performance. The sapiential tradition thus depicts creation in a dramatic and intensely loving manner. The entire portrayal is filled with a sense of delight and appreciation both for the creator and for creation itself.

This sense of joyful divine exuberance is graphically illustrated in Zeph 3:17 where the prophet addresses the nation of Israel and declares, "The LORD thy God is in the midst of you, a Mighty One who will save; He will rejoice over you with joy, He will be silent in His love, He will joy over you with singing." The Hebrew word that is rendered as "joy" here is *gyl*, which means turning or spinning around. It is the kind of word that would be used to describe a typical Jewish celebration where dancing takes place joyfully, involving circular motions. This is how Yahweh is depicted, as a participant in the divine dance of joy of his people. To the Hebrew mind, the concept of God leaping, twirling, and dancing was clearly not an alien one. Hebrew culture was known to be characterized by the enjoyment of dancing some of which was formalized and incorporated into a rhythmical cycle of feasts. The Hebrew word for a religious dance was a *hag* which is sometimes translated as "feast" or "festival." These celebrations occurred at various times of the year—there was the *hag ha-Pesach*, the *hag ha-sukkot* and the *hag ha shavuot*—all of which marked particular occasions of importance. In the collective consciousness of Israel the activity of dancing is evidence of the redemptive work of Yawheh. Witness the words of Jer 31: 4, "I will build you up again and you will be rebuilt, O Virgin Israel. Again you will take up your tambourines and go out to dance—*machowl*—with the joyful." Once the restoration of the people has been effected and salvation once more enjoyed then the most natural visible expression of this was to dance.

However, of all the feasts in which the community of Israel participated, the feast that is most pertinent for our discussion of God's activity is the *hag-YHWH*. This phrase only occurs four times (in Exod 10:9; Lev 23:39; Judg 21:19; and Hos 9:5) and carries the sense of YHWH celebrating his own festival by dancing, inviting others to join with him. This image is echoed in the drama of salvation as the story of God's

---

97. The Hebrew term (Prov 8:30) can be rendered in a variety of possible meanings intended to convey the sense of either "caring for" or "constructing."

movement on behalf of humanity. There is a dynamic quality to the descent of Christ to earth in human form and his ascent to heaven bringing with him the redeemed community.

It is necessary here to place this depiction of the mode and manner of creation alongside that presented in Gen 1. Here the whole tone feels at first somewhat different. Creation appears to come into being as a result of divine fiat. The word is spoken and this action alone is causative in producing the material world. Yet careful attentiveness to the text reveals that even here we witness the dynamic role of the Spirit, which flutters—*merachefet*—over the face of the deep. This hovering motion indicates that this story contains far more than a crude, militaristic order/obedience mode of operation. The Spirit dynamically brings into being the desire of the creator for there to be life. And whilst we do not read the same of the same sense of ⊠delight that Prov 8 provides, we are presented with a picture of Yahweh surveying creation at the conclusion of each day and declaring that it is indeed pleasant. Whilst the writers of Gen 1 and Prov 8 bring significantly different emphases to their depiction of creation, what is common to both is the sense of delightful, responsive and sensitive pleasure in the interaction between God as agent and creation itself. Moltmann articulates this when he writes, "When we are saying that the creative God plays, we are expressing this image with the metaphysical insight that, although the creation of the world and of man constitutes a meaningful divine action, this action is in no way a necessary one."[98]

This too is the emphasis of David Ford in his essay entitled "The God of Blessing who Loves in Wisdom."[99] Ford asserts that the wisdom tradition is less concerned with categories such as event and address and draws more attention to the complex connections, continuities, and discontinuities of life. Wisdom is about discerning how and why life can flourish. Ford goes on to claim that the binary categories of love and freedom so often associated with Barth and Jüngel are, at times, unable to contain the sense of exuberance that terms such joy, glory and beauty require. Ford's proposed solution is to posit a third term in addition to love and freedom, and that is "the God of blessing who loves in wisdom." In so doing Ford attempts to articulate something of the playful mystery of a God who delights to bless. Coleridge's description of the imagination

---

98. Moltmann, *Die ersten Freigelassenen der Schöpfung*, 24: "wenn wir sagen, der schöpferische Gott spielt, so hüllt sich in dieses Bild die metaphysische Einsicht, daß die Schöpfung der Welt und des Menschen zwar göttlich sinnvolles, aber in keiner Weise notwendiges Tun darstellt." ET from Moltmann, *Theology of Play*.

99. Ford, "The God of Blessing who Loves in Wisdom," 2004.

as possessing both passive and active qualities has caused us to explore what this might mean when applied to God's engagement and interaction with the world.

God's Imaginative Symbolic Communication

The third main feature of Coleridge's view of the imagination, as we have already explored, is its symbolic nature. It is now time to approach the question of symbol from a different angle. If, as Coleridge claims, the human imagination is a repetition in the finite realm of the divine imagination, we are compelled to ask what this says about God. What is implied in the claim that God engages in imaginative, symbolic communication? Does Coleridge's concept of symbol address questions of divine ontology? We have already noted the way in which Coleridge defined a symbol as being *tautegorical,* in that a symbol participates in the very thing it also represents. Symbols not only possess the capacity to facilitate an encounter between divine revelation and human reception but for Coleridge they were, in reality, indispensable. In Swiatecka's view, commenting on Coleridge's concept of symbol, this is precisely the place where the creative work of God and humanity coincides. He writes, "language, as a symbol, is not descriptive only, it is also creative by its own power as symbol, which is the power within us which enables us to see it as symbol: but creative only when we allow that power to act."[100]

Symbolic Co-inherence

It is necessary at this juncture to explore the nature of this co-inherence between the activity of God and the activity of humankind. To do this, it is pertinent to place this discussion within the broader framework of both Coleridge's theory of artistic endeavor and the presence of the *Logos* imbued throughout the whole of creation. These two apparently disparate concepts are intimately linked in the mind of Coleridge and they are linked via his theory of symbol. Whenever an artist creates something entirely new, whether it be literature, sculpture or fine art for example, the artist is in effect expressing visually that which is hidden, namely the essence of a thing. If a truly creative artist paints a tree then this is far more than a copy of a tree; it is a symbol of its own life, its "tree-ness" as it were, which is ultimately derived from the creativity of God. Coleridge writes about this in this way in *Biographia Literaria*. "The artist must imitate that which is within the thing, that which is active through form

100. Swiatecka, *The Idea of Symbol*, 58.

and figure, and discourses to us by symbols—the *Natur-geist* or spirit of nature."[101] The artist then starts from the *natura naturata,* or the visible sensible forms, and then creates something which embodies the *natura naturans,* their true essence, which in turn points to their divine origin. There is thus a progressive hierarchy of symbols from those that possess a "lower dignity" to those that truly communicate and participate in the Logos which lies behind and within all things. To perceive symbols in this way demands a Christian *Weltanschauen* and an attentiveness to the light of Christ within. Coleridge's theory of symbol, whilst attempting to address the tangled issue of subject-object relations, a conversation that was given great impetus by Kant, ends up being profoundly Christian in its outlook. Symbols are "the tips of an ontological iceberg"[102] and are built on the presupposition that there is an eternal world, a oneness within which all things cohere. If there is nothing eternal then symbols cannot be translucent. To make a Coleridgean claim that something is a symbol is also to make a statement about the entire metaphysical structure of the universe.

It is no surprise to find therefore that for Coleridge, the divine generation of symbol is most explicitly seen in the events of the life of Christ. Swiatecka lists the way in which Coleridge argued that the acts, events, and words of Christ are symbols.

1. They are both the actions of a "man among men" and the acts of God.
2. In Christ, the invisible God is made visible; the infinite is made present in the finite and the eternal within the temporal.
3. The events of the life of Christ are the visible and historical part of an invisible and eternal redemptive plan.
4. The actions of Christ in scripture are continuous with the activity of Christ within each person.[103]

The incarnation exemplifies therefore, *par excellence*, Coleridge's understanding of symbol. Whilst Christ stood before people and revealed God to them, he did so *as God.* There was a perfect correspondence between what Christ represented symbolically and the One he represented. Much later Karl Barth stresses the same point as Coleridge when discussing the constancy of God. He writes, "Jesus does not simply speak about

---

101. Coleridge, *BL* II, 259.
102. Swiatecka, *The Idea of Symbol,* 59.
103. Ibid., 52.

God—of course He does this too—but God Himself speaks through Him in such a way that He Himself is the speaker in Him. Jesus does not simply act in obedience to God—of course He does this too—but in His act God acts, He Himself doing fully and conclusively what is to be done by the creature for God's sake."[104]

Symbol and Consubstantiality

This leads our discussion naturally towards the important Coleridgean usage of the term "consubstantiality," to which reference has already been made. When Coleridge wrote that symbols are consubstantial with the truths of which they are conductors, he consciously and deliberately borrowed the technical, theological term, "consubstantial," from the Nicene Creed. The formulation of the creed was crafted carefully to assert the same *homoousios* of the Father, Son, and Spirit, whilst simultaneously maintaining the separate economic roles that are demonstrated within the Trinity. For Coleridge to use the same term but to apply it to a whole range of symbolic contexts was a bold move. Halmi claims that by doing so Coleridge placed himself in an uncomfortable position.[105] If, for example, Coleridge were to admire a beautiful sunset and see it as symbolic of the creative imagination of the creator, then logically the sunset becomes consubstantial with the creator. There is thus no difference between nature perceived and enjoyed in the sunset and Christ who is consubstantial with the Father. Both possess the quality of consubstantiality. The distinction between nature and God therefore collapses and we are left with a shapeless pantheism. Halmi claims that by substituting the world for the Son, "Coleridge violated precisely that minimum standard of orthodoxy which the bishops at the Nicene Council had sought to guarantee by incorporating *homoousios* into the creed in the first place."[106] Once the world has replaced the Son then the Incarnation becomes impossible.

Halmi also claims that when Coleridge borrowed the term consubstantial from the Nicene fathers he fundamentally misused the word. The relation of Father to Son within the Trinity is one of both identity and difference; there is an identity of substance between the two persons of

---

104. Barth, *KD*, 2/1, 578: "Jesus redet nicht nur von Gott—das tut er freilich auch!—sondern Gott selber redet durch ihn, so, daß er selbst in ihm Sprecher ist. Jesus handelt nicht nur im Gehorsam gegen Gott—das tut er freilich auch!—sondern indem er handelt, handelt Gott, tut Gott selber vollgültig und endgültig, was um Gottes willen vom Geschöpf getan werden muß."

105. Halmi, *The Genealogy of Romantic Symbol*, 80.

106. Ibid., 86.

the Trinity but there is also a difference in form. When Coleridge uses consubstantiality with reference to symbol it is not about identity and difference but rather the relationship is one of "part-to-whole." In other words, the symbol is simply a smaller part of the whole and effectively resides within the whole, there being no real difference between substance and form. Thus Halmi makes Coleridge out to be an undifferentiated panentheist in which the distinctiveness between sign and signifier or between God and nature is elided.

Halmi goes on to apply this alleged confusion in Coleridge's thinking on symbol to a discussion of the nature of the Eucharist and in particular Coleridge's engagement with both Roman Catholic and Lutheran theology. Central to the Lutheran position were the twin concepts of synecdoche (*pars pro toto*) and ubiquity (*totus in omni parte*). Luther had insisted that the words of institution, "this is my body . . . this is my blood," are to be understood as synecdoche where a part is made to represent the whole. But Luther also asserted that the presence of Christ in the world means that he is present fully in a given place without being confined to it. This represents his teaching on ubiquity. Coleridge was fully cognizant of these views yet regarded them with some degree of contempt. In one of his notebook entries, Coleridge writes, "not indeed that transubstantiation is a doctrine of Scripture, but that it is a mistaken conception of a true doctrine, far nearer the truth . . . than the consubstantiation of Luther, which according to that ubiquity of the Body of Christ, which he deduced from the union of God with man . . . allows of no peculiarity of the sacramental elements, but applies equally to every morsel of Man and Beast throughout the Universe.[107]

In Halmi's view, Coleridge has overstated his case for the power of symbol by deploying the term "consubstantial," which he subsequently recoils from when considering the nature of the Eucharist, as the citation above appears to assert. This inconsistency in his usage of consubstantiality raises doubts over Coleridge's theory of symbol. Is his theory based on consubstantiality or is it tautegorical? According to Halmi's argument a symbol can be tautegorical or sacramental, but not both.

It is my view that it is Halmi, not Coleridge, who has overstated his case. As we have already noted, Coleridge was acutely aware of the need to make a careful distinction between nature and God. While he was influenced by Schelling, he was anxious to avoid the pantheism which Schelling's schema appeared to espouse. His doctrine of the Trinity was an orthodox one, albeit with an unusual twist, and allowed for no dal-

---

107. Coleridge, *CN* III, 3847.

liance with views that conflated together the divine within nature. An alternative perspective on Coleridge's views on the Eucharist needs to be sought, as this may allow greater entry into the function of the imagination within his sacramental theology.

One such perspective if offered by MacIntyre who makes a strong claim for the role of the imagination when considering Eucharistic concerns. MacIntyre begins his argument, unusually, with the story of King David at the cave of Adullam (1 Chr 11:15–19).[108] The context of the story tells us that whilst David was occupying Jerusalem the Philistines were encamped nearby in the village of Bethlehem. David longs for a drink from the well in Bethlehem and three brave warriors set off to fulfill his desire. At great personal risk to themselves, the warriors succeed in penetrating behind Philistine lines, draw water from the well and return unnoticed to David with the fresh water. David, somewhat bizarrely, refuses to drink the hard won water, and instead pours it onto the ground with the words, "God forbid that I should do this! Should I drink the blood of these men who went at the risk of their lives?" Had David chosen to drink the water it would no doubt have tasted like water. There is no suggestion here that the water had mysteriously turned into blood on its way back to Jerusalem for the water remained water. Neither did David say that the water represented the blood (or the very life) of his warriors in some kind of symbolic sense. The narrative suggests that in the imagination of David there was an immediate identification of water and blood without either substance losing their intrinsic integrity. This is a distinctly Hebrew way of perceiving not dependent on the sophisticated theologizing of later theologians in the Western tradition. The distinction between subject and object in this narrative concerning Kind David collapses at the point of the imaginative identification of the two substances.

When this way of seeing is applied to the institution of the Eucharist, "this is my body . . . this is my blood," the same kind of hermeneutic can be applied. The dualism between sign and signified or symbol and symbolized appears to be an unnecessary one. When Jesus took the bread and pronounced the words "this is my body," there is no sense that the bread that he held outstretched suddenly ceased to be bread. Yet, via the realistic imagination, the bread was also his body in the same manner that David's drink of water was the blood of his warriors. The point of contact with Coleridge here is that he too insisted that the chasm that exists between subject and object (at least in a Kantian world) is in fact an

---

108. MacIntyre, *Faith Theology and Imagination*, 35.

illusion. There is a prior unity within and behind all things and that subject and object are intimately related in polar orbit around one another. It is the imagination that brings them together.

Christ's use of the Greek term *anamnesis* (remembrance) is pivotal here too. To do this "in remembrance" of him is to engage in an activity that is far greater than simply recalling a past event through the use of memory. Remembrance carries with it the notion of re-living, re-entering, and participating afresh in the whole passion narrative. It is not possible to engage in *anamnesis* without the imagination. In so doing the gulf between past, present, and future ceases to exist. What happened in biblical history is now a present narrative with a future proleptic. What took place in one geographical space has an intimate connection with people in an entirely new geography. The moment of immediate identification is the moment when space and time merge and where subject and object cohere. It is this kind of imaginative use of tautegorical symbol that I believe Coleridge had in mind.

Canonical Illocution

Coleridge's view of the place of symbol within linguistic discourse locates his theory within the arena of Speech-Acts. Speech-Act theory is a relative newcomer to the theological stage although as long ago as 1932 Karl Barth wrote of "The speech of God as the act of God" ("Die rede Gottes als Tat Gottes.")[109] Whilst it is not appropriate here to explore Speech-Act theory in full, it is enough to say that the theory states that there are certain forms of speech that can be labeled as "illocutionary," in that an event actually occurs in the saying of something. To say, "I do" in a wedding ceremony, for example, is to bring something into being (namely the status of being married) by the utterance of speech. For God to say, "let there by light," is also an illocutionary act in that light is actually created.

Later developments of Speech-Act theory, notably those developed by Vanhoozer, maintain that Speech-Acts occur within a contextual milieu, one that he describes as "canonical illocution."[110] By this he means that there are a mix of factors—cultural, psychological, theological, narrative, covenantal—which combine to facilitate the execution of Speech-Acts. In other words, for the utterances of God in Scripture to be heard as the *address* of God to humankind there needs to be a point of contact

---

109. Barth, *KD* 1, 148.
110. Vanhoozer, *First Theology*, 155.

which enables that address to be perceived and apprehended. Without that perception no *response* to God's address is possible. One can fruitfully speculate whether that point of contact, the *Anknupfungspunkt* between the human and the divine, is Coleridge's concept of symbol. Whilst our discussion of symbol has so far been restricted to the natural world and to the symbolic nature of the Eucharist, the world in which Coleridge inhabited as a poet was primarily linguistic. It is in relation to the linguistic nature of symbol that Vanhoozer's concept of canonical illocution is most relevant. It likely that when Coleridge penned the definition of symbol as "the translucence of the special in the individual . . . the translucence of the Eternal through and in the temporal," what he had in mind was the work of the poet.[111] Coleridge attributed to the poet an almost priest like role as one who could be the conduit of divine grace. That other great English Romantic, Byron, held no such grandiose a view of the poet's craft. "In poetry," he wrote, "there can only be words and this illusion of depth and timelessness is a linguistic conjuring trick, a sleight of hand performed in language and inseparable from it."[112]

For Coleridge the reverse was true. By acting as a translucent window onto another world linguistic symbols possess the power to make connections between the finite and the infinite. They touched earth with the scent of heaven and as such foreshadowed the incarnation itself. Coleridge considered that language possessed this incarnational quality and wrote in a letter to Godwin that he "would endeavor to destroy the old antithesis between words and things, elevating as it were, words into things, and living things too."[113] Coleridge was well aware that this opinion stemmed from a position of faith; faith that behind the words and symbols being communicated there lay a greater reality. It was because this greater reality is truly there, that one can claim the ontological connection between language and being. He makes his position clear in *Lay Sermons*.

> The words of the apostle are literally and metaphorically true: We (that is the human race) live by faith. What we do or know, that in kind is different from brute creation has its origin in a determination of the reason to have faith and trust in itself . . . The primal act of faith is enunciated in the word GOD: a faith not derived from experience, but its ground and source, and without which

---

111. Coleridge, *LS*, 30.
112. Manning, "Byron's Imperceptiveness to the English Word," 189.
113. Coleridge, *CL* 1, 625.

> the fleeting chaos of facts would no more from experience, than the dust of the grave can of itself make a living man.[114]

Here Coleridge is staking the claim that any kind of meaning in language is predicated upon a faith presupposition not only that reality actually exists independently of our apprehension of it, but that the ultimate reality is God. Without such a presuppositional base Coleridge would have had to agree with Byron's skepticism about language's slippery qualities.

Linguistic symbols are grounded, by definition, in particular cultural and historical contexts. To portray God as a shepherd, and indeed to go further and state that the Lord is my shepherd is to deploy symbolic language embedded in an agrarian society. Such a symbol, drawing as it does upon mundane phenomena, becomes immediately accessible to humankind. Symbolic language, therefore, accommodates itself to the particularity of human experience. It makes a universal claim from a particular symbol. Once symbolic communication is defined and understood in this way one may assert that God is one who takes particularity seriously. Such a claim about one of the ways in which God chooses to communicate, namely through symbol, means that God is depicted as finding a suitable or appropriate "fit" with culture. There are echoes here of the creation narrative in Genesis once more. God "shapes" Adam from the dust of the ground; there is a molding and *gestalt* forming process in order to "fit" Adam into the newly created world. Likewise Adam's apparent loneliness appears to prompt Yahweh to find a suitable or appropriate helper, one who fits in a complimentary manner with Adam. To describe God as the One who communicates symbolically is to assert that symbolic language forms an appropriate fit with the culture in question.

An example of this can be drawn from Rev 3 and the letter to the church in Laodicea. The church is chided for being neither hot nor cold but lukewarm. To what does such symbolic language signify? The symbol of lukewarm water only possesses both communicative and revelatory power when the cultural context is understood. The city of Laodicea lay between Hierapolis with its hot cleaning and healing waters and Colossae which enjoyed cold refreshing streams. The murky water supply of the newly founded town of Laodicea was delivered through pipes from Hierapolis resulting in a lukewarm kind of sludge which benefitted nobody. It was neither healing (hot) nor refreshing (cool). The symbol of lukewarm water whilst couched in metaphorical language, epitomized

---

114. Coleridge, *LS*, 16.

the condition of the church community in Laodicea, offering neither a place for healing nor for refreshment. The linguistic symbol was entirely appropriate to the particularity of the place.

Symbolic language by its very nature is imprecise resisting closed "scientific" limitations on meaning. Paul Ricoeur, writing on the related subject of metaphor, often refers to the "surplus of meaning" that metaphorical, symbolic language permits, opening up a passion for the possible.[115] The very imprecision of symbol is suggestive of a God who enjoys and delights in possibilities. Symbols possess a dual quality in both illuminating and revealing on the one hand whilst simultaneously obscuring and confusing on the other. Symbols can both attract and repel depending on the degree to which faithful imagination is deployed. We can observe this dual nature of symbolic communication repeatedly within the biblical corpus.

Coleridge repeatedly refers to the great "I AM" when describing God and so it is necessary to turn to this text in order to inquire how the use of this particular mode of naming God contributed to Coleridge's theological and philosophical project. The denotation stems from Moses' encounter in the desert with the burning bush narrated in Exod 3. In this narrative God reveals himself in a somewhat confusing, bizarre manner. The burning bush is a symbol of God's enduring, empowering presence, but it also communicates something of both his character and his mode of interaction. The transcendent God inhabits the material world of the bush yet does not consume it. The occupation of the divine in space and time does not constitute an invasion but a co-habitation. Both the finite and the infinite can dwell together without the finite being consumed and thereby nullified. The burning bush is in this sense a foreshadowing of the incarnation itself. One can speculate whether Coleridge chose this encounter between Moses and God to illustrate one further point with which his energies had been consumed, namely the relationship between subject and object. This question had occupied the attention of Kant and his successors, as we have already explored. Coleridge was convinced that the dichotomy between the two was illusory, that the two were, in reality, held in dynamic tension in polar orbit. The burning bush account is perhaps an illustration of this; an occasion where the transcendent God (the object) engages with the "phenomenal" bush (the subject), and the two coexist together in unity. In this one symbolic image both subject and object are brought together in harmony with each other. There is no evidence in the writings of Coleridge for this speculation, although one must

---

115. Ricoeur, *Rule of Metaphor*, 3–8.

legitimately be able to draw some conclusions from Coleridge's curious, yet surely significant, reference point in his deliberations on the nature of the imagination. The task for Moses, and by implication for all subsequent generations too, was to allow such a rich symbol to become fertile with meaning. There is a multiplicity of layers of significance attached to the symbol of the burning bush and no one interpretation will suffice. The God who communicated to Moses in this way had a clear intentionality in doing so in this manner but permitted the reception and appropriation of such a symbol to take place in a rich and unbounded manner.

This form of divine speech is an example of canonical illocution.[116] The speaker is God and he utters the Word as a self-declaration of who he is. This utterance has illocutionary force in so far as it is intended to effect an event, an act. The illocution has symbolic content (the burning bush) and particular intent (a force) which in this instance is the divine empowerment and commissioning of Moses to undertake the challenge of leadership. The illocutionary act is determined by the speaker and therefore is objective rather than subjective. The final stage of this encounter is the perlocutionary response of Moses. This refers to the effect that the illocutionary act of the speaker has on the beliefs or actions of the hearer. Despite considerable hesitation, a new paradigm of God's character began to form within Moses which enabled him to accept his divine assignment.

Symbol and Surprise

The burning bush story is but one example of the characteristic of surprise that is an essential element in imaginative symbolic engagement. In the following three scriptural examples, the incarnation, the parables of Jesus, and the day of Pentecost, this quality is made further evident. Nowhere is the notion of the imaginative particularity of God more startlingly realized than in the Incarnation itself. Whilst we, with the benefit of hindsight, can draw lines of connection between Old Testament prophecies concerning the coming of a future Messiah and the arrival of Jesus in Bethlehem, for those Jews living in Israel at the time of Christ such fulfillments of the prophetic word would have been far from obvious. The imaginative creativity of God that is so apparent within the created order is demonstrated supremely in the novel, surprising, unexpected, and unpredictable intervention of God in humanity with the Word made flesh in Bethlehem. The element of novelty and surprise that

---

116. Vanhoozer, *First Theology*, 155.

the Incarnation evokes is surely indicative of the creative playfulness of the Father and Son in their mission.

This creative playfulness of Christ in the manner of his teaching has been highlighted by the work of Kenneth Bailey who has drawn attention to the way in which the parables, using symbolic language, are framed through the use of anecdotes, images, and narrative drawn from the cultural milieu of the time. In the following example one can witness the way in which the parable depicts Jesus the storyteller deliberately arousing curiosity, surprise, shock, and astonishment in the narration of a tale. The parable is found in Luke 11:5–8, "The Friend at Midnight." Popular exegesis of this parable turns around the question of the need to be persistent in prayer. Bailey offers an entirely alternative hermeneutic claiming that the text, understood aright in its cultural and historical setting, deals with the question of shame. The import of this parable pivots around the question which Bailey paraphrases thus: "Can you imagine having a guest and going to a neighbor to borrow bread and the neighbor offers ridiculous excuses about a locked door and sleeping children?"[117] To the Middle Eastern mind the obvious response would be, "No, I couldn't imagine such a thing!" The reason for this is that the parable hinges around the question of a sense of honor and the blamelessness of the man who is asleep. Bailey points out that the guest who arrives at the house after having being on a journey would have been considered to be the guest of the whole community and not just the individual. Thus the entire community was responsible for his welfare. The significance of the passage lies in the Greek word *anaideia*, which, in contrast to many modern translations, has the negative connotation of shamelessness and is used here with reference not to the man who knocks on the door but to the man who is asleep. Once this is clear the parable takes on a new meaning. It is because the sleeping man wants to avoid shaming the entire village community by failing to provide sustenance for the traveler that he will, of course, get up and provide bread. The parable thus deals with the *nature of God* rather than an injunction to persist in prayer. Bailey summarizes the impact of the story thus: "The parable said to the original listener, 'When you go to this kind of a neighbor everything is against you. It is night. He is asleep in bed. The door is locked. His children are asleep. He does not like you and yet you will receive even more than you ask. This is because your neighbor is a man of integrity and he will not

---

117. Bailey, *Poet and Peasant*, 119.

violate that quality. The God to whom you pray also has integrity and he will not violate you either."[118]

Such teaching, drawing upon simply everyday imagery readily understood by his hearers, points to a form of theological expression that was highly imaginative and symbolic in its presentation. The parables of Jesus were intended both to illuminate and confuse, to attract and to deter. They remain an oblique, playful form of speech and as such provoke endless fascination.

The events of the day of Pentecost may offer further illustration of the category of surprise. The inauguration of the church is accompanied by the outpouring of the Holy Spirit witnessed as "tongues of fire" resting upon those gathered in the upper room.[119] This revelation of the Spirit to those gathered in Jerusalem elicited an inexorable curiosity which produced a subsequent receptivity to the message proclaimed. According the Coleridge's view, these tongues of fire were far more than a visual aid enabling the onlookers to perceive the works of God anew. The fire was a symbol that participated in the actuality of the Spirit's essence. The fire was not merely a symbol; it was actually the presence of the Spirit. That this was the most appropriate symbol to be deployed at this moment in history is testament to the fact that the message of empowerment for the fledgling church was what was most needed. The symbol of fire was not only descriptive of the presence and character of the Holy Spirit but also creative in effecting substantial change in the lives of those present on that day. For Coleridge, the Bible offers "copious sources of truth and power, and purifying impulses . . . words for my inmost thoughts, songs for my joy, utterances for my hidden griefs, and pleadings for my shame and feebleness."[120] It was precisely because of the symbolic language of scripture that the texts possessed this communicative power to transcend the localized and particular contexts from which they were generated.

The communicative capability of symbol in the narrative of the day of Pentecost rested up its sheer unexpectedness. The interruption of the traditional celebration through the outpouring of the Holy Spirit was so surprising that the attention of the crowd of worshippers was immediately arrested. It was an event that at first appeared to be totally without precedent, an invasion of the divine in a so perplexing a manner that produced a discontinuity with any previous narrative of God's actions

---

118. Bailey, *Poet and Peasant*, 129.

119. Acts 2:3 "They saw what seemed to be tongues of fire that separated and came to rest on each of them."

120. Coleridge, *CIS*, 10.

in history. The apostle Peter's ensuing sermon begins by acknowledging this apparent discontinuity to the bemused crowd of onlookers yet he goes on to explain the profound continuity that does in fact exist by drawing upon the prophetic tradition from the book of Joel. The events of the first day of Pentecost as an illustration of surprise do not stand alone. Indeed one does not need to look far in scripture to observe how frequently the expectations of God's engagement with humankind are constantly confounded. Surprise as a theological category thus possesses the incarnational power of interruption offering a subtle balance of the new together with the continuation of the old. It is through surprise that God awakens humanity from its slumbers with the demand that new paradigms of interpretation are found.

The Dramatic God

Coleridge's appreciation of the seminal significance of the dramatic was, as we have noted, displayed in his admiration for the work of Shakespeare and the narrative poetry of William Wordsworth. Both writers drew Coleridge into their worlds such that he could not remain a passive on-looker merely observing their dramatic skill but became a participant in an unfolding piece of narrative theatre. If this is a feature of the human imagination, then it becomes highly suggestive and fertile ground for a further exploration into the "dramatic" ontology of God. Whilst Coleridge hinted at such a possible perception, the notion of "drama" when applied to the nature of God remained for him an undeveloped theme. It is not until the much later work of Hans Urs von Balthasar that we witness a serious engagement with theology as drama. For our purposes here the second volume of his *Theodramatik* is the most pertinent for it is here that he puts forward a range of possible dramatic perspectives.

The Epic, the Lyric and the Dramatic

The first of these is the *epic* perception of events. This is akin to the attempted objective journalistic reporting of an incident as a detached observer. The reporter may not have been a witness but gathers up information with integrity in order to construct a comprehensive, coherent and plausible narrative, one that is marked with objective maturity.[121] The second type of perspective is the *lyric*, which is distinguished by a far more personal investment in the narrative. The story may indeed possess

---

121. Wells, *Improvisation*, 46.

strong resonances with the storyteller's own world which allows the lyrical storyteller to engage in a powerful, emotionally laden narrative. Concern for detached objectivity is less of an issue in this instance. The third possibility, *the dramatic,* synthesizes the strength of both previous approaches. It recognizes the emotionally involved role of the subject whilst simultaneously respecting the requirements and necessity of objectivity.

When we apply this template offered by von Balthasar to the biblical account of Nathan and David (2 Sam 12) with which we began this whole journey, it is possible to witness all three forms of dramatic engagement. Nathan begins his tale in *epic* fashion. He approaches King David ostensibly to tell a tale in a detached objective manner. It is a simple story of two farmers and a visitor who appears at nightfall. There is nothing particularly interesting or unusual about the narrative yet as the story unfolds David is drawn into the events in *lyrical* fashion. There is a resonance between the parable being narrated and the David's own experience in his childhood of growing up as shepherd, intimately knowing each member of his flock. David remembers the concern and love that he lavished upon each newborn lamb, how he ensured their survival in the face of danger. The narrative, in the skillful hands of God's prophet Nathan, is moving from an epic to a lyrical tale. David no longer hears the story dispassionately but becomes emotionally engaged at a deep level. The denouement comes when Nathan joins the *epic* and the *lyrical* together in one swift move by declaring to David, "You are the man!" In so doing this conjunction moves the narrative to a *dramatic* level, synthesizing both perspectives. The synthesis occurs within the imagination of both the storyteller and the listener. It is only at this *dramatic* stage that the full import of the story is realized. Bailey, commenting on this passage, notes the nature of Biblical storytelling. "A biblical story is not simply 'delivery system' for an idea. Rather the story first creates a world and then invites the listener to live in that world to take it on as part of who he or she is. Biblical stories invite the reader to accept them as his or her story."[122]

Once we assert with Karl Barth that "God is who he is in the act of his revelation" ("Gott ist, der er ist in der Tat seiner Offenbarung"),[123] then this biblical account reveals a God who communicates himself as One who is intrinsically dramatic. The form of communication in this account is sensitive to the particularity of the context. The prophetic parable is couched in the agrarian world of the ancient near east and the deployment of lambs as a central metaphor was highly pertinent to David's

---

122. Bailey, *Jacob and the Prodigal*, 51.
123. Barth, *KD* 2/1, 288.

own autobiography. Here we witness God's revelation of himself uniting the particular with the universal in dramatic style. Not only is this a parable intended for King David but it also carries, by its inclusion in the biblical canon, a much wider validity across both cultures and time.

That God can only be identified in and through divine words and actions is axiomatic in theological discourse. We must assert therefore that God is known through narrative events that take place in time and space. To locate God's identity within narrative is to propose that it lies within the dramatic coherence and tension of the unfolding story.[124] God's identity is given to us only within the framework of a dramatic genre. Without this paradigm with which to offer a hermeneutic of biblical narrative, divine action remains too conflicted and obscure to refer to the same person. The integrity and consistency of God's identity can only be asserted if we determine that biblical drama coheres at the point of resolution, in other words, at the end. God's identity is assured by the outcome, the configuration, of the events of the unfolding drama.

Dramatic Improvisation

When one deploys the notion of God as "the One who dramatically improvises," the hermeneutical results are surprising. We may take, by way of example, the story of Jesus' encounter with the "Canaanite" woman in Matt 15:21–28. Here we witness a dialogue between Jesus and a distressed woman whose daughter was seriously ill. The unfolding tale makes uncomfortable reading for it appears that Jesus is both racist and rude. He appears to deny the woman access to the grace of God and only grants her wish under duress as a result of her great persistence. Only when he sees her determined faith does he change his mind and allow her to taste the grace of the kingdom of God. How can such behavior be accounted for? If Jesus is both the revealer and the revealed, in Barthian terms, the portrait of the God that we are presented with is contradictory at best and repellent at worst. Jesus here seems to contradict his own welcoming invitation given in Matt 11 to all those who are weary and heavy-laden to come to him for rest. If ever there was a case for a weary soul to find rest surely it is here in the story of the "Canaanite" woman.

An alternative school of interpretation has argued that this is an example of Jesus' own growth as a human being. He initially displays all the accepted prejudices and stereotypes of his day by excluding the land around Tyre and Sidon from the orbit of the gospel and by freely adopting the commonplace derogatory language of "dogs" to describe

---

124. Jenson, *Systematic Theology, Vol.* 1, 64.

those living in that district. It is only when he meets the woman that his perspective begins to change. "The episode is cast as a turning point in Jesus' own understanding of his identity and his mission," writes Barbara Reid, "he would have shared his own people's sense of boundaries marking them as God's own chosen ones . . . this gospel invites readers today to embrace a Jesus who had the ability to change his perception of the outsider."[125] The problems with such an interpretation are acute. Jesus is portrayed as person who, until that moment, had lived his entire life in Galilee merely absorbing the unreflective racism of the prevailing culture. He needs the face-to-face exposure of a gentile woman to awake him from his slumbers for only when this happens does he begin to realize the full culturally subversive import of his own mission. It depicts a Jesus who appears to accidentally find himself in foreign territory which serves eventually to broaden his previously limited horizons. Such a view of Jesus seriously weakens his capacity to reveal the true nature of God to humankind. His revelatory role is made impossible if he is cast in the role of "a man of his time," influenced and imbued with restricted notions of the scope of the kingdom of God and the precise quality of the grace of God extended towards humanity.

Alternatively, a hermeneutic of dramatic improvisation offers a more subtle rendering. Jesus goes to the region of Tyre and Sidon intentionally. All of his actions and speech were intent on furthering the purpose of his mission. In this foreign land he is suddenly confronted with an urgent demand and he immediately uses the situation to great ironic effect. Kenneth Bailey offers a rhetorical analysis of the conversation based on an understanding of Middle Eastern culture.[126] The dialogue has three phases, each of which provides a challenge to the woman. In the first phase, "Jesus pretends indifference as he sets the stage for his dialogue with his disciples and with the woman."[127] This feigning is crucial to the outcome of the conversation. It is not a form of devious, manipulative posturing, designed to entrap or confuse. Rather it is a piece of rhetorical drama intended to provoke and expose. It can be observed for example in the story of the conversation on the road to Emmaus between the resurrected Jesus and some of the forlorn disciples. Luke records that as they neared the end of their journey, "Jesus acted *as if* he were going further."[128] It was this *appearance* of intent which elicited the urgent

---

125. Reid, *The Lectionary Commentary*, 91.
126. Bailey, *Jesus through Middle Eastern Eyes*, 217–26.
127. Ibid., 221.
128. Luke 24:28.

response from the disciples for him to remain with them without which, one is left to assume, the sense of urgency would not have arisen.

No less is true in the story under consideration here. The "feigning" on the part of Jesus towards the "Canaanite" woman gives the appearance of disinterest. He appears to adopt the stance that one would expect from a Jew who meets a gentile woman and the disciples, observing him from a slight distance, would have understood and approved of his non-response. These disciples, eager to be rid of such a nuisance, are thereby gradually drawn into the dialogue no longer merely observing a private conversation but actively participating and urging Jesus to send her away. Middle eastern readers of Matthew's account would by now be eager to discover the outcome as the sense of dramatic tension begins to rise. Is the woman sent away and her impudence rebuked? How will Jesus handle this persistent intercessor? What began as a simple request has become a piece of drama played out before a wondering audience. The roles of the actors are played by the woman, the disciples and, most crucially for our purposes here, Jesus himself. Jesus appears to be dealing solely with the woman yet in reality is covertly dealing a devastating blow to his own band of disciples providing them with an education into the true nature and scope of his mission.

In the second phase of the conversation Jesus begins to address the woman but in so doing he chooses to adopt the theological presuppositions of his disciples pressing them to their logical and absurd conclusion. He articulates publicly the truly shocking nature of their prejudice and deploys the derogatory term "dogs" as a description of the woman who presents herself before him. His interrogation of her provides a stiff test of the authenticity of her faith. Yet each time he presses her she comes back with renewed determination, undeterred by the severity of her examination. By his use of the term "dogs," Jesus entices his disciples to step yet further into the unfolding drama. Bailey suggests that Jesus is, in effect, saying, "I know you think Gentiles are dogs and you want me to treat them as such! But—pay attention—this is where your biases lead. Are you comfortable with this scene?"[129]

The third and final phase offers the extraordinary ironic twist. Jesus responds to the evidence of persistent faith and declares that her healing has come. The outsider has been included, the "dog" has become a member of the family and the onlookers and disciples are, no doubt, astounded that the grace of God extends beyond the land of Israel. Jesus has taken the accepted stereotypes of his day concerned with land and

---

129. Bailey, *Jesus through Middle Eastern Eyes*, 224.

human worth and used them to great dramatic effect by improvising with both the people and the context. In doing so he communicates a radically subversive message exposing both the latent racism of the disciples and the secret surprising faith of the "Canaanite" woman. This story is an example of the extraordinary dramatic improvisory capacity of Jesus in which improvisation is turned into drama to effect a profoundly new and significant theological paradigm. Walter Brueggemann writes of drama in this way, "the biblical drama teaches us that God is a genuinely other character who takes a decisive role in the drama and that we are 'others' to God."[130]

The Divine Performance

The drama of Scripture is not merely to be construed as the normative narrative nature of human existence. Biblical drama demands that God himself is viewed as not only the director and producer but one of the players too. If God is one of the performers on the stage of the redemptive story then the church has been given the mandate to "perform" the gospel in addition to merely proclaiming it. Nicholas Lash has argued exactly along these lines stating that Christian witness to the veracity of the gospel consists in the interpretative performance of scriptural texts. It is not enough, he argues, that the church simply possess sacred texts as letters and symbols printed upon paper. Such texts need to be embodied within a living community of persons who, by the nature of their mutual interaction and relationships, illustrate the significance of the ancient sacred narratives. His argument proceeds by way of analogy drawn from the American constitution. This founding charter lays down the values and aspirations of the new nation but unless such words on paper become embodied they remain unexpressed and unfulfilled. The American constitution is "performed" every day whenever American society embraces those ideals in action. When American politicians articulate sentiments referring to "our dream" or "our destiny," they are in effect calling the people to continue to embody and perform in daily life that which was laid down in print by the founding fathers.

It is no different, considers Nash, with the script of Scripture. It is not so much the script, the mere existence of ink on paper, that is holy, writes Nash but the people, the company who perform the script.[131] One may argue that the Acts of the Apostles is nothing more than the attempt

---

130. Brueggemann, *The Bible and Postmodern Imagination*, 68.
131. Lash, *Theology on the Way to Emmaus*, 42.

by the fledgling Christian community to enact the significance of the risen Christ, often requiring a capacity to improvise as new situations and challenges emerged. The council of Jerusalem, described in Acts 15, is a good example of such improvisation. Here the apparently conflicting demands of Jewish tradition and Christian freedom needed find a place of reconciliation. Questions of the continuity of theological testimony together with the discontinuity and interruption that the resurrection provoked rose rapidly to the surface. There was an urgent need to take the "familiar" script of the Hebrew Scriptures with the "unfamiliar" event of the risen Christ and the subsequent full inclusion of the Gentiles within the orbit of God's grace and to improvise a solution under the guidance of the Holy Spirit. As soon as we assert however that Christian expression demands collective dramatic improvisory performance, then we are forced to consider the character of God who searches for a reciprocal response to his initiatives. If authentic Christian discipleship is intrinsically dramatic, then this presupposes a God who chooses to engage in a dramatic way.

The dramatic nature of God's being is witnessed in Israel's discourse about God's engagement with his people. God does not stand apart and aloof from Israel, observing their struggles with covenant obedience. What God does to Israel he does to himself. We observe this dynamic in the account of the exchange between the angel of the Lord and Abraham in Gen 22. The angel appears as a messenger "of" God, yet also declares that this angel "is" God: "But the angel of the LORD called out to him from heaven, 'Abraham! Abraham!' 'Here I am,' he replied. 'Do not lay a hand on the boy,' he said. 'Do not do anything to him. Now I know that you fear God, because you have not withheld from me.'"

God presents himself in the text not simply as an observer of the dramatic encounter, but as one of the players. He inhabits the stage on which Abraham and Isaac play out their respective roles and appears at the conclusion to offer resolution to the dramatic tension. In this discourse, God is understood to be a "settled" participant in the story, yet is more than merely a player.[132] God remains God in absolute freedom, yet indwells the human stage, choosing to enter into the suffering and the contingencies of finite existence. This is the testimony of Israel too on the occasion of the dedication of the temple during the reign of Solomon. The Lord appears to Solomon to say, "I have heard the prayer and plea you have made before me; I have consecrated this temple, which you have built, by putting my Name there for ever. My eyes and my heart will

---

132. Jenson, *Systematic Theology, Vol. 1*, 76.

always be there."¹³³ God is again understood not only to be utterly other, but to also be utterly present, indwelling the arena of human theatre. As Robert Jenson expresses it, "God is identified with Israel in that he is identified as a participant in Israel's story with him."¹³⁴

Yet our discussion of the dramatic nature of God himself needs to be broader than this consideration of narrative storytelling. Drama and improvisation are not merely concerned with delivering a propositional, cognitive message in a creative way. Drama is not simply about words and how words are used; it is as much about the spaces between words—the silences and the actions—as well as the actual script. Drama requires a context, a stage, a backdrop and an audience. All these components are required if the desired dramatic impact is to be achieved. The story in Matt 15, which we have just considered, depends for its dramatic effect upon Jesus' initial silence as well as the action of healing the woman's daughter at the end of the encounter. These silences and deeds are as much a part of the theatre as the dialogue itself. Taken all together they contribute to the impact of revelation of God in Christ. This is the import of the work of Ivan Khovacs, exploring the theological outcomes of the work of von Balthasar.¹³⁵ "We would do ourselves a disservice," states Khovacs, "if we understood the communicative, affective engagement in the drama as merely the backdoor entry into the sobriety of cognition." The dramatic approach to cognition is not to be understood as a slightly quirky approach deployed to achieve a cognitive result. Drama offers a way of knowing that is neither entirely cognitive nor solely impressionistic, yet provides access to truth that could not otherwise be achieved.

The Language of Seeming

At this point we need to return to an early version of Coleridge's poem *Frost at Midnight* published in the *Poetical Register* quoted earlier, for it is there that we find the language of *"seeming"* that is pertinent to our discussion here on the use of the dramatic.¹³⁶

> Haply hence,
> That still the living spirit in our frame,
> Which loves not to behold a lifeless thing,
> Transfuses into all things its own Will,

---

133. 1 Kgs 9:3.
134. Jenson, *Systematic Theology*, Vol. 1, 77.
135. Khovacs, "Robbing Peter to Pay Paul," 2002.
136. Coleridge, *PW*, 241.

> And its own pleasures; sometimes with deep faith,
> And sometimes with a willful playfulness
> > that stealing pardon from our common sense
> > smiles, as self-scornful, to disarm the scorn
> > for these wild reliques of our childish thought,
> > that flit about, oft go, and oft return
> > not uninvited.[137]

Coleridge here plays with possible ways of arriving at truth and in doing so searches for a third route which goes beyond, as it were, the stark choice faced by Hamlet in his famous soliloquy; to be or not to be. Is this all there is, muses Coleridge, a simple dualism, a brutal choice? Coleridge toys with a third option, the language of "as if," an intermediate world where nothing belongs to fixed categories and the possibility of play is permitted. It is a world in which "the willing suspension of disbelief" is necessary.[138] In the lines of this poem Coleridge gives weight to two apparently contradictory tendencies in human beings to animate the inanimate. Sometimes it is done with deep faith and at other times with willful playfulness for both are permitted. As Gavin Hopps explains,

> What is important for now is simply that Coleridge's explanation as a whole corresponds perfectly to the paradoxical logic of superstition. He knows very well that such behavior must "steal pardon from our common sense" and may well be a "wild relique of childish thought," yet nonetheless he continues to do so and even "sometimes with deep faith". . . On this reading the language of seeming would signify something that looks like but ultimately differs from agnosticism, since it is not a hovering noncommittally between, but rather a simultaneous attachment to two extremes.[139]

This third option, the land of "seeming" opens up a space not possible in a simple world of "being" or "not being." This space which is neither "in jest nor in earnest" allows for new possibilities to emerge. It is a tentative, provisional place which allows for response and dialogue. It is a place where "yes" and "no" are not the only options available, where "maybe," "as if," "perhaps," and "seeming" are just as valid modes of exploration. The dialogue between Jesus and the "Canaanite" woman in Matt 15, which we have just been considering, displays exactly these qualities. Jesus appears to show no interest in her at first. He seems to

---

137. Coleridge, http://historyofideas.org/stc/Coleridge/poems/Frost_at_Midnight.html.
138. Coleridge, *BL* II, 6.
139. Hopps, "The Playful Devotions of Byron and Coleridge," 15.

have other priorities which he defines in terms of taking the gospel only to the Jews. This game of "seeming" is neither fully comic nor entirely serious but it is profoundly curious, intriguing, inviting. This is the way of such language, to seem to be saying and doing one thing whilst simultaneously exploring the possibilities of another. It is the world of "as if," a kind of invited feigning, which entices the "other" into a dialogue in order to illustrate and expose. The subtlety of this interchange stands in stark contrast to the reductionism of Enlightenment thinking. Hartley's associationism to which Coleridge was so deeply attracted initially made no allowance for the playfulness of such discourse. It permitted only crude and superficial certainties. Coleridge's project attempted to point to another world in which perception and apprehension occurred as if by accident, as a by-product, full of mystery and surprise. It is this almost inexpressible quality that Karl Barth perceived in the music of Mozart when he declared that at the heart of such sublime music there lay a resounding God-gifted *Yes!* to life in all its fullness.

We have already explored how the mystery of the Eucharist can be understood as "immediate identification," to use Macintyre's phrase, via the imagination. The notion of "as if" is particularly applicable in this context too. On reception of the bread and wine the believer knows that what is held before him is indeed bread and wine yet on faithful reception of the elements acts "as if" they are other than they appear to be. Such appearances are not considered to be illusory or the result of a wild flight of fancy. On the contrary, it is the only way to receive the bread and wine, to make this sacrament real. To quote Hopps again, "This is because whilst in contrast, on the one hand, to Platonism, for example, Christianity upholds the value of the material order, on the other hand, in contrast to Materialism, for example, it is prepared to countenance a mysterious depth to which things give way."[140]

The practice of "as if," and the use of the language of seeming, is akin to the world of play where normal rules of engagement are suspended for a while so that another world may be explored.

The notion of the dramatic God who communicates in freedom and love with creation at times in dramatic fashion, deploying the language of seeming is the destination that Coleridge's divine imagination has taken us. It points us towards the ultimate dramatic narrative, that of the story of reconciliation itself. A dramatic story has an origin, the source of its action, but this origin is usually the subject of threat. The positing of threat introduces dramatic tension which keeps the story alive

---

140. Ibid., 27.

and maintains movement and life. The resolution of conflict or tension is the final outcome of the process of reconciliation. This is the pattern of dramatic discourse: action, threat, tension, and resolution. The biblical material is replete with examples of such dramatic improvisation.

Yet it is also possible to describe the economic Trinity in equally dramatic terms. Robert Jenson explores this notion of dramatic reconciliation in God. "The only history of God that is actually enacted is the one the constituting reconciliation of which is the Lord's crucifixion and resurrection. Staying with this reality of God, we may describe what happens with Christ's death and resurrection as the maintenance of God's unity with himself, through the conflicted history with us which is his only actual history."[141]

God's dramatic engagement with us has as its intention the completion of the drive towards reconciliation. We have witnessed how this action exhibits the qualities of improvisation, surprise, irony and playfulness. The source from which such characteristics flow is surely from within the Trinitarian web of relationships that has risked all for the sake of securing a reunification of all things in Christ.

The Imaginative I AM

We have now returned full circle in our investigations in to the imaginative ontology of God and the journey brings us back to original starting point, the definition of the imagination that Coleridge offered in *Biographia Literaria,* which delineated this human faculty, "as a repetition in the finite mind of the eternal act of creation in the infinite I AM."[142] Coleridge consciously uses the term "I AM who I AM" with particular reference to God's imaginative creative activity. What did he have in mind in making such an assertion? What is this "eternal act of creation"? The question pushes us to explore how this creative activity is articulated in the biblical accounts.

The Hebrew term that the priestly redactor of Gen 1 used was *bara,* a word reserved solely to describe the creative activity of *ex nihilo*. It was most likely used instead of *asah,* meaning "to make," which carried with it associations of human activity.[143] *Bara* was something that only God could do. God chose, out of nothing, to create something that pleased him such that, upon reflection, when he observed creation he could declare that it

---

141. Jenson, *Systematic Theology, Vol.* 1, 162.
142. Coleridge, *BL* I, 202.
143. Botterwick and Ringgren, *Theological Dictionary of the Old Testament,* 246.

was *tob*, pleasant and good. God's creativity is thus declared to be fundamentally different to human creativity. We can only create out of that which has been given to us; God's creativity flows from within himself. Out of the limitless possibilities that are available the resultant creation has the effect of giving God "pleasure." The conclusion that the Hebrew storyteller invites us to draw from this account is that God creates out of sheer good pleasure without an apparent utilitarian intention in view.

The Hebrew word that is translated as "imagination" furthers this image of creative delight. Our first encounter with the imagination of God is in Gen 2:7 where the writer uses the term *yatsar*. This account of creation depicts God forming or shaping Adam from the dust of the ground and breathing life into his nostrils. It is a tender, gentle, creative image of a God who carefully shapes into a form. The readers of this creation account are invited, through the skill of the storyteller, to imagine God taking the rough clay from the earth and molding it much as a potter would do into the shape of a human being. It is the image of an artist, a sculptor at work. The same portrayal of God is presented by the prophet Jeremiah where he uses the illustration of the work of the potter. The Lord appears to Jeremiah (chapter 18) and instructs him to visit the home of the potter. This Hebrew term is based on the same root verb we have already encountered in Gen 2 (*yatsar*). In this context it means that Jeremiah is to visit the home of "the one who fashions" or the "fashioner." It refers to the skill of the artist or sculptor who forms and shapes the clay into a vessel which can be of use. The Lord says through Jeremiah that this is precisely how he is to be perceived and understood. His self-affirmation is as "the one who fashions," or as one might literally say, "the one who imagines." Such a designation presents the reader with a picture of Yahweh in aesthetic terms, someone concerned both with beauty and with the functional purpose of the creative process.

This shaping activity constitutes the heart of creation and is a product of God's creative imagination. When God created or shaped (*yatsar*) Adam in his own image, and endued him with the same capacity to imagine (*yetser*) he was enduing humanity with the ability to imitate God's own creativity. Adam was given the same shaping potentiality, to create something new out of the very fabric of the material world. However, the imagination afforded Adam the potential to distinguish between opposites, namely the ethical distinction between good and evil. In Gen 6:5 we read that, "God saw that the wickedness of man was great in the earth, and that every *imagination* (*yetser*) of the thoughts of his heart was only evil continually" (King James Version). The etymology of this word derives from the same root word *yzr* as the words for "creation" (*yetsirah*), "creator" (*yotser*) and "create" (*yatsar*). The allusive interplay between God's creative activity and humankind's capacity to imagine an alternative future without God is highly significant. The Jewish theologian Eric Fromm frames the context in this way: "The noun '*yetser*' means 'form, frame, purpose' and with reference to the mind, 'imagination' or 'device.' The term '*yetser*' thus means 'imaginings' (good and evil). The problem of good and evil arises only when there is imagination. Furthermore, man can become more evil and more good because he feeds his imagination with thoughts of evil or good. They grow precisely because of that specifically human quality—imagination."[144]

In the aftermath of the flood (Gen 8:21) the same term is used, this time in the noun form and is translated as "the inclinations" or the "the imaginations" of the heart which are persistently evil. The sense conveyed is that the shaping capacity of humankind is now distorted from one of gentle beauty, to evil and oppressive purposes. Yet it is fundamentally the same activity of giving form to something that is originally conceived in the mind. The human shaping is a derivative of the divine shaping both requiring the deployment of the imagination. It is the human imagination that has become distorted and is in need of redemption. Yet this discussion about the creativity of God in relation to humanity needs to engage not only with the creative processes depicted in the Genesis accounts but also with the curious usage by Coleridge of the term "I AM," instead of the more straightforward "God." Is this a deliberate choice of words by Coleridge or an accidental rhetorical flourish?

Our dialogue with Coleridge up to this point would suggest that there is nothing accidental at all about his use of language. We have already explored the nuances of this term in relation to the theological significance of the present moment—the "now" of God. Yet the word has perhaps further allusive references. Tellingly, Moltmann quotes the character Pallieter, in the novel by Timmermans, who one day was leaning against a tree contemplating the rays of the sun. When asked by a passer by, "what are you doing?," Pallieter replies "I am."[145] Moltmann uses this incident to make the point that our existence is of worth, value, and great beauty, simply because "it is." He writes, "unser Dasein ist gerechtfertigt und schön, bevor wir etwas machen oder versäumen."[146] We are because God simply "is." The "I AM" of God is a statement not only of the precious value of "now," but also a declaration of the non-utilitarian nature

---

144. Fromm, *You Shall Be as Gods*, 126.

145. Moltmann, *Die ersten Freigelassenen der Schöpfung*, 28.

146. Ibid., 28.

of creation. By deploying this designation, Coleridge strikes a blow at the utilitarian perception of God that Kant espoused, that the notion of God served as a useful base from which to urge moral rectitude. Whilst the existence of God was beyond human cognition and therefore of no value in the realm of understanding, the idea of God was useful in the ethical sphere as a source of practical reason. Coleridge's usage of the term "I AM" subverted such a functional conception of deity, by placing an intrinsic value on existence. Moltmann writes of this purposeless creation in this way: "And so the so-called end purpose of history is, according to the Christian conception of the end, no purpose, but the freeing of life from the law of purpose and performance to the all pulsating joy of God."[147]

Naturally such statements raise eschatological questions. If the final purpose of history is the re-engagement of the whole of creation with the intrinsic joy and delight that God enjoys then the challenge is to re-imagine God in such playful terms. The primary analogies that Christ uses to describe the nature of the coming kingdom are drawn not from the world of politics, government, or justice but from the realm of childhood.[148] When Jesus describes the kingdom of God with reference to children, he is asserting that it is not only the simplicity of childlike trust that is profoundly necessary but the capacity to re-connect with the purposeless playfulness of children that is the hallmark of those who are truly able to enter the kingdom of God. If God delights in purposeless play as our earlier exploration into the biblical sapiential tradition has exposed then Coleridge's simple usage of "I AM" points us towards this quality at the heart of God's being.

George MacDonald, the Scottish theologian and poet who drew such inspiration from Coleridge, once preached a sermon entitled "The Child in the Midst," in which he explored the theme of childlike play in relation to the character of the kingdom of God. In answer to the question, "what is the kingdom of Christ?," MacDonald writes: "if then to enter into this kingdom we must become children, the spirit of children must be its pervading spirit throughout . . . If God is represented (to humanity) in Jesus, and Jesus is represented in the child, therefore God is represented in the child, for that he is like the child. God is child like."[149]

---

147. Ibid., 41: "So ist denn auch der sogenannte Endzweck der Geschichte nach christlichem Bedenken des Endes gar kein Zweck, sondern die Befreiung eines nach Zwecken und Leistungen vom Gesetz unterworfenen Lebens zur alles beschwingenden Freude Gottes."

148. Matt 19:14.

149. MacDonald, "The Child in the Midst," 4.

MacDonald does not pursue the assertion that God is child-like very far. One aspect that he does refer to is the characteristic of wonder, drawing on an observation from Bacon that, "wonder, that faculty of the mind especially attendant on the child-like imagination, is the seed of all knowledge."[150] Yet what MacDonald does do is point to a way of perceiving the kingdom that was radically different from anything that his contemporaries would have permitted. For God to be described in such terms is to allude to the realm of play which this thesis has attempted to survey. It is to George MacDonald's credit that he was sufficiently prescient to realize that the playfulness of God would one day need to be explored in much greater detail.

We have not however exhausted our exploration into the Coleridgean usage of the term "I AM who I AM." Luke Wright has argued cogently that Coleridge's "project" was a "vitalist" one.[151] Vitalism was a philosophical position that emerged in the sixteenth and seventeenth centuries in reaction to the mechanistic explanations of natural phenomena that were beginning to take hold. This distinctly Cartesian view of the world sought to explain questions of biology in purely mechanical terms. Vitalism argued that living organisms were fundamentally different from the inanimate world in that they contained some kind of life giving "fluid" or distinctive "spirit" that made them alive. The vital spirit is a substance that infuses bodies causing them to be different in nature and essence to non-living matter. Coleridge, it is argued by Wright, integrated a vitalist natural philosophy with his systematic theology by asking the question, "what is the essential spirit that infuses all life? From where does it come and what is its nature?" Coleridge was thus paving the way to argue that the ground of all being is that life is a gift stemming from the ultimate source of life. This personal life-giving God, must be conceived of as transcendent and supra mundane not the world-god of pantheism.[152] It is for this reason that Coleridge writes, "this, this is what I have so earnestly endeavored to show, that God is *Ens super Ens*, the ground of all Being, but herein likewise absolute Being, in that he is the Eternal Self-Affirmant, and the I AM in that I AM. And that the key of this mystery is given to us in the pure idea of the Will, as the alone *causa sui*."[153] Coleridge here is stressing that at the heart of creation there is a divine heartbeat which is eternally self-affirming. It has no functional intention but due to its essential centrifugal

---

150. MacDonald, "The Imagination, its Function and Culture," 9.
151. Barbeau, *Coleridge's Assertion of Religion*, 59.
152. Coleridge, *OM*, cxxiv.
153. Ibid., cxxiv.

nature continually moves outwards in self-giving towards creation. Our "purpose" as human beings is merely to recognize the source of our being and to keep in step with the rhythm of this heartbeat. It is therefore "purposeless" in that it contains no intrinsic functionality or utility. The way in which Coleridge himself understands the divine declaration of being in Exod 3:14 is beautifully illustrated in this extended quotation from *Opus Maximum* in which he writes that the origin of our being:

> is both more sublimely and more adequately conveyed in the Hebrew words "I am in that I am" or rather in the literal translation of the words "that which I will to be I shall be." For the future, which involves, a fortiori, the past and the present, is used as the fittest symbol of an eternal act, to God an all comprehending present and to every finite being a future in which nothing past is wanting or left behind . . . The sublime enunciation might be paraphrased thus, the whole host of heaven and earth, from the mote in the sunbeam to the archangel before the throne of glory owe their existence to a Will not their own . . . What I will be I eternally am, and my Will is the being in which all that move and live have their being.[154]

This quotation from the *Opus* is a natural extension of Coleridge's earlier references to the "I AM" found in *Biographia*. There, Coleridge had refuted the Cartesian statement of personal autonomy and insisted instead on a quite different formulation. "I am, because I affirm myself to be; I affirm myself to be, because I am."[155] A few paragraphs later he picks up this theme again and states, "we begin with the "I know myself," in order to end with the absolute I AM. We proceed from the self in order to lose and find all self in God."[156] Coleridge's usage of the biblical I AM predicates all that follows in his thinking. One might dare to paraphrase Coleridge's thinking by claiming, "because God is, we are." All human attempts at self-affirmation are made possible and validated by the prior fact that God is. Self-knowledge is achieved not via observation of the thinking process (cf. Descartes) but is through an act of self-affirmation and this act is based on God's own *causa sui*, the eternal, divine I AM.

---

154. Ibid., 189.
155. Coleridge, *BL* I, 275.
156. Ibid., 283.

CHAPTER 6

Conclusion

Imagination and the Playfulness of God

THE FOREGOING EXTENDED DISCUSSION has at its root the intent to determine our place in God and God's place within us. In so doing we have taken care to avoid the controversial and ultimately fruitless controversies concerned with the extent to which the grace of God can be resisted or his purposes frustrated. We have thus trodden along a more blurred landscape where the boundary between God and his creatures is more *perichoretic* and less well defined. Our guide along the first stretch of this route has been the paradigmatic imagination introduced and explicated (at least partially) by Samuel Taylor Coleridge. Once we crossed the bridge from the human imagination in all its mysterious wonder and headed into another land towards the yet more mysterious divine imagination, we did not so much as leave Coleridge behind but rather continued in the direction to which he pointed.

That direction is articulated by Coleridge in his definition of the primary imagination. This human faculty, possessed by all, is none other than a reflection of the "eternal act of creation in the infinite I AM."[1] Imagination is thus, for Coleridge, both the *mode of being* and the *modus operandi* of the Trinitarian God. When God creates by the spoken word in Gen 1—"Let there be . . ."—he does so imaginatively. When he forms and shapes with his "hands" in Gen 2, he does so imaginatively. When God affirms his own identity to Moses as the "I AM," he communicates imaginatively. What he is within himself—Father, Son, and Spirit—he is in imaginative interpersonal communion. These are the implications

1. Coleridge, *BL* II, 202.

of Coleridge's daring claim and this book has sought to tease out what such implications could mean. Let us now attempt to draw the threads together.

Our discussion began with the question of knowability. This was the import of the Kantian Copernican Revolution and the locus of knowing was re-configured by him and his successors to lie within the subjective "I." Anything beyond this vantage point could not truly be known with any degree of assurance. We could never be sure of the true final status of the *Ding-an-Sich*. In addition to the quest for certainty in knowing, Kant's project grappled with the question of "practical reason," or ethical behavior. His search for an ethical basis for the construction of community drew him towards the notion of "God" as the means by which moral standards could be instilled and applied. "God"—as a concept rather than as a person—served a useful purpose in guaranteeing and monitoring ethical choices. Yet Kant's pursuit of truth in the realm of human knowing came to an abrupt halt in the face of the sublime. How could the experience of beauty discovered in a sublime form be explained or understood? Precisely what was this profoundly disturbing human phenomenon of "awe," that one felt, unbidden, in the presence of that which is sublime? Kant thus addressed a range of questions which can here be subsumed under the headings of "truth," "goodness," and "beauty."

These same questions were adopted with alacrity by Coleridge, who, while being significantly influenced by the Kantian project, developed along his own, very different, path. That path pointed inexorably towards an engagement with the Triune God, in whom questions of truth, goodness, and beauty could all be addressed. Coleridge's astute reflections on the nature of the Trinity led him to conclude that, with reference to God, "Will" is prior to "Being." By this he drew attention to the fact that God is constituted in intentional, relational acts of volition. God's nature is rooted in personhood or, to use a Coleridgean term, in "personeity." This has significant theological ramifications. If God is understood to be persons-in-communion as distinct from an abstract "Being," then this permits the space for divine hospitality and human participation. The Trinitarian nature of God means, above all, that he is knowable in that he is within himself known. All three persons of the Trinity know and are known by each other. The Son is known through the Spirit by the Father. The Spirit enables the Father to be known by the Son. The Father and the Son know the Spirit. It is an unending cycle of reciprocal knowing each another. Within this circle of knowability others are invited to share and participate. From this Trinitarian dance accommodation and inclusion of others can occur without loss or distortion of the divine life. Indeed, God is able to ensure a distinction between himself and others not via a process of exclusion and the erection of boundaries but by inclusion in the divine embrace. Robert Jenson describes this as God being "roomy," it is his openness to participation, to making space for others, that characterizes his essence.[2] The evidence for this "roominess" is the act of creation itself for it is by this action that God announced his intention to include and to welcome. The inherent knowability of God is the guarantor of all knowability. The quest for truth finds its origin and its end in the Trinity.

That humankind is able to participate in the roominess of God is due to the *imago Dei* that is imprinted within us. The distinctiveness of that image is located not so much in our volitional capacity nor in moral virtue. These two poles have been the fault lines along which many a theological battle has been fought. Rather, the image is found in the fact that creation begins with the *Logos*, the creative spoken word of God, the Speech-Act that causes life to begin and flourish. In the whole of creation it is only to humankind that the Word of God is addressed and a response invited. This address-response capacity is, of course, the foundation of all prayer and is indicated in the human drive to seek for that which is "other." The longing for self-transcendence, to seek the face of another-who-is-not-me, is the vestigial evidence of the creative act. Coleridge appeared to intuitively know this to be true. His belief that the imagination was either a part of or, indeed, the main substance of the *imago Dei* demonstrates that he placed himself neither in the volitional nor the moral virtue camp. Whilst the imagination for him was an aesthetic function and was essential in the artistic realm, it was also far more than that. Coleridge knew that the drive towards self-transcendence demanded that the imagination not only seek restlessly for God (in the Augustinian sense) but also achieve the transcendental unity of apperception that Coleridge had learned from his reading of Kant.

If the interpersonal communion between Father, Son, and Spirit is mutually, reciprocally imaginative then what form of language may one use to describe the nature of this inter-personal exchange? Some have argued[3] that this can best be articulated in aesthetic terms. God is beauty, one may say, and the interplay of relationships within the Trinity transcends the notion of "goodness" in that these relationships have no other point of reference other than for their own sake. The exchanges are therefore simply "beautiful," rather than functional, and as such they "sing."

2. Jenson, *Systematic Theology Volume 1*, 226.
3. Ibid., 235.

There is a sublime musical quality about them that eternally invites others to freely enter into the divine enjoyment. It is thus akin, writes Jenson, to a divine "fugue,"[4] where more voices and further instrumentation are constantly added. This musical analogy, adopted by Jenson at the conclusion of his *Systematic Theology*, is entirely understandable. It reflects a search for appropriate language with which to describe the "space" that God occupies, and how that space can include and accommodate others. The difficulty that has often arisen in the formulations of Western theology may stem from its over-dependence on a purely linguistic framework of thought. How can the Father, Son, and Spirit coexist within the same "space" without one or other being consumed or elided? Yet with the intra-Trinitarian relationships no such competitive atmosphere is found. The Three can coexist together in perfect mutual harmony, each remaining distinct and each supporting and "liberating" the others. It is this mutual occupation of the same space that language struggles to articulate adequately. The analogy of music, therefore, offers an alternative mode of hearing and perceiving and the simple experience of hearing a three-note chord illustrates this perfectly. The three notes inhabit the same aural space, producing one sound yet with three distinct and separate tones.

An example of this can be drawn from the work of sixteenth-century composer, Thomas Tallis, who was known as a master of polyphony. One of the finest examples[5] of this is the motet *Spem in Alium*, written for forty different voices split into eight choirs of five. The beauty of this work stems from the way in which each voice enriches the others and enables them to be truly free. The presence of forty voices is entirely non-competitive; indeed the reverse is true in that each voice is required to sing their distinctive part so that the whole may be enhanced. Although each voice occupies the same auditory space, the blending of musical contributions is the source of what, in the skillful hands of Tallis, becomes something sublime.

Whilst this musical analogy is very rich and attractive, it is my view that it needs to be subsumed under a larger parameter. It is the paradigm that Schiller proposed when he explored the role of the *Spieltrieb*—that drive, within all, which searches for beauty and which unites all other drives together. When one makes music, one plays, for music cannot be "commanded" in response to some higher fiat. For music to be music and not mere noise, the appropriate conditions need to be in place, a habitat of freedom, delight, pleasure, and harmony. Music cannot, therefore,

---

4. Ibid., 236.
5. I am indebted to Prof. Jeremy Begbie for this illustration.

be forced and can only be played in freedom, for play is the ultimate expression of freedom. Maybe it was this very freedom that Furtwängler afforded to his musicians that enabled his orchestras to produce music of sublime quality. It is this language of "play" that offers an alternative form of expression that may adequately describe not only the being of God within himself but also his mode of engagement with creation. This book has sought to argue that the category of "play" not only provides an alternative discourse about God but actually demands to be heard with intense seriousness. Playfulness is too important to be taken lightly.

The linguistic hurdle that this presents is not insignificant. Play can be seen as a frivolous, ornamental, a decorative addition to human activity. This is precisely the objection that Schiller anticipated and against which he wrote in his letters: "For a long time you may have been tempted to argue that beauty, when it is defined in the language of play, has been debased and becomes an expression of all those frivolities that we associate with it."[6]

It is commonly perceived that play is what we do once the serious and important work of making a living has been completed. Play can thus easily be relegated to the sphere of leisure, an activity which only those in developed Westernized democracies have the luxury to pursue. Yet play, as we have already explored, is far more existential and innate to human existence than that. To play is to give oneself permission to explore possibilities, to experiment with new configurations, to re-draw the boundaries of legitimacy, to allow for freely given and freely accepted forms of inter-relationship. Play opens up rather than closes down. Play is intrinsically imaginative, willingly suspending disbelief to make space, or room, for newness. Schiller was persuaded that the *Spieltrieb,* to which Coleridge was so profoundly attracted, was the route by which the elusive goal of the apprehension of beauty and the sublime could be attained.

It should come as no surprise therefore that the kingdom of God is depicted with reference to children. Play is the enduring and often perpetual activity of children such that when Jesus calls humanity into the newness of the coming kingdom he does so by inviting us to re-enter the world of the child. To inhabit the kingdom is to enter a world of play which God himself inhabits. This "purposeless" activity is the cause of delight and joy. As a by-product it opens the space for imaginative

---

6. Schiller Brief 15 http://www.kuehnle-online.de/literatur/schiller/prosa/aestherzieh/15.htm: "Wird aber, möchten Sie längst schon versucht gewesen sein mir entgegenzusetzen, wird nicht das Schöne dadurch, daß man es zum bloßen Spiel macht, erniedrigt und den frivolen Gegenständen gleichgestellt, die von jeher im Besitz dieses Namens waren?"

creativity and engagement with others. This is why "play" or "playfulness" are terms which may legitimately permit us to re-imagine God. In using Coleridge as our guide, this journey has, at times, followed the path of the poet, at others the way of the philosopher and at still others through the world of the biblical exegete. For Coleridge, the stepping-stone is in many ways immaterial for the final destination of the exploration of the imagination is always the same. It lies in the sublime beauty and mystery of the Trinitarian God whose ways are not our ways and who constantly engages in the surprising, the dramatic, the unexpected and the playful, in order to bring about the final unity and reconciliation of all things in and through the eternal incarnate *Logos*.

Appendix

Coleridge, the Imagination, and George MacDonald (1824–1905)

THE SCOTTISH AUTHOR, POET, and Christian minister, George MacDonald, is best known for his fairy tales and fantasy novels which include *Phantastes, The Princess and the Goblin, At the Back of the North Wind,* and *Lilith*. What is perhaps less well known is that he made a major contribution to British theology in the nineteenth century, particularly through the publication of his sermons and a collection of musings entitled *A Dish of Orts*. During his formative years he was exposed to Scottish Calvinism as well as the Celtic tradition from the Western Isles. In his later life he counted the poet William Wordsworth, E. T. A. Hoffmann, Goethe, F. D. Maurice, and Coleridge amongst his main literary and theological influences. It was from this amalgam of sources that he developed a sophisticated and nuanced theology of the imagination and as such was unique amongst his contemporaries. There are strong similarities between the thinking of Coleridge and MacDonald on the subject of the imagination in addition to a few significant differences in emphasis.

Integral to the thinking of MacDonald was the influence of the Celtic tradition with its deep Trinitarian foundation. MacDonald claimed that the "secret of the whole story of humanity is the love between the Father and the Son. That is the root of it all. Upon the love between the Father and the Son hangs the whole universe."[1] MacDonald's affirmation of the triune relations led him to seek an understanding of the imagination in their light. Understanding God as the Trinity, with the Father and Son bonded together in the overflowing love of the Spirit, caused MacDonald to assert that the creative imagination is first and foremost an attribute of God, a derivative of his love. The imaginative interplay between Father and Son which is eternally new is the spring from which

---

1. MacDonald, "Knowing the Risen Lord," 67.

all other expressions of imaginative creativity find their source. The prime manifestation of the power of God was therefore to be seen as "loving creativity," rather than "sovereign will."[2] This marked a significant departure from the Calvinism of MacDonald's youth. By placing an emphasis on the divine imagination MacDonald was determined to preserve the freedom of God to act in such a way that the call of redemptive love was answered. In so doing MacDonald wanted to avoid any sense of mechanical necessity being placed upon God.

There have been relatively few theologians who have taken up the challenge of constructing a bridge between a theology of the imagination and the ontology of God. George MacDonald was one of the few who has attempted to do so. His seminal essay, "The Imagination, its Functions and Culture," in his book, "*A Dish of Orts*" addresses this very question. In it he writes, "the imagination of man is made in the image of the imagination of God. Everything of man must have been of God first."[3] This is indeed a bold claim. MacDonald is, in effect, making two daring statements. Firstly, he asserts that imagination is to be considered as one of God's attributes. Many orthodox theologians have produced lists of divine attributes but one would scarcely expect to find "imagination" listed amongst them. Yet this is precisely what MacDonald is demanding; that the very being of God needs to be constituted as one in which the imagination is a central part. In second place, it is important to notice where MacDonald locates the *imago Dei*. It is not in man's rationality nor his sociability nor in his volitional capacity nor even in his moral character. Rather the *imago Dei* is to be found primarily in the imagination, linking it firmly to God's original creative activity.

MacDonald was careful however to distinguish between divine creativity and imagination and that possessed by humanity. God always takes the radical initiative, creating out of a void, bringing order and harmony. Humanity, by contrast, only creates in response—not as an initiator—for our creativity works only with that which has already been given. We simply re-fashion into new shapes and forms; we do not create anew. He writes, "the imagination . . . can present us with new thought forms, new that is as revelations of thought. It has created none of the material that goes to make these forms."[4] In this respect MacDonald places the emphasis firmly on the *difference* between divine and human creativity. Coleridge would perhaps have trodden a more theologically

2. MacDonald, "The Imagination, its Function and Culture," 2.
3. Ibid., 3.
4. Ibid., 10.

risky path emphasizing the truly creative power that humanity possesses as a gift from God. This potential is more than simply the capacity to find, "the Trouvere," but the power to actually create.[5] MacDonald's theology self-consciously avoided the pitfalls of pantheism and he was careful to place human creativity within a bounded, limited framework. Human imagination does not exist autonomously, randomly, or self-centeredly. It is given as a gift from the Creator and is always to remain anchored to its source in the Trinitarian love of God.

Whilst MacDonald did not explore in detail what the imagination of God might look like he did make two strong assertions about it. The first of these was that because of his capacity to imaginatively empathize God is able to enter into the pain and suffering of the human condition. This allows for, enables, and often elicits an intimate response to the divine approach. Secondly, whilst God is constant in his faithfulness to creation, he is imaginative, and therefore often surprising, in his engagement with the particularity of each individual person and circumstance. His constancy is not to be equated with predictability. Even his judgment is lovingly restorative and is consistent with his character.

---

5. Ibid., 12.

Bibliography

Arendt, Hannah. *Lectures on Kant's Political Philosophy*. Chicago: University of Chicago Press, 1989.
Bailey, Kenneth. *Jacob and the Prodigal*. Downers Grove, IL: InterVarsity, 2003.
———. *Jesus through Middle Eastern Eyes: Cultural Studies in the Gospels*. London: SPCK, 2008.
———. *Poet and Peasant; and Through Peasant Eyes*. Grand Rapids: Eerdmans, 1972.
Baker, James. *The Sacred River: Coleridge's Theory of the Imagination*. New York: Greenwood, 1969.
Barbeau, Jeffrey, ed. *Coleridge's Assertion of Religion: Essays on the Opus Maximum*. Leuven: Peeters, 2007.
———. *Coleridge, the Bible and Religion*. New York: Palgrave Macmillan, 2008.
Barfield, Owen. *What Coleridge Thought*. Middleton, CT: Wesleyan University Press, 1971.
Barth, John Robert. *Coleridge and Christian Doctrine*. Cambridge: Harvard University Press, 1969.
———. *Coleridge, Keats and the Imagination*. Columbia: University of Missouri Press, 1990.
———. *Romanticism and Transcendence*. Columbia: University of Missouri Press, 2003.
———. *The Symbolic Imagination: Coleridge and the Romantic Tradition*. New York: Fordham University Press, 2001.
Barth, Karl. *Kirchliche Dogmatik 1*. Zürich: Theologischer, 1952.
———. *Kirchliche Dogmatik 2/1*. Zürich: Evangelisher, 1948.
———. *Kirchliche Dogmatik 3/3*. Zürich: Evangelischer, 1950.
———. *Kirchliche Dogmatik 4/1*. Zürich: Evangelischer, 1953.
———. *Church Dogmatics*. Edited and translated by G. W. Bromiley and T. F. Torrance. Edinburgh: T. & T. Clark, 1957.
Beer, John. *Coleridge's Poetic Intelligence*. London: Macmillan, 1977.
Begbie, Jeremy. *Theology, Music and Time*. Cambridge: Cambridge University Press, 2000.
———. *Voicing Creation's Praise*. Edinburgh: T. & T. Clark, 1991.
Beinhocker, Eric. *The Origins of Wealth: Evolution, Complexity and the Radical Remaking of Economics*. Boston: Harvard Business School Press, 2006.
Botterwick, Johannes, and Helmer Ringgren. *Theological Dictionary of the Old Testament*, Vol. II. Grand Rapids: Eerdmans, 1975.
Bowie, Andrew. *Aesthetics and Subjectivity: From Kant to Nietzsche*. Manchester, UK: Manchester University Press, 1990.
Brett, Raymond. *Fancy & Imagination*. London: Methuen, 1969.
Burwick, Frederick. *Coleridge's Biographia Literaria*. Columbus: Ohio State University Press, 1989.
Brice, Ben. *Coleridge and Scepticism*. Oxford: Oxford University Press, 2007.

Bibliography

Brueggemann, Walter. *Genesis*. Interpretation. Atlanta: John Knox, 1982.
———. *The Bible and Postmodern Imagination*. London: SCM, 1993.
———. *Theology of the Old Testament*. Minneapolis: Fortress, 1997.
Coburn, Kathryn. *Inquiring Spirit: A Coleridge Reader*. New York: Minerva, 1968.
Coleridge, Samuel Taylor. *Aids to Reflection*. Edited by H. N. Coleridge. New York: Kennikat, 1971.
———. *Biographia Literaria, 1, Collected Works*. Edited by Kathleen Coburn. Princeton: Princeton University Press, 1983.
———. *Biographia Literaria, 2, Collected Works*. Edited by Kathleen Coburn. Princeton: Princeton University Press, 1983.
———. *Collected Letters 1815–1819. Vol. 4*. Edited by E. L. Griggs. Oxford: Clarendon, 1959.
———. *Confessions of an Inquiring Spirit*. Edited by Henry Coleridge. London: Pickering, 1840.
———. *Lay Sermons*. Edited by R. J. White. London: Routledge & Kegan Paul, 1972.
———. *Lectures on Literature 1808–1819*. Edited by Reginald Foakes. London: Routledge & Kegan Paul, 1987.
———. *Table Talk. The Collected Works Band: 14*. London: Routledge & Kegan Paul, 1990.
———. *The Collected Notebooks of Samuel Taylor Coleridge*. Edited by Kathleen Coburn. New York: Bollingen Foundation, 1957.
———. *The Complete Poetical Works of Samuel Taylor Coleridge*. Edited by Ernest Coleridge. Oxford: Clarendon, 1912.
———. *The Friend. Band: 4,1*. London: Routledge & Kegan Paul, 1969.
———. *The Philosophical Lectures*. Edited by Kathleen Coburn. London: Routledge & Kegan Paul, 1949.
———. *The Statesman's Manual*. In *The Collected Works of Samuel Taylor Coleridge*. Edited by R. J. White. London: Routledge & Kegan Paul, 1972.
Collingwood, Robin. *The Idea of History*. Oxford: Oxford University Press, 1983.
Cutsinger, James. *The Form of Transformed Vision: Coleridge and the Knowledge of God*. Macon, GA: Mercer University Press, 1987.
Dearborn, Kerry. *Baptized Imagination: The Theology of George MacDonald*. Aldershot, UK: Ashgate, 2006.
Edwards, Mark. *Neoplatonic Saints: The Lives of Plotinus and Proclus by Their Students*. Liverpool: Liverpool University Press, 2000.
Empson, William, and David Pirie. *Coleridge's Verse: A Selection*. London: Faber & Faber, 1972.
Engell, James. *The Creative Imagination: Enlightenment to Romanticism*. Cambridge: Harvard University Press, 1981.
Fichte, Johann Gottlieb. *Die Bestimmung des Menschen*. Hamburg: Meiner, 2000.
———. *Versuch einer neuen Darstellung der Wissenschaftslehre*. Hamburg: Meiner, 1975.
Ford, David. "The God of Blessing Who Loves in Wisdom." In *Denkwürdiges Geheimnis: Beiträge zur Gotteslehre; Festschrift für Eberhard Jüngel zum 70. Geburtstag*, edited by Ingolf U. Dalferth, Johannes Fischer, and Hans-Peter Großhans, 113–26. Tübingen: Mohr/Siebeck, 2004.
———, editor. *The Modern Theologians*. Oxford: Blackwell, 2005.
———, and Daniel Hardy. *Living in Praise: Worshipping and Knowing the Living God*. Grand Rapids: Baker Academic, 2005.
Förster, Eckhart. *Kant's Final Synthesis: An Essay on Opus Postumum*. Cambridge: Harvard University Press, 2000.

Freydberg, Bernard. *Imagination in Kant's Critique of Practical Reason*. Bloomington: Indiana University Press, 2005.
Fromm, Eric. *You Shall be as Gods: A Radical Interpretation of the Old Testament and Its Tradition*. New York: Holt, Rinehart and Winston, 1966.
Gallant, Christine. *Coleridge's Theory of the Imagination Today*. New York: AMS, 1989.
Gibbons, Sarah. *Kant's Theory of the Imagination*. Oxford: Clarendon, 1994.
Gravil, Richard, Lucy Newlyn, and Nicholas Roe. *Coleridge's Imagination*. Cambridge: Cambridge University Press, 1985.
Green, Garrett. *Imagining God*. San Fransisco: Harper & Row, 1989.
———. *Theology, Hermeneutics and Imagination*. Cambridge: Cambridge University Press, 2000.
Gunton, Colin. "Creation and Re-creation: An Exploration of Some Themes in Aesthetics and Theology." *Modern Theology* 2 (1985) 1–19.
Gunton, Colin. *The One, the Three, and the Many: God, Creation, and the Culture of Modernity*. Cambridge: Cambridge University Press, 1993.
———. *The Promise of Trinitarian Theology*. Edinburgh: T. & T. Clark, 1997.
———. *The Theology of Reconciliation*. London: T. & T. Clark, 2003.
Halmi, Nicholas. *The Genealogy of Romantic Symbol*. Oxford: Oxford University Press, 2007.
Halmi, Nicholas. "When Is a Symbol Not a Symbol? Coleridge on the Eucharist." *Coleridge Bulletin* 20 (2002) 85–92.
Hamilton, Paul. *Coleridge and German Philosophy: The Poet in the Land of Logic*. London: Continuum, 2007.
Haney, David. *The Challenge of Coleridge*. University Park: Pennsylvania State University Press, 2001.
Hardy, Daniel. "Harmony and Mutual Implication in the Opus Maximum." In *Coleridge's Assertion of Religion: Essays on the Opus Maximum*, edited by Jeffrey Barbeau, 33–52. Leuven: Peeters, 2007.
Hedley, Douglas. *Coleridge, Philosophy and Religion*. Cambridge: Cambridge University Press, 2000.
———. "Coleridge's Speculative Mysticism: Reflections on Dr. Perkins's Logic and Logos." *Heythrop Journal* 35 (1991) 421–39.
———. *Living Forms of the Imagination*. London: T. & T. Clark, 2008.
Hill, John. *Imagination in Coleridge*. London: MacMillan, 1978.
Hölderlin, Friedrich. *Hyperion: oder der Eremit in Griechenland*. Edited by Walther Killy. Urach, Germany: Port, 1947.
Holmes, Richard. *Coleridge: Darker Reflections*. London: HarperCollins, 1998.
Hopps, Gavin. "The Playful Devotions of Byron and Coleridge." *Coleridge Bulletin* 25 (2005) 15–39.
Huizinga, Johan. *Homo Ludens: A Study of the Play Element of Culture*. London: Routledge & Kegan Paul, 1949.
Hume, David. *An Enquiry Concerning Human Understanding*. Edited by Tom Beauchamp. Oxford: Oxford University Press, 1999.
Hurtrez, Lionel. "Nature and subjectivity: Coleridge and Fichteanism." *Coleridge Bulletin* 18.4 (2001) 1–15.
Inge, William. *The Philosophy of Plotinus*. Vol. 2. Westport: Greenwood, 1968.
Jasper, David. *The Interpretation of Belief: Coleridge, Schleiermacher and Romanticism*. Basingstoke, UK: Macmillan, 1986.
Jenson, Robert. *Systematic Theology*. Vol. 1: *The Triune God*. Oxford: Oxford University Press, 1997.

———. *Systematic Theology*. Vol. 2: *The Works of God*. Oxford: Oxford University Press, 1999.
Jeremias, Joachim. *The Parables of Jesus*. Translated by S. H. Hooke. London: SCM, 2004.
Kant, Immanuel. *Critique of Aesthetic Judgment*. Oxford: Oxford University Press, 1911.
———. *Groundwork of the Metaphysical of Morals*. New York: Harper & Row, 1956.
———. *Kritik der reinen Vernunft*. Darmstadt: Wissenschaftliche Buchgesellschaft, 2005.
Kearney, Richard. *The Poetics of Imagining*. London: Harper Collins, 1998.
———. *The Wake of Imagination: Ideas of Creativity in Western Culture*. London: Hutchinson, 1988.
Khovacs, Ivor. "Robbing Peter to Pay Paul: Theology's Indebtedness to the Theatre with Reference to the Theo-drama of Hans Urs von Balthasar." Unpublished paper, University of St. Andrews colloquium. 2002.
Kneller, Jane. *Kant and the Power of the Imagination*. Cambridge: Cambridge University Press, 2007.
Kooy, Michael. *Coleridge, Schiller and Aesthetic Freedom*. New York: Palgrave, 2002.
Lash, Nicholas. *Theology on the Way to Emmaus*. London: SCM, 1986.
Leask, Nigel. *The Politics of Imagination in Coleridge's Critical Thought*. Basingstoke, UK: Macmillan, 1988.
Lebrecht, Norman. *The Maestro Myth*. London: Simon & Schuster, 1991.
Lewis, C. S. *The Collected Poems*. Edited by Walter Hooper. London: Fount, 1994.
———. *The Screwtape Letters*. New York: Macmillan, 1961.
MacDonald, George. "Knowing the Risen Lord." In *Proving the Unseen*. Edited by William Peterson. New York: Ballantine, 1989.
———. "The Child in the Midst." In *Unspoken Sermons*, 13–23. New York: Cosimo, 2007.
———. "The Imagination, its Function and Culture." In *A Dish of Orts*, 2–28. Charleston, SC: BiblioBazaar, 2007.
MacIntyre, John. *Faith Theology and Imagination*. Edinburgh: Handsel, 1987.
McFarland, Thomas. *Coleridge and the Pantheist Tradition*. Oxford: Clarendon, 1969.
McFague, Sallie. *Models of God: Theology for an Ecological, Nuclear Age*. Philadelphia: Fortress, 1987.
Manning, Peter. "Don Juan and Byron's Imperceptiveness to the English Word." In *Byron*, edited by Jane Stabler, 180–93. Longman Critical Readers. London: Longman, 1998.
Masson, Scott. "Repeating the Act of the Infinite in the Finite: Theological Anthropology in Coleridge's Opus Maximum." In *Coleridge's Assertion of Religion: Essays on the Opus Maximum*, edited by Jeffrey Barbeau, 145–62. Leuven: Peeters, 2007.
———. *Romanticism, Hermeneutics and the Crisis of the Human Sciences*. Aldershot, UK: Ashgate, 2004.
McGrath, Alistair. *Iustitia Dei: A History of the Christian Doctrine of Justification*. Cambridge: Cambridge University Press, 2005.
Meurs, Nora. "Resisting the Silence: Coleridge's Courtship of the Sublime." *The Coleridge Bulletin* 25 (2005) 40–45.
Moltmann, Jürgen. *Die ersten Freigelassenen der Schöpfung: Versuch über die Freude an der Freiheit und das Wohlgefallen am Spiel*. Munich: Kaiser, 1981.
———. *Theology of Play*. Translated by Richard Ulrich. New York: Harper & Row, 1972.
Newlyn, Lucy. *Cambridge Companion to Coleridge*. Cambridge: Cambridge University Press, 2002.
Orsini, Gian. *Coleridge and German Idealism: A Study in the History of Philosophy*. Carbondale, IL: Southern Illinois University Press, 1969.
O'Siadhail, Michael. *Poems 1975–1995*. Newcastle upon Tyne, UK: Bloodaxe, 1999.

Pederson, Ann. *God, Creation and all that Jazz: A Process of Composition and Improvisation.* St. Louis, MO: Chalice, 2001.
Perkins, Mary. *Coleridge's Philosophy: The Logos as Unifying Principle.* Oxford: Clarendon, 1994.
———. "Logic and Logos: The Search for Unity in Hegel and Coleridge." *Heythrop Journal* 32 (1991) 192–215.
Perry, Seamus. *Coleridge's Notebooks.* Oxford: Oxford University Press, 2002.
———. *Coleridge and the Uses of Division.* Oxford: Clarendon, 1999.
Plato. *The Republic.* Translated and with an introduction by Reginald Allen. New Haven: Yale University Press, 2006.
Plotinus. *The Ennead.* Online: http://oaks.nvg.org/sa1ra6.html.
Plotkin, Bill. *Nature and the Human Soul.* Novato, CA: New World Library, 2007.
Polkinghorne, John. *Faith, Science and Understanding.* New Haven: Yale University Press, 2000.
Reid, Barbara. *The Lectionary Commentary.* Edited by Roger Van Harn. Grand Rapids: Eerdmans, 2006.
Reid, Nicholas. *Coleridge Form and Symbol.* Aldershot, UK: Ashgate, 2006.
Richards, Ivor. *Coleridge on Imagination.* London: Routledge & Kegan Paul, 1962.
Ricoeur, Paul. *Oneself as Another.* Chicago: University of Chicago Press, 1992.
———. *Rule of Metaphor.* Toronto: University of Toronto Press, 1977.
Santner, Eric. *Hyperion and Selected Poems.* New York: Continuum, 1990.
Schelling, Friedrich. *Sämmtliche Werke.* Vol. V. Stuttgart: Cotta, 1856–61.
———. *Zur Geschichte der Neueren Philosophie.* Darmstadt: Wissenschaftliche Buchgesellschaft, 1978.
Schiller, Friedrich. *Briefe über die ästhetische Erziehung des Menschen.* Online: http://www.dreigliederung.de/gliederung/schillersbriefe.html.
———. *Essays: Aesthetical and Philosophical.* London: Bohn, 1884.
———. *On the Aesthetic Education of Man.* Edited by Elizabeth Wilkinson. Oxford: Clarendon, 1967.
Schwöbel, Christoph. *God: Action and Revelation.* Kampen: Kok Pharos, 1992.
Simmons, Jack, ed. *Letters from England. Robert Southey.* Gloucester, UK: Sutton, 1984.
Smart, Nicholas. *Nineteenth Century Religious Thought in the West.* 2 vols. Cambridge: Cambridge University Press, 1985.
Stabler, Jane, editor. *Byron.* London: Longman, 1998.
Suurmond, Jean-Jacques. *Word and Spirit at Play: Towards a Charismatic Theology.* Grand Rapids: Eerdmans, 1994.
Swiatecka, Jadwiga. *The Idea of Symbol: Some Nineteenth Century Comparisons with Coleridge.* Cambridge: Cambridge University Press, 1986.
Vanhoozer, Kevin. *First Theology.* Downers Grove, IL: InterVarsity, 2002.
Vlasoplos, Anca. *The Symbolic Method of Coleridge, Baudelaire and Yeats.* Detroit: Wayne State University Press, 1983.
Watson, Jeanie. *Risking Enchantment: Coleridge's Symbolic World of Faery.* Lincoln, NE: University of Nebraska Press, 1990.
Welch, Claude. "Samuel Taylor Coleridge." In *19th Century Religious Thought in the West.* Vol. 2, edited by Ninian Smart, 1–28. Cambridge: Cambridge University Press, 1985.
Wells, Sam. *Improvisation: The Drama of Christian Ethics.* Grand Rapids: Brazos, 2004.
Wordsworth, William. *The Complete Poetical Works Of William Wordsworth.* Vol. 1. Whitefish: Kessinger, 2007.
———. *The Poetical Works Of William Wordsworth.* Boston: Houghton Mifflin, 1982.
———. *Selected Poetry.* Edited by Mark van Doren. New York: Modern Library, 2002.

www.ingramcontent.com/pod-product-compliance
Lightning Source LLC
Chambersburg PA
CBHW051742230426
43670CB00012B/2129